PRAISE FOR JULIE

An Innocent Bystander

The Killing of Leon Klinghoffer

"The human side of a harrowing tale…Behind every act of terrorism are ordinary people—those who are the victims, those who are the perpetrators, and those who watch from the sidelines—and Salamon's goal is straightforward: to present all of the actors, the Klinghoffers, the hijackers, White House aides, and others, as real-life husbands, wives, sons, and daughters, instead of symbols or stock characters in a political drama…Salamon's book's greatest contribution is the way that it humanizes the political ordeal…*An Innocent Bystander* offers valuable insight." —Tara McKelvey, *New York Times Book Review*

"Heavily researched…Julie Salamon sheds fresh light on the tragedy… In a book that reads like a spy thriller and a closely observed narrative of the Israeli-Palestinian conflict, Salamon asserts that Klinghoffer was shot not because he was a Jew but because he was an American. *An Innocent Bystander* is based on Salamon's access to newly unclassified material and interviews with many of the key figures who are still alive—including several who hadn't spoken out previously." —Sandee Brawarsky, *Jewish Week*

"Leon Klinghoffer's death became a symbol for many of the costs and fears of terrorism. Julie Salamon has written a book about that moment and the human threads that followed in a way that depicts the Israeli-Palestinian conflict."

—Scott Simon, National Public Radio

"*An Innocent Bystander* tells the awful story of Palestinian terrorists hijacking an Italian cruise ship. It also explains how competing governments, complicated treaties, and outright lies kept the four attackers from ever facing American justice…Julie Salamon strives to be scrupulously fair. Her book focuses not only on the captives but also on the captors."

—Jacqueline Cutler, *New York Daily News*

"A gripping, profoundly moving, and insightful examination of the *Achille Lauro* tragedy from multiple perspectives."

—Saul David, author of *Operation Thunderbolt: Flight 139 and the Raid on Entebbe Airport, the Twentieth Century's Greatest Special Forces Mission*

"Julie Salamon's *An Innocent Bystander* is an empathetic and deeply researched account of how families across the globe deal with the loss and pain born out of the Israel-Palestine conflict."

—Moustafa Bayoumi, author of *How Does It Feel to Be a Problem?: Being Young and Arab in America*

"Salamon's elegantly constructed account of the *Achille Lauro* hijacking and its bitter aftermath illuminates how the specter of modern terrorism has sown hostility throughout the world. Yet the book is at its most poignant when exploring the personal rather than political: Salamon's ingenious storytelling deepens our understanding of how human beings find the strength to cope with the incomprehensible."

—Brendan I. Koerner, author of *The Skies Belong to Us* and *Now the Hell Will Start*

"Salamon plucks the story of the killing of one man out of the rush of history and holds it up for nuanced consideration. In so doing, she shows us how the events around a single murder continue to ripple outward, through the families of both the murder victim and the man who set that murder in motion. An illuminating, necessary book."

—J. T. Rogers, author of *Oslo*

"Gripping…An engrossing narrative of a notorious act of terror…Salamon adeptly reveals the parallel lives of the well-educated and privileged wife of the leader of the Palestinian Liberation Front and the successful New York City–bred daughters of abductees Marilyn and Leon Klinghoffer. Salamon's account of the strategizing of Palestinian, Israeli, and American diplomats, followed by the soldiers' captures and subsequent escapes, are as engaging as a spy novel."

—*Kirkus Reviews*

An Innocent Bystander

An Innocent Bystander

The Killing of Leon Klinghoffer

Julie Salamon

BACK BAY BOOKS
Little, Brown and Company
New York Boston London

Back Bay Books / Little, Brown and Company
Hachette Book Group
1290 Avenue of the Americas, New York, NY 10104
littlebrown.com

First published in hardcover by Little, Brown and Company, June 2019
First Back Bay trade paperback edition, April 2020

Back Bay Books is an imprint of Little, Brown and Company, a division of Hachette Book Group, Inc. The Back Bay Books name and logo are trademarks of Hachette Book Group, Inc.

The publisher is not responsible for websites (or their content) that are not owned by the publisher.

The Hachette Speakers Bureau provides a wide range of authors for speaking events. To find out more, go to hachettespeakersbureau.com or call (866) 376-6591.

ISBN 978-0-316-43310-5 (hc) / 978-0-316-43311-2 (pb)
LCCN 2018949529

10 9 8 7 6 5 4 3 2 1

LSC-C

Printed in the United States of America

To my family, as always, with love

Contents

Principal Characters

LEON KLINGHOFFER

Leon Klinghoffer, New York entrepreneur

Marilyn Klinghoffer, human resources director; Leon's wife

Lisa Klinghoffer, older daughter of Marilyn and Leon

Ilsa Klinghoffer, younger daughter of Marilyn and Leon

Jerry Arbittier, Lisa's husband

Paul Dworin, Ilsa's husband

Letty Simon, family friend who handled public relations

Charlotte Spiegel, Klinghoffer friend and fellow passenger on
    the *Achille Lauro*

Maura Spiegel, professor; Charlotte's daughter

Seymour Meskin, family friend and fellow passenger on the
    Achille Lauro

Abraham Foxman, national director of Anti-Defamation
    League, 1987–2015

Benjamin Netanyahu, Israeli ambassador to the United Nations,
    1984–1988; prime minister of Israel, 1996–1999 and 2009–

ABU AL-ABBAS

Abu al-Abbas, commander of the Palestinian Liberation Front

Samia Costandi, professor; first wife of Abu al-Abbas

Reem al-Nimer, heiress and revolutionary; second wife of Abu al-Abbas

Khaled Abbas, first son of Samia Costandi and Abu al-Abbas

Omar Abbas, second son of Samia Costandi and Abu al-Abbas

Loaye al-Ghadban, first son of Reem al-Nimer and Mohammad al-Ghadban

Reef Ghadban, second son of Reem al-Nimer and Mohammad al-Ghadban

Ali Abbas, son of Reem al-Nimer and Abu al-Abbas

Bassam al-Ashker, the youngest hijacker

Majid al-Molqi, leader of the four hijackers

Ahmad Maruf "Omar" al-Assadi, hijacker

Abdellatif Ibrahim Fataier, hijacker the passengers nicknamed Rambo

Monzer al-Kassar, international arms dealer; old friend of Abu al-Abbas

Yasser Arafat, chairman, Palestine Liberation Organization

ALEX ODEH

Alex Odeh, West Coast regional director, American-Arab Anti-Discrimination Committee, 1983–1985

Norma Odeh, Alex's wife

Helena Odeh, oldest daughter of Alex and Norma

James Abourezk, United States senator (South Dakota), 1973–1979; founder of American-Arab Anti-Discrimination Committee, 1980

Meir Kahane, founder, Jewish Defense League, 1968

Irv Rubin, head of Jewish Defense League, 1985

U.S. GOVERNMENT

Ronald Reagan, president, 1981–1989

George Shultz, secretary of state, 1982–1989

Caspar Weinberger, secretary of defense, 1982–1987

Oliver North, chair, White House counterterrorism task force, 1985–1986

Carl Stiner, major general; commanding general of Joint Special Operations, 1984–1987

Laurence Neal, lieutenant commander; naval aviator, 1975–1995

Nicholas A. Veliotes, ambassador to Egypt, 1984–1986

ITALY

Bettino Craxi, prime minister, 1983–1987

Antonio Badini, chief foreign affairs adviser to Prime Minister Craxi, 1983–1987

Fulvio Martini, Italian Navy admiral; head of military security and intelligence, 1984–1991

Gianfranco Pagano, defense attorney representing two of the *Achille Lauro* hijackers

Luigi Carli, prosecutor

OPERA

Peter Sellars, creator-director of *The Death of Klinghoffer*

John Adams, composer

Alice Goodman, librettist

My friends, I must insist upon this rule. For it is only through the sharing of the *personal* that we can see each other for who we truly are.

—J. T. Rogers, *Oslo*

PART ONE

The *Achille Lauro*

October 7, 1985–October 22, 1985

Prologue

Beirut, October 14, 1985

This was the moment that the *Achille Lauro* entered the consciousness of five-year-old Omar Abbas, younger son of Samia Costandi, first wife of Mohammed Zaidan, better known as Abu al-Abbas, commander of the Palestinian Liberation Front.

The telephone in their apartment rang and Omar heard his grandmother say, "Hello, Nabeel, did you finish your PhD?" And then his mother, Samia, told him and his older brother, Khaled, to come say hello to Baba, their father, but to pretend he was their uncle, Samia's brother, Nabeel. Omar could tell from his mother's face that this was very serious.

"Hello, Uncle Baba," he said.

The five-year-old's failure at subterfuge would become part of family lore. For Samia, the call signaled that her ex-husband, Abu al-Abbas, was safe. For Omar, the conversation was merged into the mythology that would always surround his father, a towering figure who instilled in his sons a permanent sense of longing.

The divorce had been modern, granting custody to Samia with visiting rights for their father. During the year Omar and Khaled lived with their mother in Beirut, close to their maternal grandparents, in Hamra, a lively neighborhood full of cafés where intellectuals and activists mingled to discuss poetry and philosophy and politics amid the chaos of a decade's ongoing sectarian violence. Samia taught

English as a second language close by, at Beirut University College, her alma mater.

Omar felt safe and protected, even though he knew there was a civil war and he remembered times when there would be explosions sounding like fireworks that meant his family had to hide in the stairwell with neighbors. His mom brought a blanket and snacks; for the kids, it was an indoor picnic, even though they knew the fireworks were bombs.

Hearing Baba's voice carried Omar's imagination to happy summers in Tunisia, where he spent vacations with his older brother, Khaled. That's when they saw their father and were taken care of by their Auntie Reem, their stepmother, who treated them even nicer than her own kids. Omar and Khaled considered Loaye and Reef, Reem's sons from her first marriage, as brothers.

Tunisia provided a haven for the Palestine Liberation Organization, which had been driven from Beirut in 1982, but for young Omar, it simply meant the hot chocolate Reem gave them at breakfast and a dog he loved, though it had so many fleas Auntie gave it away to a friend who had a farm. Tunisia meant watching cartoons on television when the three older boys left Omar, the youngest, behind. They told him he couldn't come because they were going to help the dwarfs fight giants, battles in which they always claimed victory. In Tunisia Omar saw the way grown-ups spoke to his Baba, like his dad was a Jedi knight. Even the cracked dry soil of the garden produced watermelons from seeds planted by his father, another sign of his strength.

In Omar's eyes, Abu al-Abbas was a hero, like Robin Hood the fox in the animated Disney film he loved to watch, always having to hide from the sheriff. Tunisia was his Baba's refuge, his Forest of Nottingham.

Back in Beirut, Omar understood that here his father had to be kept a secret—not easy for a little boy who wanted to brag about his important dad.

One day in kindergarten the teacher went around the room asking the kids what their fathers did.

Omar listened as Mahmoud said his father was a dentist and Sara said her dad was a doctor.

What does your dad do, Omar?

I can't say.

What do you mean, you can't say?

Omar knew he wasn't supposed to tell anyone that his dad was a fighter, but he was bursting to say something. Everyone was looking at him. So, he made noises like a machine gun, pretending to hold an imaginary weapon in his hands.

They didn't understand. One kid thought the sputtering sounds indicated a jackhammer and asked him if his father was a "digger."

Omar felt compelled to try again.

"My dad," he said, "when Israelis see him, they say, 'Catch that guy!'"

I

A Week Earlier...

The Mediterranean Sea, October 7, 1985

The *Achille Lauro* had a tendency to tilt toward disaster.

A disturbing sign appeared at the very beginning, before the ship was even built. Known simply as Construction 214, the luxury vessel was going to be the pride of Rotterdam Lloyd, a major Dutch nautical line. The project began in 1939 but was delayed for years by Dutch workers resisting the German occupiers of Rotterdam during World War II. Finally launched in 1946, the ship was originally named for a martyr, the great-grandson of the company founder, Willem Ruys, who was taken hostage and killed by the Nazis in 1942. A few good years followed and then air travel sent the ocean liner business into a steep decline. In January 1965, the *Willem Ruys* was sold to Lauro Lines, a Neapolitan shipping company.

The Italians replaced the name on the ship's bow with *Achille Lauro*, after its new owner, a wealthy industrialist and political force in Naples. Nothing unusual about that, except there was something unseemly about replacing an homage to a victim of fascism with the name of a Mussolini supporter who remained committed to right-wing politics. Eight months after the exchange, in the midst of a major overhaul, the *Achille Lauro* experienced a massive explosion and fire. Once again, it survived.

During the next twenty years, the *Achille Lauro* endured business troubles, fires, collisions, and a brush or two with war. In 1982, the ship's namesake died at age ninety-five, leaving Lauro Lines heavily in debt; the company went bankrupt and the vessel was seized by creditors. Early in 1985, the *Achille Lauro*, repossessed by the Italian government, was leased for three years to Chandris Shipping Lines, a substantial Greek maritime company, which agreed to charter the ship for twenty cruises each year, all leaving from Genoa.

Advertising was pitched at people who wanted to indulge in the fantasy of unattainable luxury at affordable prices. Once on board, passengers were handed a glossy brochure, decorated with photographs of sexy men and women, written in giddy prose.

"Whilst at sea you will savour the delights of the gourmet's table—with no less than six meals daily," including a midnight buffet!

"Your only problem—a happy one—will be to choose from the extravagant array of tempting dishes!"

Captain Gerardo De Rosa was at the helm when the *Achille Lauro* left Genoa early Thursday evening, October 3, 1985. The ship docked in Naples the next day, and was then bound for ports in Egypt, Israel, Cyprus, and Greece, eleven days in all.

De Rosa was well qualified. A graduate of the Nautical Institute in Piano di Sorrento, a municipality of Naples, he'd worked his way up through the ranks from cabin boy, gaining experience on freight ships for the Lauro Lines. Now, at age fifty-one, after more than thirty years at sea, he was on his eighteenth outing as a cruise ship commander.

Captain De Rosa oversaw the complex technical and safety requirements of moving the massive vessel, which was 23,629 tons, 643 feet long (almost two soccer fields), and 82 feet high (eight stories). She was powered by eight diesel engines putting out 32,000 horsepower to twin propellers.

On a luxury liner, however, seafaring expertise was merely the baseline competency. The *Achille Lauro* was both tourist resort and cargo vessel because of the sheer amount of food, drink, and linens required to accommodate guests. A sampling of job descriptions for the 383-member staff and crew reflects these needs, a mix of quotidian and indulgent: engine room and deck hand, quartermaster, cabin boy, laundry worker and cook, as well as hairdresser, photographer, barber, hostess, barboy, and cocktail waitress.

For the 673 passengers, the captain had an additional, picturesque part to play. He had to fulfill the romantic notion inherent in this kind of travel, one that required him to wear a tuxedo as comfortably as a uniform, to embrace the packaged glamour with an aura of sincerity and flirtatious good humor.

Deeply tanned with large, expressive eyes and an engaging smile, Gerardo De Rosa was born to assume just such a role. Growing up in Gragnano, a hillside town in southern Italy advertised for its excellent pasta, De Rosa was such a charming, exuberant child his mother ironically dubbed him Tristone (Sad Sack), perhaps to ward off evil spirits. De Rosa appreciated the desire of passengers to briefly experience the fiction of a carefree childhood. He described the *Achille Lauro* as "this enormous plaything, this 'Land of Toys' where everything was imagined and reimagined continuously for comfort and for entertainment."

He claimed to enjoy watching and rewatching the ritual of discovery, as passengers explored the ship's labyrinthine byways, coming upon the swimming pools (heated, both indoor and outdoor), massage spa, boutiques, movie theater, beauty parlor, gymnasium, and nightclubs, where dancers, magicians, and singers performed every evening. He liked being part of the fantasy. "A passenger expects from a cruise everything that he has ever dreamed of and even something more," he would write, "not even he knows what, but we have to try to guess what it is, so that in the end the reality exceeds the expectation."

On Sunday evening, October 6, De Rosa prepared himself for the official onboard welcome ceremony, timed to allow passengers to settle in. The ship had already been in motion for three days, having made passage through the strong tidal currents of the Strait of Messina, the narrow strip of water separating Sicily and Calabria. They were now at open sea, heading across the Mediterranean toward Alexandria, Egypt, where passengers who chose could disembark the next morning for a day excursion by bus to Cairo and the Pyramids. They would reboard the ship that same evening at Port Said.

The captain always tried to shake hands with each and every passenger. After the handshakes, he mingled some more in the ornate Salon Arazzi (Tapestry Hall) on the Promenade Deck, the second highest on the ship, where guests sipped cocktails at tables set with red tablecloths and napkins. De Rosa sought to wish everyone an enjoyable cruise, introduce his top officers, and then open up the dancing, with "The Drinking Song" from *La Traviata*. It was corny yet effective. De Rosa never deviated from the script, repeating the ritual in Italian, French, English, and Spanish. There were almost two hundred Austrians, seventy-eight Germans, seventy-one Americans, and twenty British; the rest were mainly from South America, Italy and other European countries, plus two Israelis.

On this voyage, as always, De Rosa's enjoyment was tempered by the weight of responsibility. He knew that in a group of hundreds of people, it took only one unhappy, rude, or belligerent person to create a multiplying effect of dissatisfaction.

That evening he had been distracted briefly by one passenger moving through the receiving line, a middle-aged man with thick glasses and oddly showy clothes: shirt collar too big, an out-of-style necktie. De Rosa noticed this man had been watching him with unusual attention.

The man grasped the captain's outstretched hand in both of his, then turned the captain's palm upward, and mumbled a few words. De Rosa could understand only one, the word "Allah." In the moment, this didn't strike the captain as unusual. They were moving toward Islamic countries. When he pulled his hand away, De Rosa saw the man had deposited a gift in his palm: a *komboloi*, a string of Greek worry beads. The captain interpreted the beads as a prayer object, like a rosary, or maybe an expression of affection and friendship. He slipped the beads in his coat pocket without much thought; he often received business cards or notes from people during this moment of introduction. Though he didn't catch the man's name, he would not forget their meeting.

After an evening of socializing, De Rosa was tired. Back in his cabin, as he took off his jacket, he pulled the little chain he'd been given from his pocket. He glanced at the *komboloi*, then dropped it on his bedside table, along with his cigarettes and lighter.

Normally he had no trouble falling asleep. That night was different. He had been feeling uneasy all evening—not sick exactly but filled with dread. This was not an unfamiliar feeling. De Rosa had experienced this anxiety before, during long hours he'd spent on oil tankers and freighters, always when heartache was on the horizon. It was a feeling he had the night he learned his mother had died years before, in 1978, when he was crossing an ocean. He'd had the same emotion just a few months earlier, in February 1985, a premonition about Paolo, one of his brothers. He called home to Gragnano from a stop in Trinidad, something he had never done, to discover that Paolo had died, without warning.

These memories kept him awake. Finally, he left his bed to go up on the ship's bridge, directly above his quarters, to make sure everything was in order. He was reluctant to go back to bed, so he remained in the solitary comfort of the balmy autumn night until one of his sailors approached him to see if anything was wrong. Not wanting to explain himself, the restless captain returned to his cabin.

Back in bed, he smoked one cigarette after another; this usually put him to sleep. Nothing worked, not even Halcion, the insomnia medication he rarely took but did that night. The captain dozed off at 3 a.m. only to be awakened at 5:30 by a knock at the door. A waiter was there with his morning coffee. The ship was ready to begin the docking process at Alexandria.

A few minutes later De Rosa was on deck, waiting with his crew members for a pilot, someone familiar with the local seabed, to arrive from shore to guide the ship in. The captain usually liked to start the day with a joke, something to set a sociable mood, but that morning he was out of sorts, tired from lack of sleep and a nagging feeling of disquiet.

During the hour or two it took to dock in Alexandria, he found himself looking for the passenger who gave him the worry beads.

Instead, strolling on the bridge, he found a group of American passengers and began to talk to them. He had a fondness for Americans; his parents had lived in the United States for a few years before he was born; one of his brothers, born there, still lived in New York, on Long Island.

He was expecting a quiet day at sea. Most of the passengers, 600 out of 673, were scheduled to take the one-day land excursion to Cairo and the Pyramids. Once they were safely off the ship, the *Achille Lauro* would be on its way, headed for Port Said, about 150 miles east, at the mouth of the Suez Canal, where the day-trippers would arrive by bus that evening, in time to board the ship to spend the night. He watched a young couple exit; they left their children on the ship with their grandmothers. The ones who stayed behind tended to be old or very young, or not feeling well.

The exodus of sightseers began at 7:30. De Rosa stood by the railing and watched, making sure things went smoothly. There was always something to worry about. Would someone who had left the ship have an accident, or get lost, or be late for the boat when it left Port Said at the end of the day?

Shortly before the ship's scheduled ten o'clock departure from Alexandria, De Rosa noticed several police officers gathered on the pier. Then he caught sight of a beautiful young woman, someone he didn't recognize as a passenger, walking down the *Achille Lauro* gangplank, wearing a stylish black hat and a wraparound blue dress. De Rosa barely had time to absorb this elegant image, when a young man, also nattily dressed, darkly handsome, an Arab perhaps, came toward the woman, pulled out a pistol, and fired a shot. She collapsed.

Before De Rosa could react, the woman got up from the ground and began casually chatting with another man. The captain instantly understood this was a film shoot, probably a low-budget movie, because the group quickly left the area, as though escaping.

De Rosa noticed he was sharing this bizarre scene with someone else. A man the captain recognized had been watching down on the pier. Leon Klinghoffer, one of the Americans, was easy to remember because he was the only passenger on board in a wheelchair. Klinghoffer seemed annoyed that the filming was blocking him from getting back on the ship. The captain was about to offer help when someone began to push the wheelchair back aboard. De Rosa wondered if Klinghoffer had planned to take the excursion and then changed his mind, or if he just wanted to get off the ship for a while.

As the ship left the port, the uneasy feeling that had kept De Rosa awake the night before returned. This anxiety persisted even though he hadn't yet been informed about a passenger who had abruptly decided to leave the cruise altogether in Alexandria. One of the cruise managers had dealt with the matter; she reported later that the passenger seemed agitated and confused, first saying he had to leave because of an important business matter, then he had to leave because his wife was ill. The manager took care of it, made sure the appropriate releases were signed, and watched the man depart.

No one was alarmed. "There are always a few strange people aboard every ship," De Rosa observed.

When De Rosa was trying to put the pieces together later, he realized the passenger who fled the ship was the man who gave him the *komboloi* and invoked the name of Allah. De Rosa didn't know it yet, but this man had many names—Petros Flores was one, Khaled Abdul Rahim was another.

After a quick stroll around the deck, where the remaining passengers had begun to take their place on chaise longues on the sundeck, De Rosa returned to his cabin and stretched out on his bed. He tried to read a book but could not distract himself. When a waiter knocked on the door around noon, offering to bring him lunch, De Rosa declined. He remained on his bed, lost in his thoughts for almost an hour, until he was yanked out of his reveries by another, more insistent knock on the door.

Before De Rosa could respond, his second in command ran into the room. It was a quarter after one. "I know this with chronometric precision," the captain would recall.

"What's wrong?" De Rosa asked.

When he heard the answer—"There are terrorists on board"—the words didn't register.

De Rosa responded to his fellow Neapolitan in dialect: "Giovanni, what the fuck are you saying?!"

It took a fraction of a second to realize this was not a joke.

He and Giovanni quickly went to the bridge, where other crew members were waiting.

The captain saw the crew members' instincts were to fight. Someone said they should bring out the rifles kept on board for passengers to use for trap shooting; an officer moved his hand toward the pistol he always carried.

"Do not touch the pistol," the captain told him sharply. He ordered the crew to bring the hunting rifles to him for safekeeping. He did not want to get into a gunfight with terrorists, whose weapons were almost certainly deadlier.

He and his first officer left the bridge to see what was happening on their ship. They walked past the swimming pools, then headed downstairs, from the highest point of the ship to the lowest floor.

As they got closer to the dining room, instead of hearing the normal buzz of the lunchtime crowd, there was an eerie silence. As they walked in they saw shattered glass, scattered chairs, some handbags strewn about, and a group of passengers huddled in the corner, a pair of men holding them at gunpoint. In the distance, he heard what he believed was the muffled sound of distant gunfire.

Before De Rosa could fully take in the scene, he heard an agitated voice over the loudspeaker calling urgently:

"Captain…the captain must report immediately to the bridge."

Together with his first officer, De Rosa made his way back up to the navigation room, opened the door, and found the barrel of an AK-47 pointing directly at his face.

The man holding the assault rifle was Bassam al-Ashker. At age seventeen, he was technically not yet an adult, but the weapon in his hand gave him all the authority he needed.

His journey to the *Achille Lauro* began years before his birth, after the Israeli victory in the 1948 War, when his mother and father fled their village near Zefat (also known as Safed), an ancient town near the Lebanese border that became a refuge for Jewish mystics in the sixteenth and seventeenth centuries. Ashker was born in 1968 in northern Lebanon, in a refugee camp called Nahr El Bared, under the rule of the Palestine Liberation Organization's Fatah movement, which gained power much the way Hamas would a generation later, by distributing food, running schools, providing health care. Fatah mixed business and politics, overseeing production of ceramic tiles and wood carvings decorated with the map of the country its followers called Palestine. The women in the camp embroidered kaffiyehs, the traditional checkered black-and-white scarf that became the signature of PLO chairman Yasser Arafat.

Raised in a three-room house made of stone and clay, with no running water, Ashker grew up hearing stories from his mother and father and grandfather, who had been a Thoroughbred horse breeder, about the beautiful land left behind, the bountiful life that came to an end with bombs dropped from Israeli planes, their homes mowed down by Israeli tanks. Ashker refused to say "Israeli" or "Israel," referring to the new occupants as Zionists, and the country as Palestine, and the ongoing war as the Palestinian-Zionist conflict. He was ready to die for Palestine, a country where he had never lived and that didn't officially exist.

At six he went to classes in the school built by the United Nations, operated jointly with the PLO, eager to join the older children called lion cubs, or little combatants, by teachers who taught them the usual subjects as well as how to handle an assault rifle. Classes were crowded—fifty or sixty students per room. The rumble of fighter jets was a familiar sound; the curriculum included training in what to do if they were bombed.

Though Ashker loved Lebanon, his adopted home, he yearned for *al-watan*, the homeland he had never known. "The first thing I learned was to fight to survive," he would explain.

Lebanon had historically been a cosmopolitan country, its culture a reflection of invaders who had tried to make it theirs: Phoenicians, Ottomans, Syrians, Greeks, Romans, French, Assyrians, and Arabs. The Lebanese learned to survive by adapting, and Lebanon became known in the West as the Switzerland of the Middle East because of its powerful, discreet banks. Beirut was a glamorous international capital, often described as a regional Paris. Ashker experienced Lebanon as a landscape of wreckage, since it had been bombed repeatedly in a sectarian conflict fueled by forces from both outside and inside the country.

The Lebanese civil war began in 1975, when Ashker was seven, and wouldn't end until 1990. In the simplistic version, this complex struggle was a battle between Lebanese Christians and Lebanese Muslims. But like almost every conflict in the postcolonial Middle East, this so-called civil war involved a stew of operatives from within and abroad, seasoned by historic grievances and ongoing misunderstandings, fueled by religious intolerance, power lust, and greed. The cast of players, overt and covert, reflected Lebanon's strategic location, bordered by the Mediterranean Sea on the west, Israel on the south, and Syria on the north and east. Every battle waged in Lebanon was monitored in the United States and the Soviet Union for its effect on the Cold War of the megapowers. Similarly, Lebanon was caught in the proxy war for control of the Middle East between Iran's Shia Muslims and the Sunnis of Saudi Arabia; Iran gained the upper hand in Lebanon with the establishment in 1982 of Hezbollah, a militant Shia group. Israel, defending its northern border, became a full-fledged and open combatant in Lebanon's internal war that year, invading Lebanon after a series of border fights between the PLO and the Israel Defense Forces (IDF).

The Palestinians had become everyone's pawn. After 1948, an estimated four hundred thousand Arabs fled from Israel to Lebanon, eventually making up 10 percent of the population. But Lebanon didn't embrace the refugees. Those without money or outside connections were forced to live apart in camps, denied citizenship, allowed to work in only selected occupations, and restricted from rights granted to other foreign workers who held passports from other countries.

Their subjugation became a potent political weapon. Tensions were exacerbated by the events of Black September in 1970, when PLO fighters were driven from Jordan, establishing a new headquarters in Lebanon, which they used as a base to strike at Israel and where they became further embroiled in the Lebanese civil strife, eventually playing a pivotal role in the conflict.

Ashker had watched Marwan, his closest boyhood friend, transformed from a happy child to a fighter obsessed with avenging the deaths of his mother and brother, killed by Israeli soldiers during a raid. By age nine, Ashker had learned how to handle a weapon; at fourteen he qualified as a *fedai*, a commando devoted to his childhood hero Yasser Arafat, the PLO leader he affectionately called Abu Ammar or Al Khitiar (the Old Man). In the West, Arafat had become known as a canny media manipulator, master of what would become known as "television terrorism." Only five feet two inches tall, an ascetic who didn't drink or smoke and barely slept, his head covered by his kaffiyeh, Arafat became the stubbled face of the PLO, the anti-Zionist organization founded by the Arab League in 1964 as a unifying structure for several Palestinian nationalist movements. He galvanized Palestinian anger and, through control of the purse strings, canny infighting, and personal charisma, emerged as the leader to be reckoned with. Arafat gave Palestinians a voice on the international stage; he was also a terrorist responsible for the 1972 massacre of Israeli athletes at the Munich Olympics, a revolutionary who made an appeal for Palestinian statehood to the United Nations in 1974 wearing a holster, a world figure who would win a Nobel Prize for the Oslo Peace Accords in 1994—and finally, a failure, unable to deliver statehood or peaceful coexistence to his people.

Arafat visited Nahr El Bared many times. "Abu Ammar... represented everything: the revolution, the fight, the hope in that victory that I thought sooner or later would arrive," Ashker would recall. "When the Zionists attacked the camp and the *fedayeen* responded to the fire we'd never say it was the combatants who faced the enemy, but that Abu Ammar faced the enemy." Palestinian liberation became a zero-sum game, one that entailed the destruction of the Jewish state.

In Lebanon, the fervent rhetoric of Arafat and the PLO proved more muscular than their military might; the PLO resistance crumpled when confronted by the Israeli invasion in June 1982; by late summer, led by Arafat, Palestinian fighters became part of yet another exodus as some sixty-five hundred Palestinians made their way to Tunisia, Yemen, Syria, Sudan, and Iraq.

Fourteen-year-old Ashker found himself on a boat to Yemen, where he befriended another teenager, three years older, named Abdellatif Ibrahim Fataier. They passed the time telling each other their stories. Fataier, too, was raised in a refugee camp. He said his father had been killed by Zionists; his mother urged him not to be filled with hatred, assuring him that over time they would return to their homeland.

Ashker remembered Fataier saying that after repeated incursions into the camp by Israeli soldiers, "I forgot the words of my mother and the blindest hate filled me."

His words fell on receptive ears. When Ashker learned, a month after he left Lebanon, of the brutal massacres at the Sabra and Shatila refugee camps carried out by the Lebanese Christian militia and condoned by their allies the IDF, his own hatred deepened.

In Yemen, the Palestinians were greeted as heroes and taken to a training camp in the middle of the desert. It was a difficult period for Ashker. He and the other *fedayeen* would be called on to participate in various military operations and become part of a special unit where the most secret aims of the PLO were discussed.

In the aftermath of the expulsion from Lebanon, there was increasing dissent between the PLO and the Palestinian Liberation Front (PLF), a more militant offshoot that was itself subdivided into three factions. Only one PLF group remained allied with Arafat. Its leader was Abu al-Abbas, also known as Mohammed al-Abbas, Mohammed Zaidan, and Abu Khaled. In 1984 Ashker joined the PLF, disappointed by Arafat's professed willingness to negotiate with Israel, believing at age sixteen that he had found his destiny with this more combative group. He let his superiors know he was ready to take part in a suicide mission, preferably in Palestine.

In August 1985, he was handed an envelope containing a passport and a plane ticket to Algeria. A commander there told Ashker that if he truly felt ready to make the ultimate sacrifice, Abu al-Abbas wanted to meet him in person.

Ashker remembered being led into a building guarded by PLF soldiers. He was taken to an office, where he found, sitting at a desk reading papers, a bulky, imposing man with thick dark hair and mustache, and probing eyes. When Abu al-Abbas realized that Ashker was in front of him, the PLF leader approached the youth and embraced him, then asked him to sit next to him.

Even those who declared him an enemy acknowledged that Abbas had charisma. He was a military man who could hug his young martyrs with genuine affection before calmly sending them to their bloody end. Abbas was self-made, the son of Palestinians who lived near Haifa and were expelled from their home in 1948 after Arabs declared war on the new state of Israel, while his mother was pregnant with him. He was born and raised in Syrian refugee camps, where his mother died when he was eleven. Intelligent and motivated, Abbas studied Arabic and English literature at the University of Damascus; after graduating he briefly became a teacher but was soon drawn into the martial life. A chain-smoking worldly Muslim, who occasionally drank a glass of wine and loved his family and his dog, he enjoyed reading Western and Arabic poetry and philosophy, as well as watching the occasional Hollywood movie, yet was fated by history and inclination to the life of an insurgent, a fugitive, and a fighter.

When he traveled through Palestinian military camps, people flocked to Abbas, asking favors, seeking advice. His youngest son, Ali, a movie buff, would compare his father to Marlon Brando in Francis Ford Coppola's *The Godfather*, in the way he was respected, feared, needed, and venerated by his people.

In Israel, Abbas was denounced as a ruthless terrorist, the leader who in 1979 sent commandos on a midnight raid to Nahariyya, a seaside town that lay six miles south of the Lebanon border, via rubber boats that landed on the beach. The Palestinians killed a policeman, then entered an apartment building two blocks from the oceanfront around midnight, setting off grenades. They captured an Israeli man as he was taking his four-year-old daughter to a shelter and killed them both on the beach; the little girl's head was crushed from being repeatedly bashed against a rock. A second daughter, age two, suffocated to death as her mother tried to prevent the child from crying out and giving away their hiding spot. The Palestinians were arrested and remained in jail, including Samir Kuntar, a sixteen-year-old assigned by Abbas to lead this horrendous mission.

Now Abbas was enlisting another teenager for another perilous attempt to infiltrate Israel from the sea. He asked Ashker about his training and urged him to say no to the mission if he wanted. It was his choice—Abbas made that clear. When Ashker assured the commander that he was prepared for the consequences, Abbas gave him his orders, which were deliberately vague, in case he was caught: Ashker was to go to a European country and study the language so he could use a European passport without raising suspicions.

"Our men are studying new ways to get into Palestine without having to infiltrate neighboring countries that now are serving as policemen to the Zionists," Abbas explained. He told Ashker that he would receive further instructions later.

Abbas invited Ashker to stay for lunch. They talked about many things, including politics. Ashker left the meeting feeling inspired. At the airport, one of Abbas's men handed him an envelope. Inside Ashker found a passport, some money, and a plane ticket to Italy. The passport said he was thirty-six, more than twice his actual age, but he sailed through customs.

"The first days in Rome were very confusing," he remembered. "I had just left the training camps in the desert and I had ended up in the chaotic worldliness of a Western capital without knowing anyone or a word of the language. And yet I had to act like one of many tourists. It was not easy; in my whole life I had never been a tourist."

There were many false starts, as Ashker tried to follow the vague, complicated plan. He met the others selected for the mission, who included his friend Abdellatif Fataier, the young man he had met on the boat to Yemen, now twenty years old. There were three others: twenty-three-year old Ahmad Maruf al-Assadi, nicknamed Omar; the designated leader, Youssef Majid al-Molqi, twenty-three; and one more, a guy Ashker knew only as Jarbua. Ashker recognized Molqi from the PLO camp in Algiers but didn't know him. He also met several older men in Rome, who brought them clothes and cash and gave them the latest instructions, involving a dense, seemingly chaotic web of movements and travel throughout Italy.

The five traveled separately to Pisa, Isola d'Elba, back to Rome, and stayed in assigned hotels and camping sites, calling one another on pay phones, always awaiting further instructions. They were kept in the dark about what, exactly, was happening.

"I felt moments of great despair," Ashker would recall. "It seemed that ten years would not have been enough to learn Italian. Often to understand others or to be understood I had to express myself in English, a language I studied in school and in the training camps. But in doing so, I delayed learning Italian. In the two months I was there I learned very few words."

On October 1, 1985, still in Italy, awaiting yet another instruction, Ashker received a call from his commander alerting him that PLO headquarters in Hamman Chott, a seaside town just outside Tunis, had been bombed by the Israeli Air Force, in retaliation for the murder of three Israeli civilians on a yacht anchored off the coast of Cyprus. The Israelis estimated casualties at Hamman Chott at thirty to fifty; the PLO said seventy-three people were killed, of whom sixty were civilians.

"I felt an enormous rage," Ashker said. "I felt my blood boil over in my veins."

Then he received a message in code, telling him to go immediately to Genoa, where he reunited with the other four recruits and a commander. The commander told them Abu al-Abbas wanted to meet them individually before they left, but he couldn't make it. Instead, Abbas gave them their orders in a letter through this surrogate.

There would be many different recollections of what those orders were, and when they were given. Ashker himself would change the details over time, as people do, though those accused of a crime have a special motivation to remember things a certain way. Ashker remembered Abbas informing them that they would be leaving on a cruise ship the next day, October 3. Their objective was the port of Ashdod, Israel, twenty-five miles south of Tel Aviv, with the aim of "killing the greatest possible number of Zionists." Abbas said the attack would avenge the October 1 killings at Tunis.

In one version of the story, Ashker remembered the letter instructing, improbably, that if they survived the attack on Ashdod, they were to get back on the ship, take the American, British, and Israeli passengers hostage, and demand the release of fifty Palestinians held in Israeli prisons, among them Samir Kuntar, the teenager who led the failed mission to infiltrate Israel by boat and was responsible for the murder of Israeli children.

Ashker vowed to himself that he would not get back on the ship no matter what. For him, it was an honor to die on the soil of his homeland.

The commander more or less apologized for the rush. He said Abbas intended to give them a year to learn Italian, so they could travel on this Italian ship without notice. "The attack in Tunis though changed everything," he said. "You will be leaving immediately.... We have no choice."

He asked them again if they wanted to drop out. This time one of them did, the young man called Jarbua. Now this formidable mission was in the hands of four, not five, fighters, whose zeal far outstripped their experience.

The commander gave them precise instructions for the mission, pinpointing the true beginning not at Genoa, where they had boarded, but at Port Said, the docking point before Ashdod. He said that passengers who had gotten off in Alexandria to tour the Pyramids would take a bus to Port Said, where they would reboard the boat. There had been several scouting trips over the past year—Molqi, their assigned leader, had been on one of them. They knew that six Mossad agents regularly got on board at Port Said, with the permission of Egyptian authorities, to give the ship a thorough security check. They were adept at finding hidden weapons, the commander said. He urged the group that when they reached Port Said, they should keep the bags holding their weapons with them at all times, even when they left their cabin for meals.

When they arrived in Ashdod, he said, all the passengers would be on the ship, including those who had taken the Pyramids tour. When they began to disembark for a planned day of touring in Israel, he said, that was the moment to strike.

"Each of you will have a Kalashnikov and a hand grenade," the commander told them. "The machine gun, loaded and charged, will be kept hidden in your bag. One of the hand grenades should be kept armed and ready in your left hand."

If there were metal detectors that went off, the commander said, they were to kill as many people as they could, but try to avoid shooting passengers, though how they were to make this distinction in battle conditions was unclear. In this version, Ashker remembered the commander telling them that if they themselves survived, they should also capture as many Zionist soldiers as possible as hostages, take them onto a vessel of any kind, and head toward Syria.

He showed them pictures of the port that had been taken on previous reconnaissance trips aboard the *Achille Lauro*, the ship that would be transporting them.

Before he left, the commander promised he would take care of their families if they died during the mission, a likely outcome, given the ambition and lack of specificity of their marching orders.

Then they went shopping.

Ashker bought two pairs of pants, one black and one white, a white shirt and a checkered one, a green jacket and a blue. He bought a striped tie and two pairs of shoes. That evening, in the hotel, Ashker put on a fashion show for Fataier, trying on the new "touristic" clothes in front of the mirror. As he tried on the outfits, Fataier said to him, "You know, I think it's a pity to die in clothes so beautiful."

Ashker agreed. "It had been a waste to spend a bunch of money," he recalled.

They tried to cheer each other up, but Ashker couldn't stop thinking about his mother, and the grief his death would cause her. He remembered her tenderness and her desire for him to study and become a doctor.

That evening, October 2, Abu al-Abbas called them to wish them luck. He told them their family of Palestine would be there to await their return as heroes, which was irrelevant to Ashker, who did not expect to survive the mission.

The following day, the day of the departure, Ashker and Fataier got their hair cut. "We wanted to look like real tourists, orderly and elegant," he remembered. "The others, too, made themselves look right." At noon they all met and went to a restaurant for lunch with the commander. By then, Ashker said, it felt like they were "a group of old friends."

At the end of the lunch, the commander distributed the tickets for the cruise, money, and their passports—two Argentinian, one Portuguese, and one Norwegian. Ashker's name was now Antonio Alonso, born in Buenos Aires in 1965. At least the birth date was in the ballpark this time, just three years off. A few hours later, in the taxi on the way to the port, he looked at the passport again, and had the stray thought that he didn't speak a word of Spanish.

"But it did not matter to me," he recalled. "From that moment on there was only one thing that mattered, and that was Ashdod. Everything—my brain, my feet, everything—was geared to take me to Ashdod. I was born to die in the port of Ashdod."

He and the others boarded the ship in Genoa without incident, their weapons hidden in carry-on bags. They became increasingly anxious over the next few hours, as they realized how little prepared they were for cruise ship rituals. They may have known how to shoot an AK-47 but were baffled by the assigned tables in the dining room. If the situation weren't so dire, the stakes so high, their initiation might have seemed like a comedy routine. They felt conspicuous, being younger than most of the other passengers, and worried that surely someone would notice that they had classic Arab features.

That first evening, right after leaving Genoa, when a friendly young female hostess tried to help them find their table, checking the names on their passports, she began chatting in what must have been Norwegian to Fataier, who was carrying the Norwegian document. Alarmed, he just walked away.

Unnerving incidents continued to happen. Some Portuguese waiters began talking to them in Portuguese; apparently someone had told them one of the four carried a Portuguese passport. The Palestinians wondered: Were the waiters just being friendly or were they suspicious? Either way, none of the four spoke a word of Portuguese. By the second day, they stopped going to the dining room for fear of running into someone whose language they were supposed to speak but did not. In Naples, they left the ship to shop for food, which they kept in their cabin.

Ashker and the others felt certain their aloofness was attracting attention. The four of them discussed throwing their weapons into the sea and getting off at the next port, then decided that they couldn't bear the shame of abandoning the mission.

Ashker found Omar al-Assadi particularly troublesome. He had been tense from the beginning, even before they got on the boat. Ashker was worried that Omar's nervousness would betray them, a concern shared by Fataier. The fear of being discovered became overwhelming. They began carrying hand grenades in their pockets when they did venture out of the cabin. When they heard gunfire, they almost ran out guns blazing, only to discover that some passengers were shooting clay pigeons for sport. Once again, they discussed getting rid of their weapons and getting off the ship when they docked in Alexandria.

Their nerves were further frayed when, as they drew closer to port, they heard calls in Arabic, saying "Get off the ship." Was this an invitation to surrender? They took their weapons out of their bags, prepared to attack anyone who came for them. Then Ashker ventured out on deck and saw Egyptian workers disembarking, and realized the call was for them, not for him and his companions. When he returned to the cabin, they stuffed their weapons back in their suitcases. One zipper broke and the bag wouldn't stay closed. They jammed it between the closet and the bed, so it couldn't be opened.

They were in this panicky state when someone from the cleaning crew came into the cabin they shared. Ashker and the others decided these people kept showing up because they were suspicious of them, not understanding that it was probably quite normal to have someone regularly clean the cabin, bring fresh towels, make the bed. When the cleaner picked up the suitcase jammed between the closet and the bed, the assault rifle's muzzle popped up from between the clothes covering it. The cabin boy mumbled something and left, and the group felt certain they'd been discovered.

They closed the door and began an urgent strategy session. It was in that overwrought state, Ashker would insist, that they made the decision to hijack the ship and ask the captain to take them to a friendly Arab state that would give them asylum.

They grabbed their weapons and left the cabin, trying to find the command deck. They went in circles around the ship and ended up in front of the dining hall, which was full of passengers having lunch.

"We were perhaps more surprised than they were," recalled Ashker.

Seeing the guns, some passengers began to scream and run, and then the Palestinians fired shots in the air. Everything went quiet. Leaving Fataier and Assadi to watch the passengers, Ashker and Molqi went to find the captain.

Now they were standing face-to-face.

A few yards behind Ashker, Molqi stood in the doorway between the navigation room and the wheelhouse, pointing a gun at the first officer.

It struck De Rosa, even in the midst of his shock, that the young men looked like an image lifted from a magazine cover: picture-perfect terrorists, wearing tank tops, jeans, and sneakers, guns slung over their shoulders.

They conferred in Arabic and then Ashker told the captain, "We don't have a problem with Italians."

Ashker, speaking in passable English, added that if the captain or crew made a single wrong move they would be killed. Ashker assured De Rosa that he and his men were prepared to die. The captain heard the young man warn him that if they did not obey, the ship would be blown into the air with everyone on board. Ashker said more than twenty fighters were scattered around the ship.

The captain and others were herded back to the restaurant—a trek that seemed endless, walking down stairs, across one deck, down another staircase, across another hall. The group moved in silence.

This time De Rosa registered the shocking sight. What he had glimpsed before sank in: the upended tables, the broken glass, the chairs flung all over. He saw blood on the floor, from a sailor wounded in the leg. Ashker allowed the Italians to call the ship's doctor, and then agreed to let the crew member be taken to the infirmary.

As De Rosa looked around, he felt he was in a hell pit, a circle from Dante's *Inferno:* one of the Palestinians was standing on a table waving his AK-47 back and forth menacingly. By this time adults were crying and yelling, small children were screaming; he remembered the young couple who had gone on the excursion, leaving their children on the boat with their two grandmothers, one paternal and one maternal.

At that moment, De Rosa was most worried about his crew. Many of them were Neapolitans, romantic, hotheads, he knew well. He spoke sternly to them—again in dialect, so they would understand him fully: No false heroics. Don't get any ideas, he told them. Don't even sneeze.

The Palestinians ordered De Rosa to help move the passengers and crew to the Salon Arazzi on an upper deck, closer to the command center of the ship, a place easier for them to control. In a haunting reprise of the welcome reception, just the evening before, De Rosa addressed the passengers in one language after another, but now he issued a warning: "Do not move, obey orders, do not attempt any act of rebellion."

The transfer was surprisingly orderly; terrified people tend to do what they are told. More than four hundred people—seventy-three passengers, the rest staff and crew—sat on the floor in silence, broken only by a shiver of fear that spread throughout the room when Ashker yelled at the captain in English, telling him to order the crew to bring tanks of gasoline in the hall.

As De Rosa looked at the souls in front of him, he realized that the terrorists had everyone on the ship under their control. He was no longer in command, yet he hadn't relinquished his duty to the crew and passengers who depended on him. Responsibility without power was a sickening combination, a condition he hadn't anticipated and for which he hadn't been trained.

Ashker took the captain back up to the bridge, leaving the other hijackers to deal with the passengers. "I will do exactly as you say, don't worry," De Rosa assured Ashker.

The captain saw the young man's expression change to anger.

"You should be worried, not us," Ashker said, sharply. "We are ready to die; you are the ones who want to live."

De Rosa apologized, explaining that "don't worry" was just an expression. He understood that language itself held an explosive charge when the person talking had everything to lose and the one listening was so despairing he felt he had nothing to lose at all. A misspoken word could ruin everything.

As De Rosa looked at Ashker and the menacing AK-47, it sank in again that this hallucination was terribly real. So, the captain obeyed when Ashker made radio contact with Port Said and told De Rosa to confirm that the *Achille Lauro* had been hijacked. He complied when the seventeen-year-old hijacker ordered him to change the ship's destination from Port Said to Tartus, a coastal city in Syria.

A short time later, De Rosa transmitted a new message, in English, that Ashker wrote for him on a piece of paper: Palestinians had hijacked the ship in order to secure the release of fifty prisoners in Israel, including Samir Kuntar, "the great man of Nahariyya," a reference to the sixteen-year-old leader of the raid in which the four-year-old girl and her father were brutally slain.

Then, as instructed, De Rosa turned the radio off. It was six in the afternoon, October 7, 1985, less than five hours after he had been awakened from his nap.

2

The Ones Waiting Back Home

New York City

As the *Achille Lauro* sailed toward Tartus on October 7, 1985, Ilsa Klinghoffer was settling into her Monday morning routine in New York City, seven hours behind the eastern Mediterranean time zone.

She had a general sense of well-being that fall, a vision for how the contours of her life might be filled in. She was twenty-eight years old and still lived with her parents, but now—finally—she was more than ready to create her own home.

It wasn't as if she hadn't tried to leave before, the way her friends had. Upon graduating from Boston University in 1978, she planned to stay in Boston—to begin her life as an adult, to be independent, to see what it felt like to rely on herself and no one else.

Then her father had the second stroke. Ilsa had been only eight years old when Leon, then forty-nine, was laying a new floor in their kitchen and had the first stroke, from which he recovered almost completely. The second one, thirteen years later, was different. This time Leon was immobilized. Even after intensive therapy and biofeedback, it became clear that he would no longer dance with his wife, Marilyn, hang shelves for his daughters, or be able to run his appliance manufacturing business the way he was accustomed to, though he continued to go to work almost every day. This supremely physical being was trapped in a wheelchair, unable to walk more than a few steps, and only with the help of a cane. Leon had never been much of a talker; now he could barely communicate at all, either unable to get words out or saying something that didn't make sense, like "Pass the tree" instead of "Pass the ketchup." He would become so frustrated he would simply point, rather than confront his inability to speak.

Burdened by her own overdeveloped sense of responsibility fed by love for her parents, Ilsa returned to New York. She moved back into her family's apartment in Greenwich Village and applied to the master's program in public service at New York University.

A couple of years passed, and she was still in graduate school and still living at home with her parents. Her situation depressed her. She felt trapped in childhood. When she told her parents that she wanted to move out, they were perplexed. "Why would you want to do that?" they asked. "Our apartment is large, and we are gone almost every weekend." They had bought a modest condominium on the Jersey Shore a decade earlier, when Ilsa left for college; there they had developed a large network of friends whom Ilsa and Lisa, her older sister, affectionately referred to as the Beach People.

Their parents loved the sea. When Lisa and Ilsa came to visit them at the condo, Marilyn would walk them across the road to the Atlantic shoreline. Gazing at the water, Marilyn waved her hands, as though she were lighting the Sabbath candles. "Girls, breathe in the sea air," she said every time. "Breathe it in."

Wearing a brace around his foot, Leon could make his way to the sand without the wheelchair, descending the stairs from the boardwalk by gripping the railing. In the evening, he and Marilyn had a little sunset happy hour on the beach, sipping cocktails with their friends as they gazed at the dramatic horizon, the ocean glowing in the fading light. It became a hallowed place, where they could pretend that things were the way they had always been.

The beach became the latest chapter in Marilyn and Leon's great romance. Their family legend began with the story of how the first time he saw her she took his breath away No surprise: Marilyn was noticeable. It didn't matter that she was tiny—five feet tall, with a size five shoe. In photos of her as a young woman, she seemed to know how sexy she looked staring into the camera with a cigarette hanging off her lower lip, a provocative premature silver streak in her dark hair. She was ten years younger than Leon. He had been married before, briefly—the marriage annulled within a year. But she was more sophisticated and every bit as tough as he was, though her iron core was wrapped in a softer substance than his. In those old photos, Leon still had a head of thick, curly hair. He wasn't tall either, but he was muscular, unafraid to get his hands dirty, a Mr. Fix-It. After he and Marilyn married, she kept a special soap dispenser in the bathroom with a strong solvent to remove the grease that was always on his fingers.

Leon's story was a familiar New York Jewish narrative: a Lower East Side childhood, five kids squeezed into a tiny apartment behind the family hardware store. Pinkas Klinghoffer, their father, known as Papa Peter to Leon's friends, died in 1929, probably of heart disease, when Leon was thirteen. After that, when he wasn't in school, Leon was working at the store, along with his mother, Lena, and the rest of his siblings. Marilyn was a college graduate, with a degree from Philadelphia's Drexel School of Business Administration. She grew up more prosperously, in a New Jersey suburb, the daughter of a haberdasher. But she, too, had a direct line to hardship. Her mother, Rose, was an infant when Marilyn's grandparents immigrated to the United States from Odessa, Russia. Marilyn was raised on the story of that saga, how Rose got sick on the voyage and almost died on the way to America.

Leon and Marilyn married in 1949 and Lisa arrived in 1951, then Ilsa six years later. The sisters spent their early years living on the Lower East Side, right across from the Klinghoffer Supply Company.

Leon and his brother Albert operated on impulse and bravado, dreaming and inventing new products that could take them beyond the family hardware store. Their business wound up in Chapter 11 bankruptcy on more than one occasion. In 1955, one of their inventions paid off. The Roto-Broil 400 was a hit! Thirty years later, a *New York Times* food columnist would describe the appliance: "What's a Roto-Broil, you might ask? Only the ultimate modern kitchen appliance of the 1950s. Dubbing itself 'the electric kitchen,' this snazzy chrome countertop contraption promised to facilitate cooking everything from a healthy breakfast to an elaborate dinner party roast. (For 'healthy,' read 'cholesterol-inducing and high-calorie.')"

Despite the nonstarters and occasional fiascoes, and notwithstanding the arguments between Leon and Albert, the Klinghoffers prospered. The notoriety and commercial success of the Roto-Broil 400 had changed the family fortunes. Leon and Marilyn moved with their girls into Stewart House on East Tenth Street, a gleaming white-brick apartment building constructed in 1960 on the site of the old Wanamaker Department Store in Greenwich Village. Stewart House exuded a sense of prosperity, with uniformed doormen, a circular drive, and a sleek, futuristic lobby.

Ilsa loved that building and she loved her parents, but she needed to separate—if for no other reason than to convince herself that she was an adult. On December 8, 1980, she moved into a studio apartment she subleased from a friend, just a few blocks away, near Gramercy Park. The sublet was cramped and had thin walls. Ilsa spent every night listening to her neighbor, a teacher named Rhoda, sobbing into the telephone.

At the end of the year, when her sublease was up, Ilsa decided her experiment at independence had failed. It was silly to waste the money. She moved back in with her parents, still not happy but at least she had a chance to save some money.

Being single bothered her. She wasn't thinking about having children; she'd received her master's degree in 1980 and was absorbed in her career as a health care administrator. She just wanted somebody.

Her older sister, Lisa, met her husband when they were still in college. How many times had Ilsa heard their meet-cute story! Ilsa was only in middle school at the time and had lived through it. Lisa was home on winter break from the Tyler School of Art at Temple University, the middle of her sophomore year. A friend of hers from art school named Sid came to New York with a friend of his, a skinny, long-haired guy named Jerry, who was wearing aviator glasses and a long overcoat. The young men stopped by the Klinghoffer apartment. Lisa barely remembered their conversation; Jerry Arbittier always said he remembered every word. He had never met a girl like her, who knew so much about art and theater and who shared his passion for Barbra Streisand.

Though he was from outside of Philadelphia, with Lisa he felt like a rube. His father, a wholesale food broker and a gambler, had dropped out of school in sixth or seventh grade. Jerry liked to compare his up-bringing to the popular 1970s television show *All in the Family*, with his father cast as Archie Bunker, the lovable conservative, and he, Jerry, as Meathead, Archie's long-haired, liberal son-in-law. Jerry had come to New York with Sid just to get out of the house.

Back at Temple University, Jerry wrote Lisa a letter, inviting her to two concerts—one with Carole King and James Taylor, the other with Joan Baez. It was 1971.

The families were different but also similar. They were Jewish, and Jerry's father was an adventurer like Leon, an entrepreneur who wasn't afraid of losing big. As Marilyn had been doing for Leon for many years, Jerry's mother managed his father's business.

When Lisa left for a year abroad in Rome that fall, Jerry wrote to her every day. Baffled by the onslaught, she wrote to him once every two weeks. She was relatively innocent. There had been dates and a few short-lived boyfriends, but no one had pursued her in the way Jerry did. It was flattering and confounding. During that winter break, Jerry and Sid went to Europe and the three of them traveled around together on Eurail passes. When Lisa returned from Italy in the spring, about to start her senior year, Jerry proposed. A year later they married.

Ilsa was sixteen at the time. Jerry quickly became like a brother, as well as the son her father always wanted. Jerry and Lisa lived in a cheap apartment on Grand Street; most of their friends were artists. But they had keys to the Klinghoffer apartment and visited all the time. When Lisa and Jerry quarreled, and Jerry took off for Philadelphia in a huff, Leon drove down to bring him home. Ilsa assumed someone would cross her path the way Jerry had found Lisa.

Despite the six-year age gap, the sisters were unusually close, and there was the weird similarity of their names. (Leon wanted to name a son after his father, Peter, so much that he and Marilyn didn't even consider girl names. Marilyn's father, named Isador, died when she was pregnant with Ilsa, so her name became an homage to both her grandfathers—Ilsa for Isador and the middle name of Peta, after Peter Klinghoffer.) Yet there was no reason to think the two would find romance in the same way. They were very different from each other. Ilsa was left-brain—logical and methodical. Lisa was right-brain, an art school graduate struggling to succeed as a painter.

Ilsa's introduction to Paul Dworin wasn't quite a fairy tale meeting, but it was good enough. A friend had invited her to a holiday party, celebrating Christmas of 1984. Ilsa didn't want to go. She was sick. Her friend was gay; she figured there wouldn't be any men there for her. But her mother wasn't interested in excuses. Though Marilyn never pushed Ilsa toward marriage, she saw her daughter was unhappy. "Just go," she said. "If you're not having fun you can take a cab home."

The host's boss was there. He was five years older than Ilsa, divorced, a journalist, relatively new to the city. Like Ilsa, he was sick, so sick he had skipped a business trip he was supposed to be on. He had come to the party grudgingly, just to make an appearance.

Early in the summer of 1985, Paul and Ilsa were engaged. She and her mother began talking about where they should have the wedding, though her mother was preoccupied planning a trip she was taking in October with Leon and their friends from the beach. Marilyn had been studying brochures from luxury ocean liners, making sure the doors were wide enough to allow Leon's wheelchair to glide through. Finally, she found the perfect candidate. It wasn't the newest vessel, or the most elegant, but it was accessible.

Ilsa was delighted they felt able to go. Her mother had spent the past year undergoing treatment for colon cancer. She had reassured her daughters that the experimental therapy had been effective. The cancer was in remission, she told them, so there was much to celebrate—including her fifty-ninth birthday on October 6.

On October 7, 1985, Ilsa walked home from work as usual. She stopped at a deli to pick up something for dinner. As she stood by the cashier, she heard a news report on the radio.

The words didn't fully penetrate, just enough for fear to grab her in a menacing clutch. "Hijacking," she heard. "*Achille Lauro.*"

That was enough. She ran home to check the itinerary her mother had left for her and Lisa. There it was. *Achille Lauro*. That was the ship.

Ilsa immediately called her sister. In the brief time it took Ilsa to call Lisa, to tell her that she'd heard about the hijacking, and for Lisa to travel the short distance from her apartment on Grand Street to Stewart House, a throng of media had arrived. Lisa found pandemonium outside the building: photographers, journalists, sound trucks, and screams of "Lisa! Lisa! Could you tell us? How's Leon? How's Marilyn?"

Upstairs Lisa found the apartment already filling with relatives and friends. Everyone was trying to find out what was going on, who was on the ship and who was on the excursion. Maura Spiegel, daughter of their mother's best friend, Charlotte, who was also on the cruise, was on the way from Vermont, where she was teaching at Bennington College. Her sister Jill, a physician, was already there. Another family friend, Letty Simon, had rushed over from her office at Cooper Union, just a block away. Simon was involved in a neighborhood preservation project and had worked in city government before that. She understood how public relations worked.

Beginning right then, Simon would become indispensable to the Klinghoffer daughters. Simon was a dynamo, pint-sized but an alpha operator. She walked into the apartment, assessed the situation, and took charge.

The living room was crowded, like any Klinghoffer gathering, packed with people who had been embraced and entertained by Leon and Marilyn. Letty was part of this expansive circle of savvy, mostly Jewish, New Yorkers. Her parents had met Ilsa and Lisa's family on the Lower East Side, through Charlotte and Sam Spiegel. Charlotte and Leon were childhood friends.

The Spiegels were liberal Democrats, enmeshed in neighborhood politics. Sam was a Surrogate Court judge, who built his career defending the rights of drug addicts, welfare recipients, and women seeking abortions. Charlotte was a Democratic district leader for eighteen years, and then the first woman to run the Manhattan Democratic machine historically known as Tammany Hall.

Though Leon initially was the connection to Charlotte, the friendship continued because of Marilyn. The women were soulmates—they knew it the minute they first met in Leon's hardware store and burst into laughter when they saw they were wearing identical fur coats. The Spiegels were more intellectual and political than the Klinghoffers, but they all liked to party and enjoyed one another's company. Their children became unofficial cousins; they called one another's parents aunt and uncle.

For Lisa and Ilsa, the Spiegels were their social conscience. Through them, the Klinghoffer daughters participated in almost every political campaign that involved the couple, directly or indirectly. They passed out flyers, knocked on doors to galvanize voters, went on protest marches. In high school, Ilsa interned in Washington for Congressman Ed Koch; now the mayor, Koch lived a couple of blocks from the Klinghoffers.

After Sam Spiegel died of a heart attack in 1977, Charlotte and Marilyn became even closer. Charlotte accompanied her friend upstate to Rochester for the cancer treatments and now they were together on the *Achille Lauro*.

It was a trusted, familial network. Therefore, when Letty Simon told "the girls," as everyone called the Klinghoffer sisters, that they needed a communications strategy, they listened. Simon knew how appealing the two sisters were: attractive young women who seemed strangely innocent for born-and-bred New Yorkers, unapologetically sweet. Though they had no experience in public speaking, Letty coached them on how to talk to the media and what to say.

That first evening, every two hours, they went downstairs, and someone spoke to the reporters, either Letty or the sisters or Jerry or

Paul, exchanging scraps of information as they arrived. In New Jersey, children of the other Beach People were also talking to reporters; the groups checked in with each other periodically to see what they had learned.

"They were not versed in foreign affairs or the intricacies of the Middle East," Simon would recall. "I said to them, they're going to ask you a lot of other questions about politics, what do you think about this guy or that. "Just say, 'We are not experts. This is our family.'"

For Simon, there was only one message: We want everyone home safe.

Tunis, October 8, 1985

REEM AL-NIMER was having her morning coffee, sitting on the balcony overlooking the garden of her two-story home, flipping through the morning newspapers, when the telephone rang. A Palestinian Liberation Front official was on the line, looking for her husband, Abu al-Abbas. She muttered, "I don't know." She told the man that Abbas was scheduled to return home that day from a PLO conference in Amman, Jordan, and got off the phone. She didn't mention that she and her husband had had a huge fight before he left, and she hadn't spoken to him for three days. His last words to her had been, "Go to hell, if you want a divorce, I'll give you a divorce."

She'd responded by flying to Paris to visit her sister. Now she was back in Tunisia, ready to make up, but she wasn't going to explain all this to the PLF man on the telephone. During their brief conversation, she was distracted by the television, which was tuned as usual to Rai Uno, the Italian network, because she couldn't tolerate the heavily censored, state-controlled Tunisian station, and she liked looking at the styles worn by elegant Italian women. Reem didn't really understand Italian but it was obvious from the pictures and excited chatter that something significant had happened. When bold letters flashed on the screen across the image of a brochure for a cruise ship called *Achille*

Lauro, she felt a bolt of fear. This must be connected to her husband, because the brochure shown was exactly like ones he had left around their house, one in the bathroom, another one on the night table next to their bed.

Reem intuited her husband probably wasn't planning on taking her on a Mediterranean cruise. Nor had she inquired too deeply about the mysterious gold-plated Mercedes-Benz automobile that appeared at their house a couple of weeks before, a car she believed belonged to Abbas's old friend Monzer al-Kassar, an international arms dealer.

Reem saw Kassar as a necessary evil, a hazard of her husband's occupation. "As a military man," she said, "he had different relationships with different people and one of them had to be an arms dealer." But Monzer was more than a business acquaintance. Abbas and Monzer had been present at each other's wedding.

Reem was nervous about the Mercedes, which stayed at their house in Tunisia for three days. "What is this, do we own this car?" she asked her husband when he took her for a drive. (Later, she would learn that the Mercedes transported the weapons that were used on the *Achille Lauro*. The connection between the car and weapons and Monzer was an assumption—Reem couldn't say for sure. That was the kind of detail Abu al-Abbas kept to himself.)

After three years of being together, she had learned not to ask too many questions. "I wasn't digging into his personal and political or military life," she would recall. "At home I saw a lot of photos and documents and papers and weapons and letters. I never looked into his things, I never asked about certain things....I was never this wife who would ask why did you talk to this person, who is this on the phone, why is this in your pocket, why is your ex-wife sending you letters?"

By then Reem had learned that the stuff of romance, the very qualities that drew her to Abbas—his bravado and utter devotion to the Palestinian cause—made for a difficult marriage. They fought a lot about things that might sound mundane in light of the high-stakes cloak-and-dagger schemes that her husband masterminded. But these issues were important to a wife living in a new country, taking care of her two young children from a previous marriage. For example, Abbas would call to tell her he would be home for dinner in a half hour. The half hour would stretch out to an hour, and another hour, and then she would call the office and they would say, "Oh, he had to travel with Yasser Arafat. They called him and told him you have to be at the airport in ten minutes."

Reem and her husband were both fiercely proud Palestinians, yet their backgrounds were radically different. His achievements were entirely self-made, born of struggle, ambition, commitment, and daring. Reem, the descendant of powerful advisers to the Ottoman Empire, was born into privilege. Her father, Rifaat al-Nimer, was a prominent banker in Beirut. Her mother, Rabiha, was part of the Masri family, which had been landed aristocracy in Palestine; Rabiha studied at the Jerusalem branch of the Friends School, opened by the Quakers in 1869, with a special emphasis on the education of women.

Reem's childhood photographs look remarkably like those of Lisa and Ilsa Klinghoffer; in fact, born in 1952, she was a year younger than Lisa. Her mother, like theirs, was a striking, confident woman who enjoyed relaxing with a cocktail in her hand and didn't hesitate to speak her mind. Like the Klinghoffer sisters, Reem was educated in progressive private schools and indulged by a father who would do anything for his children. Like Lisa, she came of age in the 1960s—adored the Beatles (her parents took her to London to see them perform live), wore bell-bottom jeans, smoked Marlboros, loved a good party. For her sixteenth birthday, her father gave her a sports car, an Alfa Romeo, which he confiscated when he learned that his free-spirited daughter had been drag racing by the sea with friends.

As part of Beirut's sophisticated upper class, the Nimer family embraced Western culture. Reem took ballet and piano lessons, playing standards like Bach's Minuet in G, and Beethoven's "Für Elise," along with Arab classical music. Her guilty pleasure was a burger at Wimpy, the U.K. chain that had an outpost on Hamra Street. They were worldly people, affiliated by culture and heritage to Islam, but not observant of religious strictures. That was modern, internationalist life in the bubble of Ras Beirut, an upscale part of the city where the Nimer family lived peaceably among other affluent people of all religions or no religion.

Yet Reem's sensory memory was infused with Palestinian ingredients, the traditional dishes her mother prepared, like *msakhan*, spiced chicken spread on flatbread, seasoned with cumin and sumac, wrapped with onions, and garnished with pine nuts. There was an ongoing counternarrative, one that spoke to her family's allegiance to the Arab world and to her father Rifaat's lifelong yearning for his childhood home. Rifaat grew up in Nablus, about thirty miles north of Jerusalem, in a mansion built by his family when they were agents of the Ottoman Empire. His early youth was spent in luxury, his home surrounded by gardens and fountains, with three stables for horses. But the family fortunes were in decline. His birth in 1918 coincided with the end of World War I and the collapse of the Ottomans following the Allied victory.

Rifaat's upbringing was dominated by the effects of the British mandate, the 1922 authorization by the League of Nations giving Britain control of Palestine. The mandate incorporated the promise made a few years earlier in a letter from British Foreign Minister Lord Balfour to the prominent Zionist Lord Rothschild. The Balfour Declaration of 1917 offered assurance that the persecuted Jews of Europe, those fleeing from pogroms and discrimination, could find a haven in their Holy Land.

"His Majesty's Government view with favour the establishment in Palestine of a national home for the Jewish people, and will use their best endeavours to facilitate the achievement of this object," Balfour wrote Rothschild.

This guarantee set the stage for a century of struggle between two nationalisms with conflicting narratives. The Palestinian national movement emerged in reaction to the Zionist movement, which regarded Palestine as a backwater Ottoman province that excited Arab passions only after Jewish claims to part of the land. From the Arab viewpoint, the Zionist quest for a national home ignored the reality on the ground: a solid Arab majority at the onset of the mandate with an estimated 738,000 Arabs (657,000 Muslim and 81,000 Christian) and 58,000 Jews. The Jewish narrative maintains that by the turn of the century, Jerusalem already had a Jewish plurality, buoyed by the Zionist *aliyahs* (Hebrew for "going up") to the land of Israel, that transpired in the late nineteenth and early twentieth centuries. The Arabs saw these newcomers as colonialist settlers intent on usurping their lands.

The claims and counterclaims exploded in riots and sporadic violence in the interwar period, an Arab rebellion in the 1930s followed by a virtual British ban on Jewish immigration, and then a U.N. partition in 1947 of the mandate region reflecting a division that was by then roughly one-third Jewish and two-thirds Arab. This triggered a two-phase war in 1947–1948 between Israel and the Palestinians and five Arab nations, which ended in Israeli victory and the founding of the Jewish state. For Arabs, this was the Nakba, the Catastrophe, which drove 700,000 Arabs fleeing to neighboring lands, creating a Palestinian diaspora where many languished for decades in grim refugee camps that heightened the pain and despair created by uprootedness and dispossession. The subsequent Six-Day War in 1967 led to the current Israeli occupation of the West Bank and a further refugee crisis. It was these conditions of bitterness, animosity, and revanchism, with two opposing narratives that virtually excluded the reality, much less the validity, of the other's claims, that provided the backdrop for the seizure of the *Achille Lauro.*

Reem's father, Rifaat al-Nimer, grew up in the postmandate struggle between Arab and Jew; he was expelled from school after the British imprisoned him for three months for supporting the Arab revolt of 1936–1939 of Haj Amin al-Husseini, the Grand Mufti of Jerusalem, who fled to Nazi Germany, where he spent World War II after the rebellion was crushed. However, even though the Nimer fortunes had eroded, Rifaat was part of a well-connected family able to help him finish his studies and find a prosperous career. After completing university, he entered the banking business; by 1947 he was married and dividing his time between Amman, Jordan, and Nablus, where Reem was born and which would remain under Jordanian control until the Six-Day War.

Caught up in internecine Arab politics, Rifaat moved the family to Saudi Arabia in 1957. In 1961 they settled in Beirut, where he became CEO of the Beirut Bank of Commerce, which served as financier for the newly minted Palestine Liberation Organization, founded in 1964 to conduct guerrilla warfare against Israel.

As a girl new to Beirut, Reem felt stigmatized by the Lebanese for being Palestinian, though her family's wealth protected her from the harshest realities. While most Palestinians couldn't work or become citizens of Lebanon, the Nimers traveled on Jordanian passports. Still, she felt looked down on. It was as if the city's ethnic patchwork quilt of Muslims, Druze, Christians, and Jews stratified people more than it united them—even the Muslims fought one another, Shia versus Sunni. On the surface, the girls in her elite private school appeared to be welcoming, heterogeneous, a mix of Muslims and Christians, and a single Jewish student. Still, everyone wanted to know where you fit in.

"In school people always asked, 'What are you?'" she said.

By the time she turned sixteen, in 1968, Reem was caught up in the antiestablishment fervor infecting students around the globe. She hung posters of Mao Zedong and Che Guevara in her bedroom and joined Yasser Arafat's Fatah movement while still in high school. On weekends she visited military camps in southern Lebanon, where she wore army fatigues, did calisthenics, and learned how to shoot a rifle. These escapades were exciting, appealing to her wilder side. But a deeper transformation took hold when she volunteered in the refugee camps on the outskirts of Beirut and encountered unfiltered misery. The hopelessness she saw there changed a thirst for adventure into compassion, and then compassion morphed into outrage; she was unable to accept the gaping discrepancy between her life and theirs.

From that point forward, Reem's life became bifurcated between West and Middle East, between the lure of her family's bourgeois comfort and the intoxication of revolution beyond it.

"I was a Palestinian and a communist," she would write about her youthful self. "Still, my father had money and I loved to have fun."

Once she entered Beirut University College, still living at home, she became even more politically radicalized. She left Fatah for the Popular Front for the Liberation of Palestine (PFLP), enticed by the organization's Marxist-Leninist rhetoric. There she met the handsome young man who would become her first husband, Mohammad al-Ghadban.

Their politics aligned, and she was impressed by his intelligence. He was well-read and a good writer, although Reem admitted the main attraction was chemical, not cerebral. "He definitely made my heart flutter," she said.

Her father disapproved. Rifaat may have been a champion of Palestinian rights, but he was also a blue blood. Status mattered to him. "My parents saw Mohammad as a poor boy from the slums of Beirut who lacked initiative—not a suitable match at all," Reem said. Reem's infatuation with Mohammad was inseparable from her passion for the Palestinian cause.

They eloped and went on the lam—running not because they were young radicals in love, but because her father had connections everywhere in Syria, Jordan, Iraq, and Lebanon who had the power to arrest her husband and send Reem home. So they fled to East Germany. Shamed by her rebellion, her father disowned her, even blamed her for the death of his older brother, who had a stroke right after he learned about Reem's forbidden marriage.

Rifaat relented enough so the couple could return to Lebanon without fear of being seized by one of his powerful friends. They arrived back in Beirut in 1974; within a year the civil war broke out and their first child was born, a son named Loaye. The couple continued their political work, which included everything from fund-raising to robbing two banks (something Reem never confessed to her father to the day he died). They were involved in organizations that conflated Palestinian nationalism, communism, and utopian theory. They were not merely anti-Israeli, but antiauthoritarian, and soon they became wanted by the Syrian and Lebanese governments.

The next few years were complicated, lives of constant movement, fake passports, difficulty—and finally, dullness. By 1978 the pair was living in the Ivory Coast, now with two children, estranged from family, trying to make a living (helped by Reem's mother, who sent money to her daughter behind her husband's back). Mohammad had turned out to be less exciting to Reem in reality than in her imagination. In 1980, the couple returned to Beirut, ready to call it quits, tired of living in exile and of each other.

After they separated, Reem resumed a more ordinary life—as ordinary as it could be in a country living under the shadow of violence; the civil war had become a numbing presence. Bombs and gunfire and walking through rubble had become part of everyday existence. Reem lived with the children in an apartment in her parents' building, took classes at the university, and hung out at cafés with old friends and acquaintances.

One of these acquaintances was Abu al-Abbas, a PLF commander who had once helped her and Mohammad during their wanderings. Soon he was confiding in her about his marriage, and he asked Reem to visit his wife, Samia, who had recently given birth to their second son and was suffering from postpartum depression. The two women became friends, bonded by their complaints about their husbands and by their boys, who played together while they talked.

Beirut

SAMIA COSTANDI had much in common with Reem: both had been strong-willed girls, educated in English-language private schools; both grew up in upper-crust Palestinian families with emotional ties to the mythologized homeland; both felt a strong intellectual and cultural connection to the West. The two were born just a year apart and even resembled each other: beautiful women who tried to keep their nails manicured and their makeup fresh even in the midst of war. Samia's father, Kamel Bichara Costandi, was a broadcaster who worked as an actor and director for the British-financed Near East Broadcasting Station in Cyprus, where Samia was born; he was known to listeners as "the man with the golden voice." Samia spent two years of preschool and kindergarten in London, when her father worked with the BBC Radio's Arab department. One of her three brothers was born there.

But there were crucial differences as well. Samia's family was Christian not Muslim, and more religiously observant than Reem's. And, most significant, unlike Reem, Samia had not been drawn to politics or revolutionary organizations.

"I wanted independence of thought, to be free," she said. "I didn't want the stigma. The parties were dogmatic a lot of the time."

Still, with Palestinians as with Israelis, it is rare to find someone more than one bloody degree of separation from the conflict. In 1973, an admired relative of Samia, Kamal Nasser, a journalist and author who had become spokesman for the PLO, was killed in his Beirut apartment by Israeli commandos, led by future Israeli prime minister Ehud Barak, who was disguised as a woman. The assassination was part of a large-scale targeted retaliation for the deaths of the eleven members of Israel's Olympic team, who were taken hostage and eventually killed by a militant offshoot of the PLO during the 1972 Olympics in Munich. Samia's uncle, a physician, did the autopsy, removing seventy bullets from Nasser's body.

Even as a girl, living a comfortable life, Samia felt that her status in Beirut was tenuous. While her family had a wide circle of friends—their home was filled with poets, writers, and intellectuals—and she wanted for nothing material, she felt conflicting pressures. Some were the pressures of privilege—her fear of not achieving as much as she felt she should, living up to the expectations of a beloved father who trained her to recite Shakespeare at the age of four. Others were subtler, part of her growing awareness that as a Palestinian she wasn't accepted fully by other Lebanese Christians. At her private school she was the only Palestinian. Her first language had been English; Arabic was now the language at home, though at school she made sure to speak in Lebanese dialect, not Palestinian. She became adept at code switching between the two.

On graduating from the American University of Beirut, she took a bookish job, working in the publications department of the Institute for Palestine Studies, a nonprofit Arab center devoted to research about the Arab-Israeli conflict.

When a young man from the PFLP came looking for someone to translate pamphlets into Hebrew, Samia was able to find someone who could. The man then invited her to come to the PFLP offices to do some Arabic-English translation for the group. She dropped by and heard people denouncing Yasser Arafat, the head of the PLO. This heresy was frightening and exciting. It was 1974; Samia was twenty-three years old.

She began volunteering at the PFLP offices on Sundays, doing translations. One day a very tall, handsome man arrived at the office. Though at twenty-six, he wasn't much older than she was, Abu al-Abbas already had a commanding presence. When he walked into the room, everyone stood up, so Samia did, too. She felt self-conscious; everyone else was wearing army fatigues while she had on a retro 1930s-style dress decorated with red and pink flowers that nicely accentuated her slender waist. When Abbas started shaking hands with everyone, she stuck out hers, making a point to shake very firmly, thinking, "I will show him I am not a little sissy or some bourgeoisie woman."

Soon he had invited her into his office and was telling her the sad, compelling story of his childhood in a refugee camp. Then he invited her for coffee. They took a long drive and stopped at a café. The revolutionary leader looked closely at her and asked if she'd changed her hair. When she said yes, she'd put in highlights, he reached over to gently touch the lighter strands.

Then he declared his intentions. "I'm very interested in us continuing to see each other," he said, "and I have a feeling we're going to get married."

That was their first date. Samia soon learned that with Abu al-

Abbas everything was about the cause, even courtship. He introduced her to a side of Palestinian reality that was just across town but a universe away from her comfortable life. The emotions stirred by the hardship she saw with him as her guide became entangled with her intense attraction for the man who took her there.

When her parents realized that the infatuation was becoming serious, they invited their daughter's suitor for lunch. Her mother was charmed, her father was not, fearful of what the future would hold for an avowed revolutionary like Abu al-Abbas. After the couple announced their engagement, Samia's parents demanded they break it. In response, Abbas sent his future in-laws an apology for not consulting them first, noted that he and Samia had made their decision "scientifically," and concluded by saying, "I hope you forgive me when I say that the parents have the right to discuss their children's decisions but not to make them." Samia's parents succumbed; what choice did they have?

Yet his letter did not calm their fears, as their daughter's fiancé explained the path he had chosen at a much earlier age, between fulfilling his own ambitions and devoting himself to the Palestinian cause. "The decision was very clear to me," he wrote. "I chose homeland."

The young couple defied some conventions, wearing jeans to their marriage ceremony, and adhered to others. Because Samia didn't renounce her Christianity, her father had to give permission to the sheikh who presided (Lebanon, like Israel, does not recognize civil marriages). As her disapproving father reluctantly gave his written approval, he said to his future son-in-law, "Not only are you marrying my daughter, but you want me to sign also?"

Samia should have anticipated the life she had signed on to. In his wedding vow to her, Abu al-Abbas said, "For you I will make history." The difficulties became apparent within a few months, and they were much worse than she could have imagined. The civil war in Lebanon had broken out. Just before Samia became pregnant with their first child, Abbas told her they had to leave Beirut for Iraq because he was being pursued by both the Syrians and the Israelis; there were supposedly seventy-two execution orders directed at him. By then he had become the head of the Palestinian Liberation Front.

They stayed in Baghdad almost a year. In September 1977, when Samia was in her seventh month, Abbas returned to Beirut and Samia went to London, to be with her parents and give birth there. Three months later, she received a letter from her husband, describing an apartment he'd found for them and expressing his hopes and fears for his baby son. "I will try to give him the right to be a child," he wrote. "I will not force him to skip life and step into it as an adult all at once. He will live two childhoods, his childhood and my childhood, which I did not live. And he must not forget he is the child of Palestine."

But the warmth of these sentiments was offset by references to "strikes against the enemy," by the assassination of a friend by the Syrians, and by Abbas's promise, "We will never forgive them for their crime and we will avenge him when the time is right."

When she returned to Beirut with their infant son, Khaled, in early 1978, Abbas showed her the apartment he'd chosen for them, which he had described as "big and beautiful," while acknowledging "it needs a lot of cleaning and the glass, walls and decoration need some fixing, too." Samia was in despair when she saw the fixer-upper he had chosen. Located in the crowded Palestinian section of the city's al-Fakhani quarter, not far from the refugee camps of Sabra and Shatila, the place was unpainted and poorly furnished, with no latches on the doors; even the water was dirty. Something fundamental about her husband sunk in. "He was a nomad," Samia said. "He didn't care about places or objects."

The depression she struggled to submerge reasserted itself. Samia's father explained to Abu al-Abbas the apartment needed to be refurbished. The revolutionary leader listened to his father-in-law and fixed the place up. Samia and Khaled moved in—only to flee a couple of months later, to stay with an aunt in Athens, when her husband told her he'd received a security report that their building, which also housed the PLF headquarters, had been targeted by one of his enemies.

Samia left with the baby on Tuesday, August 8, 1978. That Sunday she received a call from her parents in England; the BBC reported that 175 people died and 80 were wounded in a massive bombing in Beirut, attributed to a rival PLO group trying to assassinate Abu al-Abbas.

Abbas had escaped only because he was out with a friend. Samia returned to Beirut with Khaled. Within two years, she became pregnant again, even as she found herself increasingly unable to cope with the duality in her husband's nature and the ever present fear created by his calling.

"Abu al-Abbas had a very soft side to him," she would recall. "As a husband, as a lover, he was very gentle, very kind, very soft-spoken. He never shouted at people. It was enough for him to raise his voice just a notch for people to listen, because he had authority when he spoke. He was compassionate, but he could be brutal with people he considered were criminals or had done horrible things."

After their second son, Omar, was born in 1980, Samia suffered a deep depression. "He didn't understand, he just couldn't understand," she said of her ex-husband. "He didn't believe in depression. He thought, 'Just pick yourself up and move on.'"

Despite her friendship with Samia, Reem didn't feel guilty when her relationship with Abu al-Abbas became a romance. "He was complaining to me about her and she was complaining to me about him," she said. "They were quarreling." Even though she acknowledged that he instigated the divorce, not Samia, Reem was impressed by how he treated the woman who became his ex-wife. "He was a real gentleman," she said. "That brought me closer to him."

She brought him home to meet her family. Her father reacted very differently to Abu al-Abbas than he had to her first husband, Mohammad. Abbas, too, came from humble origins, but now, at age thirty-two, he had established himself as a contender in the complicated hierarchy of the Palestinian revolution. Unlike Mohammad, who hadn't finished university and didn't enjoy engaging in intellectual discussion, Abbas brought imagination, accomplishment, and charisma to the table.

Besides, said Reem, her father was mellowed by their years of estrangement and his love for his grandchildren. "He just wanted me to marry and to settle down and to have a place for my kids," she said. "And I think they [her parents] loved him [Abbas]. It was as simple as that."

She would soon learn what Samia knew quite well: nothing was simple with Abu al-Abbas. Reem admired him, and never stopped loving him, yet she came to realize that he would never belong to a person: not to his wife, not to his children, not even to himself—he belonged to the Palestinian cause.

Yet he had been irresistible. Their courtship took place on drives over rutted roads through the darkened western section of Beirut, where Abu al-Abbas was staying, in the al-Ramleh al-Bayda district overlooking the Pigeons' Rocks, the giant formations in the sea that welcomed visitors to the city—the same place Reem had gone drag racing with her friends, just a few years earlier. Abbas reignited Reem's revolutionary spirit. He reinforced the notion that the status quo had to be disrupted, in order to reach a better future, even if the process meant wrecking the city she loved.

No sooner had they married, in 1982, than Reem was in exile again, part of the expulsion of the PLO from Lebanon following the Israeli invasion. She and Abbas moved to Tunisia with hundreds of other Palestinians, to discover there a genuine feeling of being home. The Abbas family moved into a comfortable house with a garden, and Reem enrolled her boys in a French lycée, thinking that if she returned to Beirut they could easily make the transition.

Reem became occupied with taking care of her household, perfecting her cooking, watching over her children and her husband, and doing volunteer work with the local Palestinian community. They visited friends, together with their kids. After the chaos of Beirut, the homely routine became pleasurable.

Yet this normalcy was a façade. Her husband was a military

commander wanted by the Mossad and by Syria, among others, who worked in secrecy most of the time. Abbas and the PLF were collaborating with Yasser Arafat and the the perennially ad hoc administration established under the umbrella of the PLO by Arafat, financed by the Palestinian diaspora and friendly Arab governments. Headquarters in Tunis were set up in the five-star Salway Beach Hotel. Thomas Friedman, then a *New York Times* reporter covering Lebanon, visited Tunis shortly after the evacuation. "It was a strange scene," he wrote. "PLO officials lodged in a 200-room hotel featuring an arboretum filled with strutting peacocks in the lobby and waiters serving endless rounds of Arabic coffee to retired guerrillas playing endless rounds of chess and Ping-Pong."

Abbas was in constant motion, talking to the press, meeting with *fedayeen* and commanders in training camps, and traveling to destinations unknown to Reem. He kept his wife in the dark because that's how he operated, but also for her safety, should she be captured by Israelis or other enemies.

Yet even with the mysterious comings and goings, the absences and persistent undertow of danger, she would look back on those three years as a peaceful interlude.

Then came the news of the *Achille Lauro*.

3

Big Guns

Washington, D.C.

In October 1980, five years before Leon and Marilyn Klinghoffer boarded the *Achille Lauro* with their friends, presidential candidate Ronald Reagan unwittingly was laying the foundation for his response to the hijacking.

Two weeks before the 1980 election, the telegenic former movie star paid $150,000 for a prime-time spot on CBS, betting on the American public's infatuation with heroes, real or manufactured. His fans had adored Reagan playing a secret service man (*Code of the Secret Service*), World War II pilot (*International Squadron*), and doomed football half-back (*Knute Rockne All American*). Now he and his backers hoped that his warmth and trustworthy affect would convince voters that he was a better choice than incumbent Jimmy Carter for the real-life role of commander in chief. Fear of terrorism was Reagan's ace in the hole: Carter's administration was being crushed by its failure to bring back the fifty-two Americans who remained in captivity in Iran after being taken hostage in the aftermath of the Islamic Revolution.

Using the lofty rhetoric that creates the illusion of substance, Reagan assured the nation that, if elected, he would achieve "peace through strength." Turning to the issue of international terrorism, he flexed his considerable oratorical muscle. The candidate promised that if he were president, the United States would take the lead in curbing the phenomenon he deemed "the scourge of civilization."

Reagan blithely talked past the inconsistencies in his message by doing what politicians do, even those not trained in Hollywood: he promised the American people that they could have it all. He assured them he would bring about an arms reduction while increasing defense spending and effectively combating terrorism, though the details were gauzy.

An accomplished speaker who knew how to connect with his audience, Reagan backed his intentions with the Bible, a reliable, catchall source of inspiration, though a questionable guide for managing geopolitics in the twentieth century. "Throughout Scripture, we see reference to peace-makers—those who through their actions—not just their words—take the material of this imperfect world and, with hard work and God's help, fashion from that material, peace for the world," he said.

Reagan's strategists understood their candidate's emotional appeal. Even people who didn't think him capable of the job were attracted to him personally. Writing on the opinion pages of the *New York Times* the morning after this "scourge of civilization" speech, columnist Anthony Lewis observed, "Traveling with Ronald Reagan, as I have just done for a few days, deepens the impression that he is a genuinely nice person: friendly, considerate, without malice. Up close, the genial politician of the television screen looks to be the real man."

Nevertheless, the journalist was not reassured by the candidate's amiable disposition or his experience as governor of California. "People who have tried to plumb his views on sophisticated diplomatic questions have found it hard to get past a surface statement that seems to reflect a limited briefing," he wrote. Lewis predicted that "a man with so little personal knowledge of the world would be in serious danger of becoming a captive of his advisers."

Those advisers were the establishment personified: Republicans, senior citizens (like their president, who was sixty-nine on entering office), veterans of World War II. They were Cold Warriors bred on stark notions of good and evil, honor and disloyalty, allies and enemies, and of conflict played out on familiar battlefields by recognizable states. For the Reagan team, foreign policy was defined in relation to the Soviet Union. They were wealthy capitalists whose political and economic inclinations aligned with anti-Soviet strongholds like Israel, while appeasing the conservative Arab oil-producing countries of the Gulf peninsula. Secretary of State George Shultz and Secretary of Defense Caspar Weinberger both came to government from the Bechtel Corporation, a multinational defense contractor; William Casey, director of the Central Intelligence Agency, was a corporate lawyer before serving in the Nixon administration as head of the Securities and Exchange Commission and as undersecretary of state. Reagan himself was more intuitive than informed; he believed (with good reason) that he was blessed with "the luck of the Irish" and left the details to his staff. Luck, however, did not fully explain the gift he was handed as he entered the Oval Office. In Tehran, the Ayatollah Khomeini released the U.S. hostages the day of Reagan's inauguration, a gesture widely believed to be the Islamic leader's final show of contempt for Jimmy Carter. This unearned triumph subsequently inspired repeated volleys of tough talk from the new Republican administration, proclamations of swift and effective retribution against Iran and refusal to negotiate with terrorists.

However, the Reagan team would soon discover, just as Carter had, that the war on terror was a slippery, frustrating business and happy endings are harder to come by when you can't fire the scriptwriter. During the eight years of the Reagan presidency, there were 636 hijackings, bombings, and other attacks designated "terrorist incidents" against American targets. The administration retaliated by military means in just two cases. There were numerous problems preventing a more muscular response, such as lack of hard intelligence, the low magnitude of casualties in many attacks, and the far-flung locations of the incidents. Besides these practical issues, a coherent response to terrorism was hampered by the bickering within Reagan's inner circle.

Despite Reagan's campaign rhetoric, his administration couldn't get a grip on terrorism either. His advisers were sophisticated, intelligent men who had studied history and knew that things change. But they lived inside the bubble of the military-industrial complex that had served them well. They were granddads trying to tune in to the latest sound; it just seemed like angry noise to them. Revolution wasn't new; it's always happening somewhere. Now the guerrilla fighters had technology on their side. News traveled faster than ever and couldn't be controlled. This wasn't a numbers game. Defeat came not by measuring death tolls but in the psychic disruption, the alarming blasts in unexpected places, with discomfiting images broadcast in real time on CNN, founded in 1980, the year Reagan was first elected. The State Department began to click on cable to see what was happening.

It would have been hard for Reagan's men to let go of their entrenched worldviews, even if they had been so inclined. No one wanted to educate a clueless public on the nuance of Middle East politics, especially once you wandered outside the somewhat familiar territory of the Israeli-Palestinian conflict into the miasma of incomprehensible Arab names and Islamic factionalism. The politicians were far less interested in understanding the roots of hatred than in crushing terrorists—if only they could find them. Years later, speaking of terrorists, Caspar Weinberger told an interviewer, "They have this ability to move around and shift around, day to day, and we have no actual knowledge of where they're going to be, because we don't know what their plans are."

It didn't help that Secretary of State Shultz and Secretary of Defense Weinberger advocated starkly different approaches. The fundamental disconnect between the two men was described by Jane Mayer and Doyle McManus, two former White House correspondents, as akin to "feuding medieval theologians debating a point of doctrine." Shultz advocated following the Israeli example, using preemptive and retaliatory military strikes against suspected terrorists, even if it meant hurting innocent bystanders. Weinberger remembered some lessons from the disastrous U.S. entanglement in Vietnam; he felt that military force should be a last resort, one used only when authorized by Congress.

Their disagreements were not just ideological. They didn't like each other. Assistant Secretary of Defense Richard Armitage, one of Weinberger's closest advisers, once suggested to Shultz, at an embassy reception in Lebanon, that he grab a six-pack of beer and take Weinberger on a lake and settle their differences. "He looked at me, he has the most piercing eyes, he looked right back and said, 'He wouldn't come,'" recalled Armitage. When Armitage repeated the story to Weinberger, telling him that Shultz said he wouldn't come, Weinberger responded, "He's right." The result, in terms of terrorism policy, was gridlock.

Robert McFarlane, assistant to the president for national security affairs, known to be nonconfrontational and collegial, had gained Reagan's trust and became a mediator between Shultz and Weinberger. McFarlane saw Israel as a valuable ally and, like Shultz, believed the United States should emulate Israeli antiterrorism tactics, moving from defense to offense. In the spring of 1984, McFarlane presented Reagan with National Security Division Directive-138, which marked a significant change in policy. NSDD-138 endorsed preemptive strikes, covert actions, and counterintelligence operations.

This was fine with CIA Director Casey, who had been chief of secret intelligence in Europe for the Office of Strategic Services during World War II. He hated the way the CIA's cloak-and-dagger activities had been clipped in the 1970s as part of the post-Watergate restraints on government surveillance and other clandestine actions. "I want to restore the earlier, good days," Casey told a reporter.

Terrorism was a distraction from Reagan's primary aim, keeping the country focused on his anticommunist crusade against the Soviet Union. On March 8, 1983, in a Bible-thumping speech given to a gathering of evangelical Christians, the American president called on Jesus, the Scriptures, and God to help him oppose a nuclear freeze with the Soviet Union, which he described not merely as an ideological adversary but as a cursed foe, "the evil empire." Overflowing with fervor, he told his receptive audience, "Let us pray for the salvation of all of those who live in that totalitarian darkness."

The Middle East combatants were not content to sit on the sidelines while the superpowers played their game of world domination. A month after the "evil empire" speech, President Reagan experienced firsthand, as commander in chief, a gruesome example of just how difficult it was to anticipate a terrorist attack. On April 18, 1983, a bomb exploded in the U.S. embassy in Beirut, killing 63 people, including 17 Americans. This was a year after the United States sent Marines to Lebanon, over Weinberger's objections, to be part of an international peacekeeping force meant to oversee the departure of the PLO from Lebanon. The country remained mired in war nonetheless and the Marines found themselves under constant assault by snipers.

"What was our mission?" a Marine would tell a reporter. "I'll tell you what our mission was. A lot of people died for nothing and then we left."

Things got worse. Six months later, on October 23, a truck rammed into a U.S. Marine military barracks at the Beirut airport, killing 241 American servicemen; in a separate attack two miles away, 58 French soldiers were killed along with the wife and four children of the Lebanese janitor who lived in the French barracks. The American casualties marked the highest number killed in one attack since Vietnam.

The United States was once again the clumsy giant, getting pounded by enemies who seemed to the White House like a bunch of gnats, sandflies with a vicious bite. These punches to the gut instilled an accumulated fury in the American president. At a ceremony honoring those who had died in the attack on the Marines, Reagan vented with bombast that could have been lifted from *Jap Zero*, a military training movie he starred in as part of his World War II service in the Army Air Force's film production unit. "Let us here in their presence serve notice to the cowardly, skulking barbarians in the world that they will not have their way," the actor-turned-president told the grieving families gathered at Andrews Air Force Base, where the bodies of the victims had arrived.

While Reagan's empathy appeared genuine, his fighting words carried no ammunition. The chief suspect in the attacks was Hezbollah, the Lebanese aggregate of Shia Muslim groups, backed by Iran, created in the upheaval following the 1982 Israeli invasion of Lebanon. (Hezbollah, which means "Party of God," would become the dominant Muslim political force in Lebanon.) Proof was elusive, however. There was no effective retaliation to be had.

Reporters on the ground understood what the State Department and National Security Council (NSC) back home seemed unable to comprehend. "Each successive power, including the Israelis, the Americans and the Syrians, has discovered that Lebanon's problems go much deeper than armies can solve," wrote Timothy J. McNulty, assessing the damage in the *Chicago Tribune*. He invoked a local term for the destruction—being "Lebanized"—and then explained: "It is part of the shorthand of language in which the name Beirut stands for violence, destruction and aimless killing."

Despite his rhetoric, President Reagan withdrew the Marines from Lebanon in February 1984. That same month the U.S. battleship *New Jersey* bombed Druze and Syrian military outposts around Beirut. "Each round fired by its gunners shook the entire city. Windows rattled, and the terrifying roar sent the few people on the streets scattering for cover," reported Thomas Friedman in the *New York Times*. A Pentagon spokesman acknowledged that the effectiveness was hard to gauge. He explained that bad weather and "observation problems" had prevented accurate assessment of damage caused by the shelling and of whether those caught in the crossfire were fighters or simply residents living in a country where the battle zone was everywhere.

The following month, March 1984, Bill Buckley, the CIA's Beirut station chief, was kidnapped, tortured, and then murdered by Hezbollah.

None of this appeared to weaken the American electorate's faith in Reagan's leadership. The chaos was happening in the remote "over there" to people who had signed on for dangerous jobs. On November 6, 1984, Reagan was elected to his second term in a remarkable landslide, carrying forty-nine out of fifty states.

Seven months later, Hezbollah handed Reagan and his team yet another horrific humiliation. On June 14, 1985, two terrorists hijacked a TWA flight from Athens to Rome, containing 153 passengers and crew members, mostly Americans. The pilot was forced at gunpoint to divert the flight to Beirut and then Algiers as the hijackers demanded that Israel release hundreds of Shia prisoners. Forty passengers, mostly women and children, were exchanged for fuel and food before the pilot was forced to return to Beirut, where a hijacker shot twenty-three-year-old Navy diver Robert Stetham in the head and threw his body onto the runway. In the subsequent confusion, other hijackers boarded the plane, which took off again for Algiers, where additional passengers were released, until 40 people remained held hostage. These passengers returned to Beirut and were transferred to a Lebanese jail, where they remained until June 30, when they were set free. (Israel released 700 Shia prisoners over the next few weeks, but claimed this was unrelated to the hijacking.)

This ritualized cycle of violence became part of the expanding portfolio of a then unknown functionary who had made a rapid ascent within the White House power structure, becoming National Security Adviser McFarlane's right-hand man. Oliver North could have been a movie star, a soulful tough guy like Mel Gibson (before the actor was reviled for a drunken, anti-Semitic rant) or Ronald Reagan, the president he served. North would soon enough become a familiar face, notorious for his role in the Iran-Contra affair, the illegal arms-for-hostage deal that became the biggest scandal to roil the Reagan administration. Already, in the summer of 1985, there had been press reports that the NSC staff, in violation of U.S. law, had provided illegal weapons and financial support to the insurgency of Nicaraguan contras battling that country's Sandinista socialist government. McFarlane, North's boss, had assured Congress that his staff had done nothing illegal.

This was an evasion, not the truth. In the spring, North had arranged military aid to the contras through an Iranian American arms dealer. By early fall he was involved in handling the logistics for arms shipments to Iran, dishonoring purported U.S. neutrality in the Iraq-Iran war; the deal was fostered by the Israeli government, which thought Iraq was the bigger enemy. That shipment led to the release of an American hostage held by Islamic militants in Lebanon.

Officially called the deputy director of military affairs for the NSC, North in fact was running a small, secretive counterterrorism unit in the White House, an offshoot of the Terrorist Incident Working Group, which had representatives from defense, intelligence, and law enforcement agencies, as well as the State Department. His mandate was to help change U.S. policy under the radar and to figure out how to implement preemptive strikes and covert operations, the aggressive agenda promoted by McFarlane, his boss, and endorsed by Shultz and Casey, but not Weinberger. The attacks on the Marines in Beirut and the TWA hijacking heightened North's intensity about his mission, aimed at giving the White House power to respond to international terrorism swiftly, without getting bogged down in oversight procedure. He saw this strategy as being effective. Others — inside and outside of the administration — would see it as going rogue.

Despite the Marine withdrawal from Beirut, North believed the Lebanon crisis had made the president a kindred spirit in pursuing terrorists by any means. "There were only two occasions when I saw President Reagan get really angry, and they both had to do with Beirut," he remembered. "The first time was on October 23, 1983, just after the terrorist bombing of our Marine barracks at the Beirut airport. The President was in Georgia on a weekend golf trip, and when the news came in he flew back immediately. He was in a white rage as he walked into the Sit Room, but he was also as alert and purposeful as I'd ever seen him."

North was encouraged by the words he heard the president say: "We'll make them pay."

Like Reagan, North was infuriated by his country's fallibility, the images on television and in newspapers that conveyed embarrassing weakness. He couldn't forget the photographs of the TWA pilot peering out of the cockpit window while a hijacker held a gun to his temple. "The terrorists wanted us to look impotent," he said, "and they certainly succeeded."

*   *   *

News of the *Achille Lauro* hijacking filtered up in the White House from the ground-floor Situation Room, where information was gathered, sifted and dispensed, 24/7. Sensitive matters, nerve-wracking situations, and red-button alerts were collected daily in a leather-bound folder, with the highlights summarized in the President's Daily Brief.

A CIA publication described the qualifications needed to work in the Situation Room: "Personal characteristics count: an even temperament, coolness under pressure, and the ability to have a coherent, professional, no-advance-notice conversation with the President of the United States." Humbleness, too, was a recommended virtue. "Just remember that there are many important people who work in the White House," the article reminded staff, "and you're not one of them."

When Michael Bohn, the director of the Situation Room, received word from the CIA at 9:30 a.m. local time on October 7, 1985, that Palestinians had possibly commandeered an Italian ship in the Mediterranean Sea, he reacted calmly, just as he had been trained. The information came from an SOS, picked up by Radio Gothenburg, a station in coastal Sweden, from the eastern Mediterranean, where it was already late afternoon.

"Here we go again," he thought. It seemed to him that every week he was adding another terrorist incident to the leather-bound file. He sent the news up the chain of command, to McFarlane and Deputy National Security Adviser John M. Poindexter, North's immediate boss. In the White House bureaucracy, what goes up, comes right back down. North was instructed to organize a meeting of his counterterrorism unit. It was his forty-second birthday. Before noon, more information came in from Israeli intelligence: the ship was *Achille Lauro* and Americans were on board.

For those promoting aggressive counterterrorism tactics, the hijacking offered an opportunity that was easy to sell in a bruised and bristling White House. Within twenty-four hours, North sent McFarlane a detailed memo, urging the use of military force to end the hijacking. In a handwritten note, scribbled in the margin, North revealed multiple motives for pursuing this strategy.

"Give this a chance," he wrote. "It may be the best opportunity we have to make the system work. On a personal note, it may be the only chance I have to survive the Contra business. Please give me that chance."

North understood there were sticky questions of maritime law, international treaties, and diplomatic vulnerability. Although there were Americans on board the *Achille Lauro*, most of the passengers were European, including many from Italy, Great Britain, and Germany. The ship was Italian and there were several other countries in the vicinity with stakes in the outcome, including Egypt, Syria, Lebanon, Cyprus, and Israel. And what would a preemptive strike look like? No one knew how many hijackers were on the ship, nor could they estimate how many hostages would die in a commando raid.

But North, like everyone in the Reagan White House, knew the president was tired of being humiliated by people with no respect for what he believed America stood for. He didn't want to watch the nightly news again and see an American held at gunpoint by some Middle Eastern no-name. It was time for a moment of reckoning.

Within a few hours a Delta Force special operations unit had left Fort Bragg, North Carolina, and was on a military transport headed for a British base on Cyprus. The State Department dispatched a twenty-person counterterrorism team to Rome. Secretary of State Shultz called Nicholas A. Veliotes, the U.S. ambassador in Egypt, urging him to keep the media away from the ship, if it landed there. The United States pressed Italian officials to ask Yasser Arafat if he could publicly assure the world the PLO had nothing to do with the hijacking. (The American afternoon was their bedtime; none of the Italians would sleep that night.) Someone asked the Israelis to keep an eye on the situation, as if they needed to be asked. Alternatives were discussed, including what the potential civilian casualties might be if Navy SEALs attacked the ship.

The State Department contacted several countries, including

Syria, asking them to deny entry if the *Achille Lauro* showed up at their ports—a request that would prove critical to the fate of Leon Klinghoffer.

Conversations ricocheted around the Mediterranean. Arafat assured the Italian government that the PLO wasn't involved in the hijacking. Greece offered landing space for military troops. The Egyptian ambassador to Italy said Egypt had aircraft monitoring the situation. The Italians sent warships into the eastern Mediterranean and helicopters carrying special forces to a British military airstrip on Cyprus.

As the diplomats, politicians, spies, bureaucrats, generals, and soldiers scrambled, strategies began to emerge. One by one, the pieces fell into place for this multidimensional game of chess.

But there could be no checkmate without the centerpiece of the game and the king had gone missing. Where was the *Achille Lauro*? After Captain De Rosa made contact with Sweden that afternoon and Bassam al-Ashker ordered him to turn the radio off, the ship dropped off the grid. Without radio contact, satellite tracking didn't connect. With a flip of the switch, four angry young men on the edge of hysteria were keeping the mightiest power in the world at bay. There were intermittent unconfirmed sightings reported, nothing reliable. The cruise ship was moving along a vast sea. As the long night slipped by, nobody could point to a map and say "there."

4
The Nightmare

Tartus, Syria

As the boat approached Tartus on Tuesday morning, October 8, someone asked Gerardo De Rosa how things were going. He offered reassurance in his calmest, most sincere voice.

"All we have to do is be patient for a few hours more," he said, adding that when the ship reached Tartus, "the nightmare will be over."

He felt hopeful that the hijacking would reach a bloodless conclusion. The Syrians would give the Palestinians asylum and the *Achille Lauro* would go on its way. "For all of us, by then, Tartus had become a kind of cliché; the end of fear," he would recall. "The terrorists would get off the ship and that is what counted."

Captain De Rosa didn't allow himself to think through the hijacker demands that Israel release Palestinian prisoners. Holding the crew and passengers hostage was their only bargaining chip. Would they be safer in a friendly Arab port, where the Palestinians could have political and logistical support?

He was overoptimistic perhaps, but not delusional. The evening before, when Ashker had allowed De Rosa to go back down to the Salon Arazzi to check on the passengers, the captain found a scene that was surprisingly calm. Most of the passengers and crew were asleep, though some were snacking on the sandwiches and pastries the Palestinians had passed around. He noticed that the children in the group had been tucked into easy chairs full of pillows and covered with blankets. A barista was playing cards with one of the hijackers.

De Rosa blanched when he saw passengers and hijackers companionably smoking. In a friendly gesture, the hijackers had handed out cartons of cigarettes to their captives. But they had also lined about ten open canisters of kerosene along the wall, with one placed menacingly in the center of the room. They warned the crew that any reprisals would lead them to light the kerosene.

The cigarettes raised another alarm for the captain. Remember, Salon Arazzi translates into Tapestry Hall; De Rosa knew the long curtains surrounding the room were upholstered with flammable material. He wanted to tell everyone to put out their smokes; however, weighing the combustibility factors, including the level of anxiety, he simply asked everyone to be careful.

Amid alternating currents of calm and agitation, De Rosa kept asking himself whether he should have led a retaliation by the crew. Then he did the math that justified his choice: an AK-47 holds 30 shots; with the second magazine the Palestinians hooked onto the rifles, 60 shots per rifle. Multiply times four and you have 240 bullets, enough for a massacre.

After checking in on the passengers, De Rosa was escorted back up to the bridge by Ashker, who was his constant companion. The teenager and his AK-47 never left the captain's side. Though the other officers navigating the ship were nearby, De Rosa felt isolated, caught in a lonely psychological duel with his guard.

The captain realized how young Ashker was when he noticed him preening at his reflection in a window. De Rosa thought of his captor as "the Arabian boy." The hijacker's youth both tugged at his sympathy and frightened him. De Rosa had two daughters. He knew from experience how easy it was to trigger adolescent rage and this teenager was holding a dangerous weapon.

At first Ashker ignored the captain's attempts at conversation until De Rosa asked about the music he played for hours, at full blast. The sound of it grated on the captain's nerves, like the rock music his daughters kept trying to make him understand. "They're love songs, just beautiful," Ashker explained. "It's the story of a young man who goes away and leaves his girlfriend."

De Rosa was relieved to hear this familiar theme. The Neapolitan songs De Rosa grew up with were also full of ill-fated love. He still heard the Middle Eastern rhythms as a monotonous drone but was comforted to think he had something in common with the hijacker. He needed to convince himself he could influence Ashker.

When De Rosa tried to unscramble his thoughts and emotions, he felt the night passing in a state of suspended animation. In his recollection, the hours unfolded as a dream play starring him and his captor, the experience heightened by the effects of almost two nights without sleep.

De Rosa would remember his prolonged encounter with "the Arabian boy" in oddly intimate terms, as they passed the time smoking and drinking coffee and talking in the dark. Ashker told De Rosa the story of his upbringing in refugee camps, and De Rosa offered fatherly lectures on how violence would only lead to more violence. Their conversation meandered through personal revelation and philosophical questioning, interrupted by brief bursts of anger, when De Rosa made one assumption too many about how far he could go.

"I don't understand the way you're going about reaching your objective," he said.

Ashker exploded in rage. "Who gives me the chance to speak?" he yelled. "The day that I come out into the open, the moment I try to speak up and convince them of something, not only would I not succeed but I would be killed."

He told the captain that Palestinians were backed into a corner. "For this conflict we are ready to give our lives," he said.

Several times Ashker repeated that he may have hated Americans more than Jews, because without U.S. support, the Arabs would have easily defeated Israel—just look at the numbers.

And so it went, back and forth, another debate on the intractable conflict, another conversation that would derail, resulting in yet another death.

At dawn, Captain De Rosa felt hopeful, with the Syrian shore just a few hours away. He was touched when Ashker asked if he could rest in the captain's room for a while. The boy noticed a pair of cuff links on the dresser and asked De Rosa what they were.

"Gemelli," the captain replied, using the Italian word, and then the English translation: "Twins." When he saw Ashker didn't understand, De Rosa said, "Brothers."

Comprehending, Ashker asked De Rosa if he could have one of them as a gift. When the captain said yes, the hijacker replied, "Why don't you join up with us?"

De Rosa changed the subject, pointing to the sunrise, which seemed particularly spectacular that morning, the fiery clouds casting a reddish tint onto the sea.

"See," he said, "the sun still rises."

Seymour Meskin woke up that Tuesday morning, October 8, having slept fitfully, slumped in a chair. His hip ached; he was seventy years old, still recovering from surgery six months earlier. At least he had a chair. Most of the other hostages were huddled on the floor of the Salon Arazzi. The large hall was not glamorous now, the air stifling from the heat rising up from bodies crammed together, the acrid scent of urine and fear wafting through the room.

Meskin was an accountant, a logical thinker by nature. Eventually he would record the events in a thirty-seven-page report, handwritten on legal paper in unemotional prose, with painstaking attention to external detail. His style was not to reveal how he felt. Meskin was interested in the events leading up to the hijacking, piecing together how men armed with assault rifles had infiltrated a passenger ship.

He had inadvertently been the founder of the Beach People, the group a by-product of a real estate deal gone sour. Meskin had gotten stuck with a condo complex on the Jersey Shore; he reduced his losses by persuading family, friends, and acquaintances to buy units there. That's how he and the Klinghoffers became friends.

Five days had passed since the eleven of them boarded the *Achille*

Lauro. The trip from New York had seemed arduous, a laughable notion now. The previous Thursday they'd arrived at the cavernous embarkation hall in Genoa, following an overnight flight from JFK to Milan and a two-hour bus ride. None of them were youngsters; they ranged in age from fifty-eight to seventy-one. At the time, the sleep-deprived group just wanted to get on the ship. They didn't worry that security appeared to be nonexistent, except for a routine passport check. Why would there be intensive screening? Cruise ships had been spared from the terrorist attacks on airplanes that had become regular occurrences in the 1970s. Their main concern was that their luggage would get lost in the shuffle, as exiting and entering passengers thronged in the ship terminal. Miraculously, all their bags ended up on the boat.

They had been enjoying themselves on the cruise, though there were complaints that the ship didn't quite meet the expectations promised in the advertising. Seymour's sister-in-law Mildred Hodes would say later, back in the United States, "If I boarded that boat in this country I would have gotten off. It was very European, not upscale, kind of a crummy boat."

If Mildred had her way, she would have never left New Jersey, but her husband, Frank, loved to travel. And it would have been hard to say no to Marilyn Klinghoffer, who suggested the trip to her friends from the Jersey Shore. Marilyn had been ill and needed help with her husband; Leon had a special kinship with Frank, who sold insurance and was a fellow World War II veteran. Frank's daughter called her father the ultimate schmoozer, someone who got along with everybody. After Leon's stroke, when other people struggled to understand his garbled speech, Frank would sit and talk with him like nothing was out of the ordinary.

Now Frank was off the ship, among the five members of their group who went on the excursion to the Pyramids. Mildred had signed up to see the Pyramids but had woken up feeling ill; she encouraged Frank to go without her.

The decision to divide up had been a practical, convivial way to manage the needs and desires of everyone. The basic tenet they'd set up for the trip was: each should follow his or her inclination while respecting the group. None of them would have missed the festivities on Sunday night, when they all celebrated Marilyn's birthday, the purpose of the voyage.

Those who remained on the ship on Monday had changed into bathing suits and had sunbathed by one of the swimming pools until it was time for lunch. Still wearing swimsuits and shorts, they had made the trek from the Lido Deck down to the dining hall five stories below. Marilyn and Leon took the elevator. It was pleasantly quiet, since most of the passengers had gone on the excursion—after all, the promotional literature promised an itinerary that would "take one's memory back to the distant time when what would become today's Western civilization was being formed."

The New Jersey friends had just finished their main courses and were waiting for dessert when they heard explosive sounds. Soon they saw men with Kalashnikovs herding people into the dining room, yelling at everyone to drop to the floor.

There was a jittery improvisational feel to the experience that informed people's memories of it. Marilyn Klinghoffer's first reaction to the muscled young men holding AK-47s was to wonder: Is this some bizarre form of entertainment?

The authenticity quickly became apparent when bullets shattered glass and the hijackers ordered three of the women to sit on the floor, briefly forcing them to hold live grenades in their hands.

People followed their instincts. Sylvia Sherman, Seymour's cousin, was an artist; she automatically grabbed a menu and drew sketches of the hijackers on the front and back. Sylvia crafted a credible sketch of a man pointing his AK-47 toward the dessert listings, the barrel aimed toward the mocha torte; she placed a hijacker's profile next to the notation for the goulash daily special.

Meanwhile, an Austrian woman hid in a cabin, where she would remain for days, surviving on two apples left from the welcome fruit basket.

Most people simply obeyed. They didn't know what else to do.

The Jewish passengers felt an ingrained response, the fear of anti-Semitism lurking even in those born in the United States. Many of the men had fought in the war against Hitler—including Leon Klinghoffer, who joined the Army Air Corps in 1942, right after America entered World War II, and was trained as an airplane mechanic. They watched the evening news and saw what was going on in the Middle East. They didn't have to be paranoid to worry about being singled out as Jews when confronted with men holding machine guns and speaking Arabic—even those like the Klinghoffers, who were mildly observant Jews, their national identity solidly American with a sentimental, familial connection to Israel. While the Holy Land was never their homeland, it was an appreciated Jewish refuge, a place to plant a tree in honor of someone who had died.

Accordingly, when the passengers had been ordered to follow the captain four flights up to the Salon Arazzi on Monday afternoon, Mildred Hodes pulled a card out of her wallet and dropped it onto a lounge chair. Seymour Meskin politely retrieved it and she threw it back down. "It's my B'nei Brit card," she whispered. "What if they want to pick out the Jews in the group?"

Meskin got her point, yanked the gold *chai*—a Jewish symbol of life—from around his neck, and threw it away.

The hijackers reinforced the sense of alarm by making some noise about Jews, but they didn't press the issue. When they collected passports to identify groups to isolate, they focused on citizens from the United States and Great Britain, choosing a dozen Americans and six British to sit apart from the others, near the entrance to the room.

At first the hijackers seemed bent solely on cowing the hostages. One of them, wearing a gold chain and a shirt that said MEN, strutted by the Americans and shouted, "Arafat good! Reagan bad!" (not that effective an insult for the Beach People, most of whom were Democrats). The hijackers shushed anyone who talked and refused to let people go to the bathroom until they realized the passengers were becoming unhinged by their bladders. Eventually, the women were allowed to line up to use the two restrooms; the men had to relieve themselves behind curtains separating two stages, where the orchestra usually played.

As evening fell on Monday, the relationship between captors and captives shifted between intimidation and accommodation. The hijackers asked waiters to pass out sandwiches, drinks, and fresh fruit and played Arab music on a radio. They allowed a woman in a wet bathing suit to go to her cabin and put on dry clothes. When the room became cool, they ordered the crew to bring blankets for the passengers. They handed out the cartons of cigarettes that would alarm Captain De Rosa and allowed people who could find chairs to sit on them instead of the floor.

Like the captain, the passengers were buffeted by alternating currents of emotion. Anger and fear became mixed with curiosity and another feeling—not affection exactly, rather a need to find a bond with their captors. Several people commented on the designer jeans the hijackers wore. They gave Ashker's friend Fataier a nickname—Rambo—after the Sylvester Stallone character in the then popular movie about a decorated Vietnam vet who becomes a vigilante antihero. Fataier did resemble the movie star; he had the same curled lip, those hurt-puppy eyes.

One of the hijackers came over to Leon, sitting in his wheelchair. The chair was parked next to Marilyn, who sat beside him on the floor. The young man covered Leon with a blanket and handed him a cigarette; Marilyn returned the kindness with a hug and a grateful kiss. "They seemed so middle class," she thought, "like people you could relate to."

The captain had explained that the hijackers planned to ask the Syrian authorities to negotiate with Israel to release Palestinian prisoners. Then the passengers on the *Achille Lauro* would be set free.

The U.S. citizens in particular accepted this scenario as plausible. Unlike the Europeans, they had never experienced a terrorist attack within the borders of their country. The Americans believed they had a right to safety, an entitlement that was implicit in the passports they carried.

*   *   *

At around eleven Tuesday morning, the ship slowed and the engines were stopped as the boat paused in the outer waters of the harbor at Tartus. The city was visible through the light fog that hung over the sea that warm autumn morning.

Within an hour, however, the atmosphere in the Salon Arazzi became charged with tension once again. There was no more joking or having congenial smokes with the hijackers. The passengers didn't know what was going on, yet it was obvious that something had changed. Their captors seemed angry and out of control.

They ordered the Americans and British passengers sitting near the front of the hall to move to a small upper deck, painted green, built on a round platform right above the Salon Arazzi. There was no elevator leading to that deck. When Marilyn began to push Leon in his wheelchair toward the steep stairs, the hijackers stopped her.

Her memory later distilled the moment to its terrible essence.

"I said, I can't leave him, please let me stay.

"They said, no, he'll be OK."

She moved toward the narrow staircase anyway, still pushing Leon.

She remembered the man telling her to leave him.

"I told them I couldn't leave him and begged them to let me stay behind with him. They responded by putting a gun to my head and ordering me up the stairs."

As Marilyn climbed the steps she was struck by the blazing midday sun. The fog had lifted. She always tried to stay in the shade; even though her cancer was in remission, she took drugs that warned against exposure to the sun. In the distance, she could see the shore, some buildings shimmering in the heat.

She saw cans of kerosene on the deck and one of the hijackers said, "You will get hit first if American commandos come."

Marilyn and the others sat broiling on the hot planks of the deck, which had no guardrails. One of the terrorists knocked Seymour

Meskin's white sailor cap off his head. Two more people were brought to the round green surface; they were elderly Jews with Austrian passports. One of the hijackers whacked the man with his AK-47. Another let them all know that the hijackers were negotiating with the British and American consuls in Syria; if the talks didn't go positively, the hostages would be killed one by one.

Marilyn grew more fearful as she realized how young the hijackers seemed. "They kept popping their guns and playing with grenades on their belts, like little kids," she would recall.

Clouds covered the sun, offering some respite.

Still, Marilyn felt sick from exhaustion and heat. When she tried to lie down, one of the hijackers smacked her with his machine gun and told her to sit up.

She would remember hearing two shots and a splash. She looked at her watch: it was 3 p.m.

She felt as though she was being watched. Glancing up, she saw the captain on the bridge staring down at her.

Her greatest concern at that moment did not foreshadow the misery ahead.

"I knew Leon would start to get worried," she recalled.

Up in the radio room, after the boat anchored, Captain De Rosa had watched Bassam al-Ashker and Majid al-Molqi go back and forth with the Syrian authorities. De Rosa didn't need to understand Arabic to know the talks were not going well; he knew the answer to the Palestinian demands was no.

"His eyes were like those of a madman," the captain would recall, speaking of Ashker. "He was trembling. He had removed the safety latch from his rifle."

The camaraderie they'd established the night before evaporated. "The boy who, in the end, was fairly levelheaded, fairly reasonable, and even open to discussion, to understanding and being understood, seemed to no longer exist," De Rosa would write. "In his place there was once again a fanatical being, frenzied, almost an 'alien.'"

With his hands shaking, Ashker threatened to kill De Rosa and the crew in the navigation room.

De Rosa became furious at the Syrians, not realizing they were being pressured not to negotiate by U.S. officials. He felt they essentially had written off the *Achille Lauro*. "They behaved as if we hostages didn't exist," he would write.

From the bridge, he looked down and glimpsed the American and British passengers arriving on the small green deck above the Salon Arazzi. He had only a partial view, which included the sight of Marilyn Klinghoffer. She and the others looked up at him; he saw desperation, or maybe he was feeling his own. The captain tipped his cap, trying to reassure them, though he was filled with dread.

Was he looking at the first victims if the Palestinians upped the ante? The Palestinians had put kerosene tanks up there. If there were any kind of attack from shore or the air, they could explode. Also, the deck was slippery and had no railing; if the sea turned rough these hostages could fall into the sea.

The discussions with the Syrians had gone on for almost three hours. Molqi demanded the release of fifty Palestinians from Israeli prisons and wanted negotiations to take place in the presence of the American, German, and British ambassadors, as well as representatives of the Red Cross. There was a deadline of two hours, then an extension, and then the Syrians asked for another.

That's when Molqi decided to act.

"We will start killing at three p.m.," he told the Syrians.

With that, Molqi left the pilothouse and stormed downstairs, entered the Salon Arazzi, and ordered a Portuguese waiter to take the American in the wheelchair to the ship's stern.

Omar al-Assadi was guarding the hostages in the ballroom alone; Fataier had left to take a shower and change his pants.

Assadi saw Molqi's rage and guessed what was about to transpire. He begged Molqi not to kill the American.

Molqi told Assadi to shut up and threatened to disarm him and make him a hostage. He accused him of insubordination.

Their argument took place in Arabic, so the passengers didn't know what it was about. Nor was it particularly alarming given the general sense of panic. The two men had snapped at each other before. On Molqi's command, Manuel De Souza, a Portuguese waiter in his twenties, pushed Leon Klinghoffer to the opposite end of the ship, far from view of the passengers and crew. Assault rifle in hand, Molqi followed them during this tortured hike past the Capri Club, the movie theater, all the way to the front deck, near the discotheque. When they arrived at the stern, as far as they could go, Molqi ordered the waiter to stand around the corner, on the opposite side of the ship, and to wait.

It was another sunny day in the Mediterranean.

The waiter stood trembling in the sea air only a couple of minutes and then he heard gunshots. Two rounds.

Molqi appeared and called for him.

De Souza confronted a sickening sight, the elderly man turned upside down still in his wheelchair, his chest covered in blood.

Molqi ordered the waiter to throw the American into the sea. De Souza tried, but Klinghoffer was too heavy. His body dropped back to the deck.

Molqi ordered the waiter to stay there, warning him that if he moved he was a dead man. De Souza wanted to cry but tears wouldn't come.

Minutes later Molqi returned, accompanied by Ferruccio Alberti, a hairdresser.

The waiter and the hairdresser didn't look at each other or at Klinghoffer as they completed their horrific task. After they threw Klinghoffer and then his wheelchair overboard, Molqi ordered them to clean up the mess. He made it clear they were to keep their mouths shut and they obeyed. Then Molqi went to the front of the ship and upstairs to the pilothouse, where Ashker was guarding the captain.

He handed Leon Klinghoffer's passport to De Rosa and said, "American, kaput!"

De Rosa did not want to believe what he had heard, but how else to explain the blood on Molqi's pale jeans and sneakers?

"Up until that point, Molqi was an officer, a lieutenant in a haphazard army that was inflicting violence upon us, intimidating us with weapons," De Rosa would write. "But he had not killed, and none of his men had killed. Now everything had changed. Now they really seemed like terrorists."

As if to underscore the point, Molqi showed the captain a second passport, belonging to Mildred Hodes, Seymour Meskin's sister-in-law, whose husband, Frank, had gone to see the Pyramids.

Pointing at Klinghoffer's passport, Molqi held up one finger. Mildred Hodes, he indicated, would be number two. De Rosa tried to reason with the hijackers, saying they had achieved their goal: they had brought the Palestinian plight to the world's attention. Then a grand gesture slipped out of his mouth, almost without thought. More killing was not necessary, he told them. If an additional sacrifice was necessary, he said, let it be him. Ashker and Molqi declined the offer. Instead, they ordered the captain to transmit a message to shore, saying they had killed not one American, but two. That would be the first lie De Rosa would be forced to tell.

He glanced down at the hostages on the green deck to see if they had registered what had happened.

"They did not seem any more unsettled or agitated than before," he thought. "A sign that they were not aware of Klinghoffer's murder." He gave special attention to Marilyn Klinghoffer and believed her expression had not changed either.

For an hour Molqi and Ashker spoke in Arabic with the shore. At 4:30, they gave a new order to Captain De Rosa to set sail for Libya, a two-day journey. They made it clear that they did not want anyone on the ship to know about the murder, and brought De Souza and Alberti, the waiter and the hairdresser, up to the pilothouse to reinforce the message.

Ashker ordered De Rosa to convey a warning: "Whatever they have done and whatever they will do, they have to remain in absolute silence; otherwise we will kill them," he said. "Wherever they are, we will kill them."

Before the ship began to move, Molqi ordered Assadi to accompany Marilyn Klinghoffer and the other American and British hostages off the deck and take them back downstairs to the Salon Arazzi.

Marilyn began asking the passengers who had remained there if they had seen her husband. A British woman said she had seen him being wheeled out on deck. "I know he wasn't feeling well," she told Marilyn. A crew member said he thought Leon was in the infirmary.

Marilyn approached Fataier, the hijacker they called Rambo. He had just come back from taking a shower. He told her he didn't know where her husband was, and he couldn't allow her to look for him. When she insisted, he pushed her to the floor with his gun.

Marilyn didn't know it, but her question had thrown Fataier into a panic. Where was the American in the wheelchair? As Marilyn continued to move around the lounge, trying to find someone who knew something, Fataier ran upstairs to confront Molqi.

Molqi's response was utterly demoralizing. With cold dispassion, Molqi said he had killed the man and had him thrown in the water.

Fataier asked him where and Molqi replied, On the stern.

Fataier asked why and Molqi did not answer.

When Fataier told Molqi he should have consulted the others, Molqi made it clear he had nothing more to say and ordered Fataier to isolate the Americans and British from the other passengers, once again.

Fataier returned to the Salon Arazzi and obeyed Molqi's orders, leading the Americans and British into an adjacent room stocked with a slide and swings, where children could play inside when the weather was bad.

New York City

THAT TUESDAY, the hijacking was the lead story in the *New York Times* and every news broadcast. Ilsa and Lisa Klinghoffer knew only that their parents were on the *Achille Lauro* and among the hostages. Their friend and public relations adviser Letty Simon arranged a whirlwind tour of a half-dozen TV news programs, which would include the major morning talk shows. Letty told them to emphasize their parents' poor health, hoping that—maybe, somehow, irrationally—the hijackers were watching the morning news.

On ABC's *Good Morning America*, Ilsa told Joan Lunden, the interviewer, "My father is a stroke victim, he is paralyzed on the right side…he needs medication daily and without this medication he will develop complications. Stress is a terrible problem with him."

Lisa, who was also on camera with her husband, Jerry, explained her parents hadn't been concerned about traveling in the Middle East, despite the recent TWA hijacking. "This is the first time this has ever happened on a boat," Lisa said. "It's unbelievable to us."

Lunden ended the interview on a sympathetic note.

"We hope to hear good news about your families soon," she said.

The segment concluded at 7:22 a.m., Eastern Standard Time. Leon Klinghoffer would be dead in less than an hour. His daughters continued to run from interview to interview that morning, hoping to rescue their parents, even after Leon was gone; not even the other passengers on the ship were aware of the killing.

Back at the apartment, Letty Simon was fielding hundreds of calls, trying to return all of them, partly because some reporters seemed to have more information than the State Department.

By midday, feeling overwhelmed by the onslaught of interview requests, Letty decided to grant semiexclusive access to one journalist. They needed to have an in-depth human-interest story published, something that might find its way to the hijackers and arouse their sympathy for Leon and Marilyn's family.

Facing the crowd of reporters in front of the apartment building who had been waiting for her periodic briefings, Letty spotted Sara Rimer. At that instant, Letty believed she had identified the perfect person to tell the tale with sympathy and credibility. She knew Rimer's byline and believed she would bring the requisite heart to the story. Most important, that byline appeared in the most influential news outlet in Letty's world, the *New York Times*. After the informal press conference, she invited Rimer to come up to the apartment to meet the family.

Rimer was in a mild panic when Letty approached her. Her editor had given her the assignment at the last minute and, even though she'd gotten on the subway near the *Times* headquarters on Forty-Third Street right away, she was late. The press conference was ending as she arrived. She was terrified of missing the story and having to face the wrath of Abe Rosenthal, the paper's volatile executive editor.

Rimer, who was thirty-one years old, was relatively new at the *Times*; after two years, the place still intimidated her. The newspaper had been part of her New York fantasy since she was a girl in Levittown, New Jersey. She'd spent almost a decade after college working toward her destination, beginning in Florida, in the Naples bureau of the *Miami Herald*, writing four or five stories a day and taking her own photographs. After that, there was a brief stint at the *Washington Post*, and then finally she made it to the *New York Times* in the late summer of 1983.

When she entered the Klinghoffer apartment, Rimer couldn't have predicted that she was about to write a front-page article that would become part of one of the biggest stories of the year. She identified with Ilsa and Lisa almost immediately. They were around her age; her family was close like theirs; she had sisters and her parents had a happy marriage like Leon and Marilyn.

The Klinghoffer sisters had many stories to tell about their father, a workaholic who would make a trip to Long Island City in Queens in the middle of the night when awakened by a phone call alert that someone had broken into the factory. If there was a job to do, he jumped in, even at the most inopportune moments. When Leon was taking Marilyn to the hospital to deliver Ilsa, a neighbor stopped him to ask whether he could help fix his front door lock, which was broken. "Wait here," Leon said to his wife, "I'll just be a minute." He fixed the lock and they proceeded to the hospital.

Though Marilyn got upset sometimes, she usually indulged Leon.

They shared a fundamental belief in action. Marilyn, too, was a worker. For years, she managed Leon's business. In 1972 she went to work for Gralla Publications, which published business magazines. Her first job was circulation clerk, paying three dollars an hour. By 1976 she was assistant personnel director and chief hand-holder for the company's four hundred employees. She wasn't one of those Jewish mothers who cooked homemade meals for her family every night. The girls remembered her coming home from work and ordering in. The Klinghoffers always gathered for Friday night dinners, but the Sabbath meal was assembled from take-out containers. Leon bought a chocolate cake or strawberry shortcake. Klinghoffers don't cook, Marilyn explained to her daughters.

The girls were privileged, but not pampered. After school, even after they moved to Greenwich Village, they still worked at the hardware store, sorting nails and screws, stocking shelves, shoveling snow off the sidewalk outside.

Leon was a brusque businessman and a workaholic with a temper, but he could be a soft touch, especially when it came to his family, they recalled. The only thing that could pry Leon from work in the middle of the day was one of his daughter's piano recitals. He made sure they knew how to ride a bike, running behind them when they took off.

Lisa and Ilsa told Rimer how their parents worked hard and then unwound with equal fervor. Almost every Saturday night Marilyn and Leon went out. This ritual was preceded by elaborate preparation. Marilyn headed to the beauty parlor to have her hair styled and her fingernails manicured. When she returned home, she took her time applying makeup, layer by layer. Her daughers saw how carefully she chose her outfits, accessorizing with just the right jewelry. When the whole thing was put together, she sealed the package with a big spritz of Jungle Gardenia, her favorite perfume.

Marilyn liked to throw parties. The Klinghoffer apartment became a gathering place for a large circle of friends and family. Some nights Marilyn, who at one time fantasized about becoming an opera singer, provided the entertainment. She played the piano and sang show tunes from all her favorite Broadway musicals; it didn't take much encouragement to get her going. Leon didn't say much, just smoked cigars and sipped some bourbon, looking content and watching Marilyn's dazzle light up the room.

After hearing about this family, Rimer understood how, even in this moment of crisis, the Klinghoffer sisters had managed to put themselves together—nice clothes, makeup, their curly hair put in place. She saw photographs of Marilyn, with her exquisite cheekbones and perfect teeth, and Leon, grown portly with age and lack of exercise, the curly hair long gone from his shiny head, but appearing full of pride in his family.

That evening she returned to the *Times* newsroom and began to type. In 1,070 words, under the headline "To Hostage Families, Waiting Back Home Is Also a Nightmare," Rimer created a warm yet efficient portrait of the Klinghoffers and their friends, offering people in the United States a recognizable connection to the hijacking. She wrote about how Leon was now in a wheelchair, introduced the "beach people," quoted Ilsa referring to her mother as "Mommy," and offered the touching tidbit that, for Marilyn and Leon's anniversary, their daughters had bought their parents new luggage to take on the cruise. The article ended on a hopeful note, with a quote from Paul Dworin, Ilsa's fiancé: "They're OK," he said. "They're OK. I just know it."

5

Lies, Then Heartbreak

Port Said, Egypt

A bu al-Abbas was barely known outside Palestinian circles and the Israeli operatives who infiltrated them. If recognized at all, his name was associated with the showman's flair that led him to concoct dramatic incursions into Israel from Lebanon by hot-air balloon and hang glider, efforts meant to demonstrate that the impregnable country could be invaded. The symbolism was vivid, the results disappointing and sometimes disastrous, ending with the death or imprisonment of his men in Israeli prisons and widely publicized killings of Israeli civilians. Within the Palestinian movement, which thrived on bold gestures and impassioned leaders, Abbas gained currency as a brave soldier who had seen combat and a shrewd strategist who had outmaneuvered numerous rivals from competing factions. As Yasser Arafat began to dangle an olive branch as one option in a multifaceted strategy, Abbas grew in stature among Palestinians as a hard-line dissident. Arafat tried to defang Abbas by making him an ally; in November 1984, almost a year before the hijacking, Arafat endorsed Abbas's election to the PLO's eleven-member executive committee.

For Abbas, the *Achille Lauro* operation was part of the long game, another necessary, if doomed, attempt to breach the Israeli seawall; the failed Nahariyya incursion had been another such attack. The idea for the *Achille Lauro* operation came to Abbas as he stood on a balcony overlooking the harbor of Algiers. It occurred to him then that a strike on an Israeli port would have devastating, symbolic impact. Ashdod was a major port and naval base, about twenty miles from Gaza's northern border.

Yasser Arafat now had different goals—at least that was his public stance. Privately, he condoned the operation when Abu al-Abbas proposed it to him after the bombing of the PLO headquarters at Hamman Chott. But Arafat told Abbas from the start that his name could not be connected to it. "Whether it is going to be successful or a failure, I'm not going to be part of that," the PLO chairman said. "Go but never mention my name." The hijacking had the potential to destroy Arafat's decade-long attempt to have the PLO regarded as a legitimate political entity seeking a peaceful solution, rather than a terrorist gang. In 1975, three years after the massacre at the Munich Olympics, Arafat had officially renounced acts of international terrorism (though the PLO persisted in its refusal to acknowledge the existence of Israel and continued to advocate "armed struggle" against the Jewish state). The PLO chairman needed to resolve the hijacking as soon as possible; he had already condemned it and offered assurances to the Italian government he would do whatever he could to find a bloodless solution.

Wanting to keep his distance, Arafat remained in Tunis and dispatched his trusted aide Hani al-Hassan and Abu al-Abbas to Port Said, to see if they could persuade the Egyptians to provide haven for the hijackers. Putting Abbas out front gave Arafat plausible deniability while sending the PLF commander a dual message: Abbas held substantial power and a modicum of Arafat's trust—for now. That could change quickly if he was unable to correct course on this failed mission.

On Tuesday evening, around three hours after the *Achille Lauro* left Syrian waters and headed west toward Libya, Abbas made the telephone call that would pluck him out of obscurity in the West and place him in the middle of the tortured debates about the *Achille Lauro* going on within the U.S. State Department as well as between America and its Mediterranean allies.

The call was to Radio Monte Carlo, an Arabic-language station in

Cyprus that was often used by Palestinian activists to broadcast messages. Identifying himself as Abu Khaled, an official of the PLF, Abbas took responsibility for the hijacking and urged the hijackers to "treat the passengers and crew well, to head for Port Said, and to maintain constant radio contact with authorities in the Egyptian port."

The message got through. Following these instructions, the hijackers ordered the *Achille Lauro* to change its destination once again, to Egypt rather than Libya. Shortly after the ship left Syrian waters, it was spotted by an Israeli patrol boat; soon three U.S. Navy vessels began shadowing the cruise ship, prepared to take action.

By nightfall on Tuesday, October 8, one group in the U.S. State Department was urging a rescue operation, while others counseled restraint. "These were very desperate people," explained an analyst in an internal report. "It would be very dangerous."

Everyone was trying to identify the mysterious Abu Khaled. Even when CIA analysts ascertained that he was Mohammed al-Abbas, no one had heard of him. "Who the hell is this guy?" Nicholas Veliotes, the U.S. ambassador to Egypt, asked officials in Washington (he never got an answer). The Egyptians whom Veliotes talked to also didn't know anything about Abbas, or so they said. The Italians had heard from Arafat that Abbas was a PLO emissary, which seemed curious after the Italian secret service issued a report that Abbas's loyalty to Arafat was questionable; that report also asserted that in fact Abbas was an active combatant, not a diplomat, and someone with strong ties to Iraq.

Someone in the State Department found the September 1985 issue of *Al-Watan Al-Arabi*, an Arabic-language magazine published in Paris, which contained an interview with Abu al-Abbas. In that article, Abbas discredited the PLO negotiations. "All the current plans do not suit our national struggle and its aims," he said. "This is the season for U.S. moves in the region, moves not aimed at solving the Palestinian issue or settling the Middle East crisis. They are aimed at liquidating the issue and ignore the main Palestinian requirements: the right to return, the right to self-determination, and the right to establish a state."

When asked about suicide missions, Abbas replied that the PLF "formed a special committee to discuss the possibility of carrying out special operations inside the occupied territories. This will be a new style of fighting which we hope will succeed in raising the morale of our people."

The U.S. effort to decipher Abbas's role and deal with the hijacking was complicated by the fact that each of America's allies had its own agenda, or multiple agendas. No one fully trusted anyone. Egypt's President Hosni Mubarak supported the 1978 Camp David Peace Accords, which led to the peace treaty signed the following year at the White House by Mubarak's predecessor, Anwar el-Sadat, and Israeli Prime Minister Menachem Begin. The treaty called for billions of dollars in U.S. aid to Cairo, but Egypt was an Arab country with conflicting allegiances to weigh.

Similarly, the Italian government balanced on a diplomatic high wire. The Italians were allies and supporters of American anti-Soviet policies and collaborators with the Israelis in previous antiterrorism efforts, while also sympathetic to the Palestinians. Prime Minister Bettino Craxi had two main objectives in foreign policy: to bring an end to the Israeli-Palestinian conflict and the terrorism it produced throughout the region and to defeat Soviet-inspired communism. Craxi had met secretly in Tunisia with Yasser Arafat several times the previous December and prided himself on having constructive interactions with Arab states. He believed that without credible peace talks, terrorism would continue to create chaos in Western Europe. Italy had made a nonaggression pact with the PLO in the 1970s, bargaining that a sympathetic stance toward the organization would dissuade it from training and supplying arms to Italian national terrorists, particularly the Red Brigades, a leftist paramilitary group infamous for antigovernment violence manifested through kidnappings, murders, and robberies. "Italy is a Palestinian shore of the Mediterranean," Arafat wrote in his diary. Craxi's foreign minister, Giulio Andreotti, a former prime minister, had long been a mediator between Italy and the PLO. Craxi was open about his sympathy for the PLO: he owned a villa in Tunis and referred to the Israeli bombing at Hamman Chott in Tunisia the previous week as "a terrorist action," not anticipating that he would soon be dealing with the repercussions of the Palestinian retaliation.

Regardless of his own leanings, Craxi could not ignore the Americans, whose displeasure could cost him dearly, and the United States was taking its cues from Israeli intelligence. Before Abbas transmitted his message to the *Achille Lauro*, Craxi met with U.S. Ambassador Maxwell Rabb in Rome, urging him to persuade Washington to be prudent and to consider "the high-risk potential in terms of human life that a military action could pose." Rabb politely expressed appreciation for Italy's cooperation before essentially dismissing Craxi's concerns. Informing the prime minister that his instructions came directly from President Reagan, the ambassador said the U.S. government believed reports that American citizens had been killed and intended to attempt a military rescue sometime Wednesday night.

With the deadline now fixed, Craxi felt even more pressed to bring the ship's hostages to safety as quickly as possible. He reached out to Egyptian authorities to grant safe passage to the hijackers, but only on one condition: it was imperative that "no acts of violence had been committed that were prosecutable based on Italian criminal law."

This seemed like an implausible demand even as Craxi delivered it. The captain of the ship had already indicated that possibly two people had been killed. How would Egypt be able to assure Italy that "no acts of violence" had occurred? That night, the only safe prediction was that a showdown was coming and it most likely would occur at Port Said.

By early Wednesday morning, October 9, the *Achille Lauro* dropped anchor fifteen miles offshore from that Egyptian city, known as the northern gateway to the Suez Canal. Abu al-Abbas and Hani al-Hassan were waiting in the Suez Canal House, where the Egyptian government had set up a command post with a radio-telephone link.

This grand old building's green Byzantine domes had provided the iconic image of Port Said for almost a century. Its colonnaded architecture commemorated the grandiose ambitions behind the 1869 completion of the Suez Canal, which provided passage between the Mediterranean and Red Seas and had opened a new corridor for colonialism, commerce, and war.

As the ship made radio contact with shore at 7:15 a.m. that Wednesday, Israeli spies recorded the conversations that took place. Transcripts reveal a jittery Molqi, reiterating his demand for the release of fifty Palestinian prisoners. He also tells an unnamed official at Port Said that a helicopter is hovering above the ship and if it doesn't go away, "the ship will be blown up and all the passengers aboard will be victims, do you hear me?"

The helicopter goes away and Abu al-Abbas gets on the line.

"How are you, Majid?" he asks Molqi, who immediately calms down.

"Good, thank god," Molqi responds.

Their friendly conversation sounds guarded, indicating that the participants were aware they had a larger audience.

"I hope everyone on board is OK," Abbas says.

Molqi replies, "All the passengers are all right; they have everything. We gave them food and took them to the bathroom. We gave them tea and coffee and took them to their rooms to take showers, wash. They are playing cards."

Abbas speaks carefully. "Listen to me well," he says. "First of all, the passengers should be treated very well. In addition, you must apologize to them and the ship's crew and to the captain and tell them our objective was not to take control of the ship. Tell them what your main objective is. Can you hear me well?"

Molqi understands. "I hear you well," he says. "Do you [want to] speak with the captain in English?"

Abbas continues, like a trial lawyer preparing his client for cross-examination. "First, I want to finish speaking with you," he said. "Our action was not directed against them but against terrorism and against hijackings. Is it clear?"

Molqi assures him, "Yes, it is clear."

"This way, everything will be fine," Abbas says. "Be very, very careful and wait for my message. We will arrive in your area shortly. Do you hear me?

Abbas assures Molqi that an "emissary" whom he will recognize will be dispatched to the ship soon, to bring the hijackers into safety. He reminds Molqi "to behave yourselves very carefully and to treat the passengers very well, all the passengers."

He tells Molqi again to apologize to the captain. "Tell him we didn't intend to behave this way, since our objective was entirely different."

Molqi agrees and puts De Rosa on the radio.

"I am now on deck with my officers and we are all well," the captain says.

Abbas asks him how he is feeling.

"I am fine and very calm," De Rosa replies.

Abbas apologizes. "We are truly sorry because we didn't intend to hijack you, but our situation was such that we had to assume control for several hours."

"I am familiar with your situation and I understand it well," De Rosa says. "We understand the Palestinians, we understand Palestinian aspirations, and for that reason we are all with you."

Abbas apologizes again. "We respect all Italians and the entire world," he says, "but this is our situation; we are sincerely sorry." They thank each other again and sign off.

Afterward, De Rosa replayed the conversation over and over in his head. "[It was] crazy in the way that the whole ordeal aboard the *Achille Lauro* was crazy," he recalled. "Two people speaking to each other, lying, knowing each other's lies and each with his own reason. Abu Khaled making sure his men would get out safely; and me, still a prisoner of armed terrorists who were forcing me to repeat exactly what they told me to say."

Marilyn Klinghoffer hadn't been able to sleep the night before and not because of the Arab music that was blaring through the sound system. She was frantic. How could Leon simply have disappeared?

In the middle of the night she crept over to Omar al-Assadi, whom she referred to "as the guy with the mustache," the one who wasn't Rambo. Assadi was guarding the line at the bathroom.

She begged him to let her to go down to the infirmary, just to confirm that her husband was there. Assadi told her that Leon was sleeping. When she kept insisting, the hijacker said he would go check for her.

She waited for more than another hour in the dark, listening to the endless music and the night breathing of her fellow passengers. Assadi finally returned. She watched him collapse onto a chair, put his head in his hands, and cry.

Marilyn was too tired to move, or perhaps too afraid. She waited until Assadi came to her.

She asked him point-blank, "Is my husband dead?"

No, he told her. "Everything is okay, madame."

Then he hugged her and kissed her.

Throughout the night, the passengers heard rumors from the crew that they were going to Port Said, or that the Israelis were acceding to the terrorist demands. From time to time the captain dropped by and told them to obey the hijackers and assured them that "everything will work out."

Sometime Wednesday morning the passengers noticed a shift in the attitude of the hijackers. They seemed "almost jovial," Marilyn recalled.

After lunch, the hijackers disappeared from the Salon Arazzi and then came back dressed as if going to a party. Their hair looked washed and carefully combed, and they were wearing silk shirts and Gucci shoes. They brought their luggage with them and asked some of the ship's officers to inspect it, to prove that they hadn't stolen anything.

Marilyn watched the young men walk around the room saying goodbye, weary and affectionate, as if they were friends leaving a wedding weekend. Several passengers reached out to embrace them.

When they walked out the door she realized it was over. They were leaving the ship. Soon she could find Leon.

At that moment, shortly after 3 p.m., a small gray tugboat flying the

Egyptian flag drew up next to the *Achille Lauro*. Captain De Rosa saw a tall man with thick dark hair and a bushy mustache on the deck, a man he would come to know as Abu al-Abbas. Over a loudspeaker Abbas asked the captain if all was well.

The captain punted, saying, "All who are on board are well."

De Rosa told himself the half truth that would appease was more acceptable than an "outrageous lie."

Molqi boarded the tugboat and spoke to the men on board.

He addressed Ashker, as always by the captain's side, over the loudspeaker.

Ashker translated the message for De Rosa, telling the captain to reaffirm that everyone was all right. The captain obeyed.

Ashker brought his hand to his forehead, as though saluting. "We're sorry for what happened," he said. "We apologize to you and the Italian government."

With that flourish, he and the others joined Molqi on the tugboat. Before he left, Ashker hugged the captain and De Rosa hugged him back. All the hijackers waved at the passengers who had come out onto the deck. Many people applauded.

Then the hijackers were gone.

It was a moment of exultation for most of the passengers, but not Marilyn. She was flooded with trepidation. As soon as the boat pulled away with their former captors, she urgently asked Seymour Meskin to help her find Leon. Though exhausted, they began to systematically search the boat, beginning on the deck outside the Salon Arazzi. They opened every door, hoping he was hiding somewhere.

That fruitless effort led them to their next desperate hope, down three flights of stairs, to the infirmary. The doctor told Marilyn, "I never saw him," and the nurse confirmed he hadn't been there—not since Marilyn had brought Leon in a few days earlier because his wrist hurt from leaning so heavily on his cane. He had been practicing so he could walk his daughter Ilsa down the aisle when she got married the coming spring.

Before they could decide where to look next, a crew member materialized and told them the captain wanted to see Mrs. Klinghoffer up on the bridge. By then, Seymour and Marilyn were joined by Seymour's wife, Viola, and sister-in-law Mildred Hodes. Captain De Rosa invited them into his office, where he had arranged for coffee and cognac to be served, as though to signal that the ordeal was over and civility was restored.

In this genteel setting, he told Marilyn that her husband had been killed. She burst into tears.

"You even hugged them!" Marilyn said to De Rosa, her voice shaking with anger as she referred to the hijackers.

Her friends took her to her cabin and the ship's doctor administered a sedative.

Marilyn had always treated life as something to celebrate and when necessary grapple with, not merely to endure, even though she also often told her daughters, "Life is an endurance test." She herself had always forged ahead, knowing that the underpinnings of existence were fragile. Her younger sister, Jan, a gentle and elegant woman, had a son, Ian, three years younger than Ilsa. He was born with atrial septic defect, a hole in his heart. The prognosis was nerve-wracking. Throughout his childhood the family hovered, trying to protect him from his inevitable fate. At age nine Ian was watching a ball game and collapsed. Just like that, he was gone. A year later, Marilyn threw a surprise anniversary party for Jan, who was forty-one. Lisa presented her aunt a portrait she'd painted of Ian. Jan unwrapped her other presents. Then she suddenly collapsed on the floor, and an ambulance took her to the hospital, a futile trip. She was gone, like her son, a victim of a damaged heart.

The sorrows piled up, yet Marilyn refused to succumb to the blows of fate. She kept trying to make it all appear fun and festive and insouciant, even after Leon had the second stroke and she got cancer. That determination to live a meaningful life, no matter what, led them to the *Achille Lauro*.

Now she crumpled. "I give up," she told her friends. "I can't fight anymore." She took refuge in the deep sleep induced by exhaustion and the tranquilizer. Her friends didn't know what to expect when she woke up. Sylvia Sherman, the artist who had sketched the hijackers on the ship's menu, stayed overnight with Marilyn in the Klinghoffers' cabin, in case she needed anything.

Elsewhere on the *Achille Lauro*, euphoria prevailed. People wept with relief that it was over, still believing the official word that there were no casualties. The radio was overloaded with messages arriving from around the globe, the captain's first realization that they hadn't been isolated at all—the world had been watching.

The *Achille Lauro* remained in the waters outside Port Said as De Rosa waited to see what would happen next. At 4:20 on Wednesday afternoon, still uncertain about whether the ship was out of harm's way, De Rosa reiterated via radio to someone in the Italian government that everyone on the ship was all right. Prime Minister Craxi decided to speak to him directly before giving a press conference to announce the successful conclusion of the *Achille Lauro* saga. This time, De Rosa reported that one passenger was missing, though he avoided the word "killed." He told Craxi the passenger's name and passport number.

At 6:30, Craxi announced that he had sent President Reagan condolences for the "sole victim" of the hijacking, "a terrible loss." Praising the Egyptians and PLO emissaries for their collaboration, Craxi called the hijacking "a terrible adventure which could have developed into a tragedy [and which] was resolved happily, at least for the majority of those aboard, with the exception of the American victim."

New York

THAT WEDNESDAY morning, when Sara Rimer looked at the *New York Times*, she was pleased to see her feature about the Klinghoffer family was on page one. It was a coup; the entire front page was filled with hijacking news (she didn't know how much of it was already out-of-date).

Rimer figured her part was done. She thought of her article as ornamentation on the international drama that was unfolding. But the foreign editor, who was coordinating the hijacking coverage, sent the feature writer back downtown to Greenwich Village for a follow-up.

Rimer arrived in good spirits. There had been early news bulletins saying everyone on the ship was safe; she was prepared to write a happy celebratory story. On the way to Stewart House, she picked up a bottle of champagne and a package of smoked salmon.

At about 11:30 a.m., Rimer witnessed Lisa get off the telephone with the State Department looking elated.

"It's confirmed," she yelled giddily. "It's over!"

Rimer had her notebook ready when Ilsa broke into tears and told Lisa to call their maternal grandmother, Rose.

"I can't believe it!" Ilsa sobbed with joy. "I'm so happy!"

The reporter stayed for the celebration, to talk and eat; the dining room table was loaded with food sent by well-wishers.

Rimer was still there after a couple of hours had passed and the telephone rang again. She was holding a glass of champagne in her hand; someone had just made a toast. As Paul Dworin held the receiver next to his ear, she watched his expression change from neutral to something foreboding. He pulled Jerry Arbittier aside and said something to him. Then one of them came over to Rimer, she couldn't remember who, and told her that a local news station had called to let them know of a report saying Leon Klinghoffer had been killed.

Stunned, she watched Jerry and Paul take Lisa and Ilsa into separate rooms. The reporter would never forget the wails that emerged.

Her first reaction was nonjournalistic. "I have to get out of here," she thought. "This is an invasion of their privacy."

She took the elevator downstairs and went outside to find a pay phone. She called her editor, who told her to go back upstairs and do her job. "This is a running story," he told her. "You have to keep filing."

Rimer had no choice. She went back upstairs.

To her surprise, Jerry and Paul made it clear they wanted her to stay, that they wanted a witness. Rimer remained until it was time to go back to the office and write the story that would run the next day under the headline "Cheers, Then Heartbreak, at the Apartment on 10th Street."

Rimer could not know she had witnessed Ilsa and Lisa Klinghoffer undergoing an irrevocable transformation. Until the hijacking, the Klinghoffer sisters' political concerns had been local, focused for the past few years on the Reagan-era climate that dealt harshly with the values they cared about. Living in Greenwich Village, a center of gay life and activism, they were acutely aware of the growing plague of AIDS that had descended on the arts and theater community. They were on alert to the violence that had roiled their city for more than a decade: in 1985 there would be 1,386 murders in New York City and 3,880 reported rapes, according to FBI statistics. New York was part of a bloody national landscape: the Justice Department reported that in the United States in 1985, there were 18,976 murders (more than double the number in 1965) and 87,671 reported rapes (more than triple), the increases in the last generation far outpacing population growth.

Suddenly all that was eclipsed by terrorism, this abstraction, this spy-novel menace. The Klinghoffers were an American family, innocent bystanders to someone else's war, yet they had been singled out and victimized for reasons they could not understand.

The day before, as part of its coverage of the hijacking, the *Times* offered its readers a catalogue of 1985's terrorism-related events called "Middle East and Violence: Summary of One Year's Toll." These few paragraphs contain a snapshot of the tit for tat that created a never-ending spiral of reprisal, a grim, violent toll of attack and retaliation.

The sampling of mayhem, biblical in its fury, begins with an anonymous phone call on January 14 from someone claiming to represent the "Islamic Holy War," warning that five Americans being held hostage in Beirut would go on trial as spies; the caller also took responsibility for the deaths of two French soldiers shot to death in their jeep while patrolling a mostly Shiite neighborhood.

In March a car bombing in a Beirut suburb killed more than eighty people; there were reports linking this massacre to a Lebanese counterterrorism unit that worked with the CIA. Two days later, a suicide bomber slammed into an Israeli Army convoy in southern Lebanon, killing twelve Israelis and wounding thirteen. The day after that, Israeli troops crossed into southern Lebanon and killed at least twenty-four people in a village; the summary doesn't say whether those killed were fighters, civilians, or a mixture of both.

Before spring was finished, off the shore of Israel, an Israeli gunboat would sink an Arab vessel deemed "terrorist," with twenty-eight people aboard; nineteen were presumed to have drowned. A suicide bomber in Kuwait tried to assassinate the emir of Kuwait but managed to kill only himself, two bodyguards, and a passerby. Two Frenchmen were kidnapped in the suburbs of Beirut, and a Jordanian airline was hijacked from that city less than two weeks later. The dean of agriculture at the American University of Beirut was kidnapped, the eighth American kidnapped in Lebanon in a year; a Lebanese airplane was commandeered by a Palestinian.

Then came the June hijacking of TWA Flight 847, taken over by two Shiite Muslims shortly after leaving Athens and forced to land in Beirut. One passenger was murdered; forty were held hostage.

The violence continued throughout the summer and early autumn. Bombs exploded at the oldest synagogue in Copenhagen, wounding twenty-seven people. In Beirut, terrorists kidnapped the operations manager of ABC News who was en route to the airport to fly to the United States. Four Soviet diplomats were kidnapped, one of whom was later found dead.

The list was brought up to date with the October 1 Israeli bombing of Hamman Chott, Tunisia, where dozens of civilians were killed along with PLO operatives in retaliation for the murder of three Israelis on a boat near Cyprus. The Israelis made the point that for years Palestinian strategy had included the murder of Israeli civilians and if the PLO headquarters was embedded among civilians, that was the price that must be paid.

In sum, the year's total deaths by terrorism was a paltry number compared with the 6,854 people who died of AIDS or the 43,825 fatalities caused by automobiles in 1985, just in the United States. The number of Americans killed in acts deemed terrorist was infinitesimal compared with the national U.S. body count by homicide.

However, "homicide" did not carry the same connotations as "terrorism." The very word conjured a random irrationality that triggered feelings of helplessness and anger, feelings that could not be dissipated by logical comparisons to domestic crime statistics—especially when that act of terrorism happened to you.

6

Cowboys and Terrorists

Port Said, Egypt

The U.S. ambassador to Egypt, Nicholas A. Veliotes, came on board the *Achille Lauro* close to midnight on Wednesday. He had flown to Port Said from Cairo, along with a physician and a political officer from the embassy. The ship remained several miles offshore; they approached by tugboat.

As the three men boarded the ship, Veliotes was struck by the deathly quiet. He felt the crew members were avoiding his eyes as he moved up through several levels to the bridge. Gerardo De Rosa was waiting in his office with the Italian ambassador. The weight of responsibility De Rosa had been carrying was obvious.

The captain approached Veliotes and handed him Leon Klinghoffer's passport. "I'm sorry," he said. "I did my best," and then he started to cry.

Without bothering to wait for a secure telephone line, Veliotes called his embassy over the ship's radio, and told his staff, "Leon Klinghoffer was murdered," he said. "In my name, I want you to call the Egyptian foreign minister, tell him what we learned, tell him the circumstances, tell him in view of this and the fact that we—and presumably them—didn't have those facts, we insist that they prosecute those sons of bitches."

The blunt message strayed from the diplomat's playbook, but Veliotes came from individualistic stock, people who believed in expressing themselves. His parents were Greek immigrants—his father a longshoreman turned grocery store owner, his mother a painter. His older brother, Johnny Otis, nicknamed the Godfather of Rhythm and Blues, called himself a black man though acknowledging "genetically, I'm pure Greek."

Veliotes, who was about to turn fifty-seven, had had a long career in the diplomatic corps, the years revealed in the lines on his face and receding hairline. His children had grown up in Italy, India, and Laos. He was no stranger to the Middle East and its troubles; he'd already served in Israel and Jordan. Egypt was the toughest, or maybe he was just worn out.

His injudicious outburst reflected the frustration he'd been feeling for the past week, beginning with President Reagan's response to the Israeli bombing of PLO headquarters in Tunisia. Reagan declared the bombing was "a legitimate response" to "terrorist attacks." Veliotes saw firsthand how the Egyptians interpreted the remarks. "Two or three Israelis were killed, and the Americans were outraged," he said. "More than a hundred twenty Arabs killed, and the Americans, in effect, said to the Israelis, 'Go get 'em.'"

The ambassador had spent the previous two days in circular debates about the *Achille Lauro* with his fellow diplomats in the region and politicians back home, each pursuing separate agendas while trying to find the common ground that would lead to a resolution. It seemed that every offer and counteroffer was being leaked to the press, complicating the negotiations. Earlier that day, Yasser Arafat—in Tunis—requested that Italy and the United States force Israel to offer "some symbolic gestures," then dropped this appeal, saying the release of Palestinians from Israeli jails was no longer required so long as the hijackers could be turned over to the PLO for trial. In New York, a Palestinian leader suggested to reporters that Leon Klinghoffer might have died of natural causes, while Benjamin Netanyahu, the Israeli ambassador to the United Nations, told the Security Council that Klinghoffer was singled out "for one thing"—because he was Jewish, though there was no proof that the Palestinians knew the religion of their victim. If there was one thing that had sealed Leon's fate, it was his U.S. passport.

The Israeli government continued to play the religion card while urging Egyptian President Mubarak to prosecute the hijackers. "Israel will not accept the murder of a Jew because he's a Jew," the Israeli minister of communications told Thomas Friedman of the *New York Times*, by then based in Jerusalem.

Friedman reported that "Israeli military analysts and officials indicated that they felt the hijacking of the *Achille Lauro* had serious consequences for Israel, both negative and positive." The negative, according to Friedman, was concern that Yasser Arafat "might be hailed as the savior of the *Achille Lauro*," considered a mediator rather than a collaborator of the hijackers.

The positive, if it could be called that, was that maybe Italian Prime Minister Craxi would reconsider his condemnation of the Israeli attack on Hamman Chott, now that an Italian ship had been attacked by Palestinians.

"Perhaps, perhaps it will teach some lessons to some countries—including those that have been doing the screaming," Defense Minister Yitzhak Rabin said on Israeli radio on Wednesday, not long before Veliotes stepped aboard the *Achille Lauro*.

Nothing had been resolved when Veliotes began his dreadful rounds. His focus was concentrated on one thing, the former hostages and what they had endured. After all, his foremost duty as ambassador was the protection of his country's citizens. He had never felt that responsibility as acutely as he did that night. As the *Achille Lauro* began moving toward the dock at Port Said, Veliotes went door to door, saying "the American ambassador" is here, realizing how ludicrous it must sound to these shell-shocked people when they asked him, "How do we know who you are?"

Mainly he listened that long night and tried to comprehend what it had been like to spend two full days on a ship next to barrels of diesel oil with half-hysterical young men threatening to throw hand grenades and blow them all up. Then, once they were liberated, finding out a fellow passenger had been murdered.

He did not knock on Marilyn Klinghoffer's door, deciding it was better to let her rest while she could.

Early Thursday morning, October 10, he joined some of the Klinghoffers' New Jersey friends for breakfast in the dining hall. They urged him to go see Marilyn. Veliotes was self-conscious walking downstairs to her cabin. In his line of work, appearances mattered, and he hadn't showered or shaved. "I must have looked like a terrorist myself," he recalled later.

When he entered the Klinghoffers' room, he took Marilyn's hand and they talked. Her hair—which she had stopped coloring during the cancer treatments—was gray and uncombed. The high cheekbones that had made her so striking now accentuated a weary hollowness. She didn't want to get out of bed.

He urged her to reconsider. "We really want you to come and be with us," he said. "All of your friends are waiting."

Veliotes left to give her a chance to pull herself together.

When Marilyn entered the dining room, Veliotes saw a different person than the frail, disheveled creature he had met just a few minutes earlier.

"I'll never forget when she walked into the room," he said. "She was a very pretty woman. She had cleaned up, made herself up, and put on a gorgeous summer dress and came in to join her friends." She greeted some of her friends with kisses and hugs but didn't say much.

By eleven that morning, Veliotes was back at the embassy in Cairo, where an aide informed him that the Egyptian foreign minister, Abdel-Meguid, wanted to see him immediately.

"I'm beat. I stink. I feel rotten. I haven't slept for three days," Veliotes told the aide. "Tell the foreign minister I'll be there in an hour and a half or so." He called his wife, Patricia, and asked her to bring a change of clothes to the embassy. When she arrived, he told her what had happened on the ship.

Patricia heard about the Beach People and how one of them stood up and spoke on behalf of the group. Veliotes told his wife the gist of what the man had said: "they had been scared to death, but they never cracked, they never crawled and never forgot they were Americans."

Veliotes had worked for Democrats and Republicans and lived in many countries for long enough to develop a strong core of skepticism if not cynicism. Hearing that speech from an older man who had suffered, spoken as though he was trying to reassure the ambassador, burrowed through to the idealistic wellspring that kept him going.

Telling the story opened a spigot of suppressed tears, just as it had for Captain De Rosa. The ambassador began to cry.

After the catharsis, Veliotes showered and shaved and went to meet Meguid. When the Egyptian foreign minister greeted him in his office as "Mr. Ambassador," the American knew something was wrong. They'd known each other for years and were on a first-name basis. Now that warm relationship felt chilly.

"How could this happen?" Meguid asked, and told Veliotes that President Mubarak was not happy.

Veliotes didn't understand.

Meguid pointed to a high pile of press reports about Veliotes calling the hijackers "sons of bitches."

"This is being broadcast, every hour on the hour, in the United States, on every radio station," Meguid said. In America, Veliotes's outburst was taken as a rallying cry; in the Arab world, his words were seen as a nasty slur.

Veliotes was defensive. "I was in no position to have secure communications," he said. "The most important thing to do was to notify my government and your government, on the assumption that you didn't know that an American had been killed. Equally important was to tell you our position, that these hijackers must be prosecuted."

Meguid responded impatiently. "Yes, but why did you have to call them 'sons of bitches'?"

Veliotes asked, "Well, aren't they?"

"Of course they are, and worse," replied Meguid. "But this has put real pressure on us."

Veliotes didn't say aloud what he was thinking—that he wanted the Egyptians to prosecute the hijackers because he believed the United States would not be able to prosecute them. "We could have brought them in tiger cages down Fifth Avenue, and then what?" he said later. "They would have been released. There would be a Jewish lawyer from the American Civil Liberties Union to defend them because, you know, of their rights in this country."

Veliotes wasn't anti-Palestinian. After a dozen years in the Middle East, he was conversant with the complexities of the Arab-Israeli situation, especially concerning the Palestinians. He understood their feelings of being oppressed by the Israeli occupation and did not condone Israeli reprisals. However, nothing excused what happened to Leon Klinghoffer and the other civilians on the *Achille Lauro.*

Realizing he wasn't getting anywhere with Meguid, he asked to speak to Mubarak.

"No," the foreign minister said, "the president isn't talking to anyone."

When Veliotes's boss, Secretary of State George Shultz, tried to reach Mubarak, he got the same answer. But soon the Egyptian president was talking to the whole world, telling reporters that the hijackers had already left Egypt the evening before, five hours after they surrendered.

"I do not know exactly where they have gone," Mubarak said. "Perhaps they have left for Tunisia."

Mubarak said the hijackers were handed over to the PLO before it was known anyone had been killed on board the *Achille Lauro.* "If the captain had told us that a passenger had been killed, we would have changed our position toward the whole operation," Mubarak embellished. "But when this emerged, we already had sent the hijackers out of the country."

Then, openly pandering to local anti-American sentiment, Mubarak questioned whether Klinghoffer was in fact dead. "There is no body and no proof he had been murdered," he told Egypt's official Middle East News Agency. "Maybe the man was in hiding or did not board the ship at all."

He sent written word to the White House, repeating the message that the hijackers had left Egypt. His cable was waiting for the Situation Room staff when they arrived early that Thursday morning, October 10.

Washington, D.C.

THE WHITE HOUSE soon realized that Mubarak had been lying: the Israeli embassy in Washington passed along reports that the hijackers were still in Egypt, at the Al Maza Air Base, thirty miles outside of Cairo.

Throughout the day, Israeli and U.S. intelligence operatives—quite likely with the cooperation of some Egyptian government officials— spied on the president of Egypt, using electronic surveillance to listen in on Mubarak's conversations in his office. They heard him tell Meguid that the hijackers were still in the country and that Shultz was "crazy" to think Egypt would turn in its PLO brothers. They learned that the Egyptian government had arranged for the hijackers to leave the country that night. The destination was uncertain, but they knew the flight number (EgyptAir Flight 2843), the tail number identification of the aircraft, and that it was a Boeing 737.

That's when the cowboys took over.

Ambassador Veliotes was sent instructions from the White House to arrange a meeting with Mubarak. He was to tell the Egyptian president that the United States knew he was lying, and that "letting the pirates go would surely rock the U.S.-Egyptian relationship," an unsubtle reminder that Egypt had received $2.2 billion in American aid the previous year. The same message was being sent to the Egyptian ambassador in Washington and to the Egyptian government through covert intelligence connections.

Few in the Situation Room expected Egypt to comply. Mubarak had cooperated with the American effort to bring the *Achille Lauro* to safe harbor. But the Washington team understood that Mubarak could not risk alienating the Palestinians and the Arab world. The Egyptian leader just wanted to get the hijackers out of Egypt without handing them over to the Americans. Then they would be somebody else's problem.

Scrambling for solutions, NSC officers working in the White House brought to bear a deep reservoir of military lore, acquired from books and experience. James Stark, a colleague of Oliver North, had done battle in Vietnam, and earned two master's degrees and a doctorate from Tufts University's Fletcher School of Law and Diplomacy. As he tried to think of a way to intercept the EgyptAir plane if it did leave the country, a potentially useful association popped into his head. He remembered Operation Vengeance, the midair U.S. commando raid that killed Admiral Isoroku Yamamoto, Japan's top naval commander, the strategist behind the surprise attack on Pearl Harbor that brought the United States into World War II. Yamamoto—who paradoxically had opposed Japan's entry into the war before becoming one of its masterminds—was on his way to inspect Japanese air units on the Solomon Islands when his destination was discerned by American code breakers and he was shot down. The copycat scenario Stark imagined would be even more of a tour de force since the Egyptians, however duplicitous, were U.S. allies and there was no official war going on. The United States could not shoot down an Egyptian plane; it would have to be forced to land somewhere sympathetic to the Americans.

Stark tried out the idea on a colleague and they took it to Oliver North, who liked the plan so much he later took credit for thinking of it. North and Stark consulted with Deputy National Security Adviser John Poindexter and Poindexter's boss, Robert McFarlane. McFarlane, who was about to accompany Reagan to Chicago, told North to "work out the details" and call him when he did.

The Yamamoto variation gained momentum during the morning, as more military and intelligence experts were consulted and decided it was credible. Secretary of Defense Caspar Weinberger was out of the loop for much of this initial discussion; he was in Ottawa at a session of the Canadian Parliament. When he did hear of the proposed plan by telephone late that morning, he thought it was utterly wrong-headed. "I'm dead set against it, interfering with civilian aircraft," he said. "We'll be castigated all over the world."

He ordered the NSC to stop everything until he spoke directly to Reagan.

By then the president had landed in Illinois and was demonstrating his unfamiliarity with delicate details. At the airport, when a reporter asked him about the PLO's offer to try the hijackers, he responded, "Well, I think that if [Arafat] believes that their organization has enough of a—sort of national court set up, like a nation that they can bring [the hijackers] to justice and—carry that out, all right; but just so they are brought to justice." (He corrected himself after McFarlane gently reminded him the United States didn't recognize the PLO's legitimacy. "I didn't mean to make a comment like that," Reagan said, "but I was so angry that I was thinking in terms of revenge and not justice.")

President Reagan's next destination was a Sara Lee plant in Deerfield, Illinois, where he delivered a speech about tax relief to factory workers, accepted a giant pound cake, and made the kind of corny joke that made him so popular: "When I take [the cake] up on Capitol Hill, can I use it to blackmail them into doing what we want?"

McFarlane received a call from his deputy, John Poindexter, who told him the Joint Chiefs of Staff believed the Yamamoto plan was feasible; however, Weinberger wasn't on board. McFarlane pulled Reagan aside and laid out the plan. The president may not have been strong on diplomatic nuance, but he knew how to deliver a quotable line. "Well, good god, they've murdered an American here," he told McFarlane, "so let's get on with it."

On the plane back from Washington, Reagan finally spoke to Weinberger, also on an airplane, coming back from Canada. They couldn't connect via secure phone systems, so they spoke over an open channel, just as Veliotes had done, using the code names "Finley" and "Rawhide" (the latter reference to the TV western featuring Clint

Eastwood, he-man icon, was a nice fit for the president, who had been a Hollywood cowboy himself). A ham radio operator overheard the conversation, in which Weinberger reiterated his concerns about hurting American relations with Egypt and other moderate Arab states, as well as his belief that interfering with a civilian airplane in international airspace might be a violation of international law.

Reagan cut him off with a crisp retort. "Cap, it is pretty cut-and-dried," he said. "This is a guilty party; we cannot let them go."

When Weinberger tried to call again to stop the operation, the NSC staff didn't let the call go through. At 4:37 p.m., Reagan, learning that the plane carrying the hijackers was leaving Cairo, signed the order authorizing action and let Weinberger know it was time to proceed. The defense secretary didn't argue this time.

Legal or not, wrongheaded or not, the coordination and execution of this mission fueled by testosterone and adrenaline was thrilling to contemplate for the pugnacious members of the president's staff, far more satisfying than the vexation of working through legal and diplomatic channels. Here was a chance to demonstrate that terrorists couldn't kill an American citizen and get away with it. It felt good to believe, as Reagan did, that "it is pretty cut-and-dried," even for those who knew better. Nothing political could ever be that simple — especially in the Middle East.

Everything snapped into place as the State Department contacted officials in Tunisia and Greece, urging them to turn back the Egyptian airplane if it tried to land there. Where should it land? Israel was rejected as being a second slap in the face to the Egyptians and a British base on Cyprus was crossed off because getting permission on short notice wasn't likely. Someone suggested the NATO base at Sigonella, Italy, on the eastern side of Sicily. The Reagan team agreed on Sigonella, deciding to delay telling Italy about the plan until it became inevitable, because the PLO-sympathetic Italians might leak to the Egyptians and ruin the whole thing. The decision was expeditious but awkward if not downright belligerent, because while Sigonella hosted both a U.S. Navy installation and an Italian Air Force base along with NATO personnel, it was located on Italian soil and was officially run by the Italians.

Above the Mediterranean Sea

FOR THE people in Washington the intercept, as it was called, was theoretical gamesmanship played out by making telephone calls and looking at maps, considering the diplomatic and political consequences. For Lieutenant Commander Laurence Neal, a U.S. Navy pilot, the maneuver was a wild escapade he would never forget, from the minute he climbed into the cockpit of his supersonic F-14 Tomcat, aboard the USS *Saratoga*, and headed into the night without a clue as to where he was going or why.

Less than a half hour earlier, he and his roommate had been hanging out watching TV. Their favorite show—a twenty-minute workout with Bess Motta, a popular Canadian aerobics instructor—wasn't on. They loved bouncing around with Bess, screaming at her, "You can't hurt me, Bess, you can't hurt me!" Their aircraft carrier was on Alert 60, the lowest state of alert in the Mediterranean, meaning you had to have the planes ready to fly in 60 minutes. Everything was tied down; they'd had dinner so there was nothing to do but relax.

Then came the call: Get to the ready room! Within twenty minutes, Neal was suited up, assigned an airplane and a back seater—the flier who acts as copilot and controls the weapons.

Right before takeoff, as Neal was about to start the motor, a junior officer climbed the ladder and offered a chilling send-off: "We don't know what's going on except you're looking for a civilian airliner and you may be cleared to fire."

Neal thought he heard "civilian aircraft" and "cleared to fire" but couldn't believe it. He asked the officer to repeat what he'd just said.

You may be cleared to fire.

The pilot couldn't face that difficult question in real time. He just hoped it wouldn't come to that.

This was Neal's second tour on the USS *Saratoga*, one of two aircraft carriers the Sixth Fleet kept on constant patrol in the Mediterranean. The American Navy had been a presence there for more than a century, originally defending commercial liners against the attacks of Barbary pirates. The *Saratoga* was a monster, carrying seventy to ninety planes, numerous helicopters, and a crew of close to four thousand.

As Neal powered up his Tomcat, he wasn't afraid because he couldn't be. His nickname in college had been Barbarian. In the Navy he was called Vert for three reasons: because he liked his plane to get vertical; because he enjoyed making his back seater turn green (*vert* in French); and for a third reason he wouldn't tell anyone—unless they'd had more than a few beers together. In ten years of service, Neal had flown thousands of miles, yet every single flight had been a drill—never combat, not once. He didn't know whether that's where he was headed now, but he felt ready. It was all about trust: believing in the ground personnel, who would be telling him what to do, and in the men flying the other six F-14s in his squadron. They were all on the same mission, whatever it was. It was about having faith in Ralph Zia, the squadron commander, who was charged with coordinating this fast-moving mystery operation, accompanying the F-14 Tomcats in an EC-2 Hawkeye equipped with powerful radar that had a range of hundreds of miles.

Normally Neal loved being up on a night like this. He couldn't believe the clarity of the Milky Way when seen at 25,000 feet during a waning moon. But he didn't dare look at the stars that night. He had to be totally focused because one of the things that keeps aviators alive is compartmentalization, concentrating on the task at hand and nothing else.

The F-14s spread out in "stations," circling above international waters south of Crete, waiting for the mysterious civilian plane to appear. To make sure its pilot wouldn't see them first, the F-14s were traveling "lights out," which also meant they were operating strictly on radar, blips in the night. The Hawkeye kept in touch from a distance of about a hundred miles.

They spotted some potential targets. One turned out to be a Libyan military jet. Two radar blips were identified as U.S. military transports.

After three hours of circling, Neal was getting antsy. Then came the blip they were looking for, EgyptAir Flight 2843, a Boeing aircraft. Zia sent one of the other F-14 pilots to approach. He got within one hundred feet of the plane, close enough to see the flight attendants through the windows. The radar operator aimed a flashlight at the fuselage, until he could make out the tail number that confirmed it: this was their intercept target.

From his remote station, Zia radioed four of the F-14 pilots, including "Vert" Neal. Zia told them to move in close and encircle the plane: Left side, right side, high, low, getting into position while flying blind at 25,000 feet, cruising next to the Boeing 737 at around 560 miles per hour. "We knew we were there but couldn't see each other," Neal said.

Zia—still one hundred miles away in the Hawkeye—had to communicate with the EgyptAir pilot because the F-14s were on a different radio frequency than commercial aircraft. The F-14 pilots couldn't hear Zia when he contacted the Egyptian pilot, Ahmed Moneeb, using the standard greeting: "EgyptAir 2843, this is Tiger-tail 603, over."

When Zia told him he was surrounded by American Navy fliers who were going to accompany him to Sigonella, the Egyptian pilot was understandably confused because when he looked out the window, he didn't see anything there, just darkness and distant stars.

Neal heard Zia come on the radio, talking to all four F-14 pilots surrounding the Boeing.

"He doesn't believe you're there," he said, and told them to turn on their lights, all at once. The F-14s' lights came on like a startling display of Christmas lights—red anticollision lights, green glow panels—right next to the EgyptAir plane as they all hurtled through the night sky in tandem.

"You've got his attention," Zia told them. "Back off a little, he's really scared."

It wasn't just the lights that got Captain Moneeb's attention. Zia told him, "If you do not follow my instructions, we will shoot you."

The Egyptian pilot tried to radio Cairo but found his radio had been jammed.

The F-14s and the Boeing 737 headed northwest toward Sigonella, about 350 miles away. Following instructions from the Americans, radioed from Zia's Hawkeye, Captain Moneeb told Italian air control at Sigonella that he had a "low fuel emergency," which would guarantee permission to land.

Neal had flown in and out of that NATO base many times and knew Sigonella could be treacherous. The airfield was fourteen miles south of Mount Etna, an active volcano; pilots didn't want to head north as they landed.

The F-14s were built for speed and flexibility; they could descend from high altitude very quickly, much faster than the 737. Captain Moneeb didn't have enough time to make a gradual descent; he overshot the runway twice. Neal and the other F-14s leveled off, watching from 4,000 feet while the EgyptAir plane finally landed and rolled toward a stop, just after midnight. Then came another surprise. A couple of airplanes appeared on the runway behind the EgyptAir liner and their lights popped on, out of nowhere. Neal snapped some photographs with an infrared camera and zoomed off. It was time to head back to the *Saratoga*.

When Neal got out of the plane on the aircraft carrier, people were saying, "Great job! Great job!"

"What did we do?" he asked.

Someone told him, "Those were the PLO guys, the *Achille Lauro*. They were taking them to Tunisia."

Neal felt proud of the mission, though he understood how easily a lights-out intercept at night could have gone bad. "Everyone could have been smoked," a friend reminded him later.

Still, it felt good to have done something that was real. "When you do what I did, flying planes off aircraft carriers, you rarely get to use your skills to accomplish something," he said.

"We were able to make a difference without firing a shot," he said. "We just did it through intimidation." Yet he was left with a persisting sense of unease.

Sigonella

WHEN LARRY NEAL looked at photographs he'd snapped from above the airfield at Sigonella, he saw the bright plume from the 737's motors and, farther down the runway, two little black dots. Those dots were in fact two very large airplanes, U.S. Navy C-141 transports that had arrived on Cyprus Tuesday morning, part of a special operations team hauling a huge load of men and weaponry—including two Navy SEAL teams of sixteen men each supported by dozens of other personnel, ten Black Hawk helicopters, six Little Bird gunships, and four Little Bird lift ships—a formidable military force. This was the Delta Force outfit—led by Carl Stiner, commanding general of Joint Special Operations—that had left Fort Bragg for the Mediterranean shortly after the U.S. government learned about the *Achille Lauro*, three days earlier.

Ever since being dispatched late Monday night, Stiner had been preparing for the challenge of a rescue operation at sea, aware that a cruise ship was the toughest target imaginable. The chance for a high number of casualties was significant. "Toughest" was a brutal reckoning from a man who had been on the road for 154 days so far that year, to fifteen countries, flying 197,000 miles, living in a constant state of war, none of it official, most of it fought deep under the radar.

Stiner, who retained the folksy manner and quiet drawl of his childhood in Appalachian Tennessee, was a cool-headed, experienced Middle East hand with a long career directing elite soldiers on hostage rescues, counterinsurgency, and clandestine killing. A decade earlier, he'd been posted in Saudi Arabia, where for two years he trained National Guard officers for King Khalid and Prince Abdullah. At a graduation dinner, he met one of the guests, Yasser Arafat, and several of his lieutenants. Though Stiner didn't like Arafat—he called him a "sleazy little killer"—the general was impressed by the men who worked for the PLO leader. Stiner described them as "well-dressed, very sharp, well-spoken and very knowledgeable about world affairs." He did not underestimate the enemy.

Stiner was in Lebanon during the bombing of the U.S. embassy and the attack on the Marine barracks in 1983 and suffered the humiliation of the TWA Flight 847 hijacking. He'd been in Vietnam, and now terrorism presented an entirely new game that required a different way of thinking. "You learned how to survive or you didn't," Stiner would write. "You learned whom to trust in a life-or-death situation and whom—by faction or religious motivation—you could not trust. You learned to think like a terrorist."

But terrorist organizations tended to be light on their feet. They weren't weighed down by the bulky apparatus—the heavy artillery, platoons of officers and soldiers, chains of command—that came with a U.S. Navy special operations mission—a massive construct that carried with it the means of enormous destruction.

As the diplomats and politicians plotted their strategies, Stiner and his officers had been studying diagrams of the *Achille Lauro* so helicopter pilots landing in darkness would know where the ship's towers and antennae were located. They had people trained to steer the cruise liner if Captain De Rosa and his navigational team were killed during the assault. Stiner's team planned to make their move on Wednesday, October 9, at 9 p.m.

That evening, Stiner learned the mission had been called off. A deal had been made with the hijackers.

Within a few hours, most of Stiner's troops were on their way back to the States. By Thursday morning, only the two C-141 cargo planes were left on Cyprus with Stiner, waiting for dark so they could head for home. Then Stiner learned about Operation Yamamoto and received an order from the Pentagon: "You are to follow the plane into Sigonella, capture the terrorists, and fly them back to the U.S. in chains to stand trial." Stiner assumed the chains were metaphoric. The C-141 carried a lot of cargo, but no chains, and he didn't see the need for any. As he saw it, if he put the terrorists in a plane with two SEAL platoons, "I couldn't think of anything more secure than that."

Stiner was in one of the two airplanes that showed up in Larry Neal's photograph, taxiing on the Sigonella runway behind the EgyptAir liner. Within minutes, the Egyptian plane was surrounded by Navy SEALs, some who were already on the Sigonella base and others who piled out of the C-141s with Stiner, who set up a "command post" under the airplane's tail.

It was a bizarre scene that got stranger every minute. Soon Stiner was underneath the plane's nose talking to Captain Moneeb by radio, though the cockpit was just a few feet above the general's head. At first the Egyptian pilot was reluctant to get out of the plane as ordered, but quickly was persuaded by the sight of the Americans and their guns. He climbed down a ladder, along with another man dressed in a business suit, carrying an Egyptian diplomatic passport.

Stiner greeted them by saying, "My orders are to take the terrorists off the plane and fly them back to the U.S. to stand trial for killing Leon Klinghoffer."

Captain Moneeb protested. "What sort of law is this?" he asked Stiner, who replied, "This is my law."

Stiner saw a couple of nervous men. The man in the business suit asked if the general had an aspirin. As it happened, Stiner knew that he did because, as his plane had left Cyprus for Sigonella earlier that night, he'd felt a headache coming on. The general hadn't slept more than a couple of hours since leaving Fort Bragg on Monday night, and now it was Thursday. The team doctor had stuffed a handful of aspirin in his pocket after takeoff; most of them were still there.

Stiner gave the diplomat several aspirin and then the Egyptian asked for a cigarette, which one of the radio operators handed him. He asked to use a telephone, to call the Egyptian foreign minister for guidance. Stiner sent him to base operations with an escort and then the general climbed on board the 737, accompanied by the Egyptian pilot and the SEAL commander.

The two Americans took a quick look around. The plane had been set up like an executive jet, with rows of seats replaced by tables. Four young men—one of them looked like a teenager—sat at one. At a second table there were eight or ten uniformed men from the Egyptian army, armed with automatic pistols; Stiner recognized them as counterterrorist force guards, trained by the United States. He saw stewardesses in their uniforms and two more men in civilian clothes. One was tall, with dark hair and Arab features; the other was shorter.

The Americans went back outside. Within fifteen minutes of landing, Italian troops began showing up in pickup trucks, on motorbikes, in cars, and on construction carts. They took up positions to form a larger circle around the Navy SEALs who had already encircled the plane. Americans from the NATO base parked trucks in front of the Boeing's nose and behind its tail; the Italians did the same around the U.S. military planes. Soldiers of the two allies, Italy and the United States, were pointing guns at one another.

The standoff reverberated with elements of comedy and terror, which Stiner described with macho insouciance. "We had the plane surrounded with two rings of about eighty to ninety heavily armed shooters and snipers positioned at strategic locations," he said. "However, the outer ring of our security was now directly facing the Italians—eyeball to eyeball. Though I figured they had us outnumbered by about three to one, I wasn't worried about them taking us on. They knew better than that. However, I was concerned that something unanticipated, like a vehicle backfiring, could cause one of their young, jumpy troops to open fire. If that happened, several people would die, mainly Italians."

No one knew what to do. William Spearman, the U.S. naval commander, showed up along with his Italian counterpart, Ercolano Annicchiarico. Stiner told them he understood the Italians had agreed to turn the terrorists over to the United States. When the Italians said they knew nothing about it, Stiner contacted Maxwell Rabb, the American ambassador.

Stiner recalled, "I explained that we had forced the Egyptian airliner down at Sigonella with the four terrorists on board and that my orders were to take the terrorists and fly them back to the States to stand trial, and it was my understanding that the Italian government had agreed to turn them over to me."

"You've done what?" Rabb said. This response told the general that the ambassador knew nothing about it either.

The Italians checked with their defense minister, Giovanni Spadolini, and discovered he also didn't have any information.

None of them—neither the military men on the ground nor the diplomats—were privy to the verbal, but no less muscular, game of cat and mouse the American president and his advisers had been playing throughout the night with the Italian prime minister and *his* advisers. Just after midnight, Craxi had given permission for the forced landing of the EgyptAir plane at Sigonella. Just a few hours later, Craxi was pushing back against his powerful ally, insisting that Italian law required that the hijackers be tried in Italy. The Americans were not happy.

George Shultz and Caspar Weinberger called their counterparts, Foreign Minister Andreotti and Defense Minister Spadolini, urging them to hand over the hijackers. Michael Ledeen, a national security consultant who was fluent in Italian and had persuaded Craxi to allow the 737 to land at Sigonella, put in another call. Craxi refused this request. "If it were up to me I'd turn them over in a minute" he said. "But it's not a political question, it's a legal matter." However rational, the response was not satisfying to the Americans, who continued to bombard the Italians with phone calls that soon became irritating. A U.S. embassy official in Rome acknowledged that Washington seemed "semi-hysterical."

Finally, at around 3:30 a.m. in Rome, Reagan and Craxi spoke directly, with Ledeen acting as translator. Once again, Reagan asked Craxi to turn the hijackers over to the United States for trial and Craxi, once again, said he couldn't because the crime had occurred on an Italian ship. When Reagan realized Craxi was not going to back down, he agreed that Italy would prosecute the hijackers, but he added that

America planned to seek extradition under the terms of a treaty signed the previous year. The president also wanted Italy to arrest the two men on the plane who were claiming diplomatic immunity; U.S. intelligence had identified them as Palestinians, possibly Abu al-Abbas and Hani al-Hassan, Arafat's adviser. Craxi said he would have to find out who they were.

After the two heads of state got off the phone, Craxi spoke to the Egyptian ambassador to Rome, who, while acknowledging that the two were PLO officials, insisted they were "diplomatic guests" of the Egyptian government and should be left alone.

Inside the EgyptAir 737

THE MYSTERIOUS "diplomatic guests" were Abu al-Abbas and Ozzudin Badratkan, the thirty-eight-year-old military chief of the PLF. (It would take some time for Badratkan, who was also known as Abu al-Izz, to be identified.) Badratkan was a Jordanian who took up the Palestinian cause and became intensely loyal to Abbas. In turn, Abbas thought of Badratkan as his good luck charm; the Jordanian had inadvertently saved Abbas's life, simply by inviting him over for dinner before the 1978 bombing that blew up PLF headquarters in Beirut, in the same building where Abbas was then living with Samia. Of necessity, Abbas trusted very few people; Badratkan was one of them. When the *Achille Lauro* mission failed and Abbas was sent to Egypt to clean up the mess, he asked Badratkan to join him.

Abu al-Abbas often told his wives that he was not afraid of dying. He said he didn't even think about death, which may have explained his recklessness. His only real fear was of water and swimming; he almost drowned when his mother was bathing him in a pond near the Syrian refugee camp where he was born.

Before they boarded the Egyptian plane, Abbas had told his men — the hijackers — that they were going to Tunis. He assured them that the ambassadors of Egypt, Italy, and Germany had signed an agreement for safe passage, and the agreement stipulated they would be tried by the PLO.

Now that plan had been nullified by the U.S. Tomcats. Abbas cursed Mubarak aloud, and said he was certain that he had collaborated with the Americans.

As daylight filtered in through the airplane's windows, Abbas called his men over and told them, "You have to get off the plane, Italy will take custody of you. There is a safe passage agreement and we will ask for your extradition."

He hugged them and said, "Do not fear, I will not abandon you."

Bassam al-Ashker and the other three hijackers would later reflect on the words of Abbas as they wondered which stories were true and which were not. Eventually they told themselves and the authorities so many versions of the events it was impossible to know exactly what had transpired. Yet it quickly became apparent that their allegiance to their cause was far stronger than their bond with one another. Even as they left the plane, under arrest and in handcuffs, they were looking at each other with suspicion and fear.

Abbas and Badratkan stayed behind, waiting while the Italians decided whether they were to be designated diplomats or terrorists, free to leave or doomed to remain in Italy and join the hijackers as prisoners.

Ashker did not take solace in the promises of his commander. He felt empty. "My legs were heavy," he said. "I was tired; it was three days since I had slept. They put me in a van, in a metal cage. I looked at the *carabinieri* seated around me. They looked at me like I was a Martian. In that moment, I thought of my life, the way I was as a child, at who I had become. I thought about my childhood, my family, my friends, the games we played, and when I was a little combatant. I closed my eyes. Everything that was happening was like a bad dream."

7

Fulminations

Santa Ana, California

While former senator James Abourezk was sympathetic to the Palestinian cause, he was outraged when he heard about the murder of Leon Klinghoffer. "When you read in the press that hijackers kill a crippled old man you hate it," he said. "I was pissed off. He was not part of the war."

As he had watched the story of the *Achille Lauro* gain momentum throughout the week, Abourezk's anger was joined by fear of reprisal against Arab Americans. The tone was set at the top, by the White House. The hijacking had become a parable of good versus evil, a bristling narrative of an elderly Jewish victim—a man in a wheelchair—murdered by fiendish pirates. And who were the pirates of ancient lore? They were Arabs—saber-slashing, bearded, bejeweled, headdress-wearing, sexually threatening, harem-owning, slave-trading Arabs.

Friday's headlines were filled with the takedown of the EgyptAir jet, with the big-city American tabloids jockeying to see who could be most provocative. "We Bag the Bums" was the *New York Daily News* entry. "'Got 'Em': U.S. Skyjacks the Seajack Murderers," countered the *New York Post*, whose article began, "The four Palestinian pirates...."

Abourezk understood this story was not dying soon. Those responsible had not yet been revealed; many questions remained unanswered. One thing seemed clear to him: there would be no happy ending.

The son of Lebanese-Christian immigrants, Abourezk grew up on an Indian reservation in South Dakota, where his father, who had begun as a peddler, settled and opened two general stores. Abourezk became a lawyer and served as a U.S. senator from South Dakota between 1973 and 1979.

He didn't feel much discrimination in South Dakota, but maybe that's because he'd learned how to take care of himself when he did. He was a human bulldog, strong and stocky and unafraid to fight. His ethnic awakening came later in life, when he was already past forty and serving in the U.S. Senate, taking a tour in the Middle East in 1973, during the Lebanese civil war. He visited the village his parents were from, a town about fifteen miles from the Israeli border. The mayor organized a reception for him near a bomb crater, souvenir of an attack by Israeli Phantom jets, which were made in the United States. "We have always thought of the United States as the protector of liberty, but American bombs have been dropping on us, killing our people," the mayor told the visiting senator, without explaining what provoked the bombing. "Now we think the United States is a dictator."

Abourezk came home with an altered perspective. He had always been an iconoclast; his previous work history included stints as a bartender, a blackjack dealer, a used-car salesman, and a judo instructor, before taking a more conventional route for a future politician, the practice of law. When he went to Washington as a Democratic senator from South Dakota, a reporter described him as "the renegade from the West, delighting the press with his outbursts yet infuriating his colleagues." He became a vehement critic of Israel; three years after leaving office, in 1982, he bought a full-page ad for $22,000 in the *Washington Post* that said, "Israel Is Killing Lebanon." At a press conference, he said of the Israelis, "[They] have imitated the methods and the means of their tormentors in Nazi Germany."

His message cost him. "Ask him who his friends are and he'll mention a dozen or so," wrote a *Washington Post* reporter. "And the enemies? Everybody else."

While serving in the Senate, he had come to despise the American

Israel Public Affairs Committee (AIPAC), a pro-Israel lobbying group. "Israel's got too much of a clench on the Congress and Congress is not going to make peace with the Palestinians no matter who is President," Abourezk said. "They frighten politicians to death, the Israeli lobby."

He was called "wacky" and "nutty" and "anti-Semitic." The name-calling hurt, but he kept following his conscience. That included denouncing what the hijackers did to Leon Klinghoffer and the other hostages. To him, a bully was a bully.

"I hate bullies," he said.

Once his indignation quickened in that Lebanese village, Abourezk turned his attention to the perception of Arabs in the United States. In the 1970s and 1980s, the issue was Arabs, not Muslims (the particular demonization of followers of Islam would come in 2001, with the September 11 attacks on the World Trade Center and Pentagon). Most Americans could not distinguish between a Muslim and a Christian of Arabic lineage, much less understand the difference between a Sunni and a Shiite or comprehend that the three countries with the largest Muslim population were Indonesia, Pakistan, and India, none of them Arab.

The one million or so U.S. Arabs—who were both Christian and Muslim—were lumped together as a monolithic breed of mercurial exotics with dubious values.

However, for people of Abourezk's generation, including Marilyn and Leon Klinghoffer, one cultural event became the touchstone for American attitudes toward Arabs, especially in the context of Israel: the 1958 publication of *Exodus* by Leon Uris. The literary version of a tank, the novel delivered a heroic, one-sided vision of Israel's founding, peopled with brave Jews struggling to establish a homeland, pitted against Arabs who "stank," who were "the dregs of humanity," a people whose children revealed "no laughter or songs or games or purpose."

For Jews who came of age during World War II and subsequent decades, the devastation of the Holocaust remained an abiding psychic wound. Uris offered an antidote to the horror of blanket obliteration: a kind of super-Jew, a noble soldier willing to fight to the death rather than be victimized again. It was a resonant theme. Even for Jews who had no desire to live there, Israel became an existential lifeline, the haven that hadn't existed for the millions who perished because of Nazi genocide and international rejection of Jewish refugees. Israel was seen as the last hope, the one place that would accept them when all other doors were shut. The enemy was no longer the Nazis, but the Arabs. In fact, the PLO wouldn't be formed until 1964, and when Uris used "Palestinian" in the novel, he was usually referring to Palestinian Jews, not to Arabs.

Exodus became the political and emotional template for press coverage of the Six-Day War of 1967, when Israel roundly defeated its Arab foes. "As a literary work, it isn't much," said Israel's first prime minister, David Ben-Gurion. "But as a piece of propaganda, it's the greatest thing ever written about Israel."

As the Middle East conflict spawned terrorist attacks and hijackings, "Arab" became equated with "violent." Rising oil prices in the 1970s, prompted by an oil embargo against the United States for its support of Israel in the 1973 Yom Kippur War, added "rich and greedy" to the mix. A real estate company in Washington, D.C., used the image of an Arab sheikh with dollar signs on his dark glasses in an advertising campaign. Arab villains began to show up regularly in movies and on television. For James Abourezk, the nadir may have been Abscam (short for "Arab scam"), an FBI sting operation in the late 1970s aimed at ensnaring corrupt politicians: it used a fake investment company owned by ersatz Arab sheikhs as bait, and the ensuing indictments were a public relations nightmare in terms of the image of Arabs in the United States.

In 1980, Abourezk organized the American-Arab Anti-Discrimination Committee (ADC), patterned after the Jewish Anti-Defamation League. The latter group, known as the ADL, had articulated its mission in terms of civil rights: "To stop the defamation of the Jewish people, and to secure justice and fair treatment to all."

Abourezk followed the Jewish organization's playbook, building a constituency by going from state to state and organizing local chapters, until finally he felt he had met most of the Americans of Arab descent living in the United States. One of them was Alex Odeh, who in 1983 became the ADC's West Coast regional director; Odeh worked out of an office in Santa Ana, California, just outside Los Angeles.

The fiery Abourezk was immediately drawn to Odeh, his opposite in temperament. Odeh, a gentle, scholarly type who almost always wore a jacket and tie to work, was fairly bald before he was forty, offsetting the loss with youthful sideburns. He and his wife, Norma, had three daughters—ages seven, five, and eighteen months, all American-born.

Born Iskander Michael Odeh in Jifna, a majority Christian town in the Ramallah district of the West Bank, about fourteen miles north of Jerusalem, Odeh was one of nine children in a large Roman Catholic family who believed in education and service. One of his brothers became a priest, one of his sisters was a nun, and another became a nurse.

Odeh was studying business and political science at Cairo University at the time of the Six-Day War; the Israeli government closed the borders and he was unable to return to his family in Jifna. Thus began his journey in the Palestinian diaspora. He lived in Amman for several years, then was encouraged to immigrate to the United States by his sister Ellen Nassab, a nurse who lived in Orange County, California, where she was manager of the department of obstetrics at St. Joseph's Hospital.

After completing his master's degree in political science at the California State University, Fullerton, Odeh became an Arabic language instructor at his alma mater and at nearby Coastline Community College, where he also taught Middle East history and politics. He joined the Orange County Human Relations Commission, an outgrowth of 1960s activism, organized a decade earlier to advocate for poor people and minority communities. In 1982, he was hired by the ADC and a year later became regional director, where much of his time was spent composing letters to the editor and writing op-ed pieces in response to articles he thought had an anti-Arab bias. He lectured frequently at interfaith gatherings, speaking about the Palestinian culture and his hopes for peace. With like-minded Jewish leaders, he formed a group called the Cousins Club, where Arab and Jews met to get to know one another.

He became a U.S. citizen but still felt the tug of home. When he was finally able to return to Palestine to see his mother, she suggested he visit the widow next door. Her youngest daughter, a teenager named Norma, was home from boarding school for the summer. Her mother told Norma to shake hands with the visitor from America. He shook her hand and then kissed her on the cheek. Three days later they were engaged, even though she was only sixteen and he was thirty-one. Within a week they were married; four months later Norma joined Alex in the United States.

When Alex returned from that trip to Jifna, he presented his sister Ellen a small bottle of dirt and said, "This is so you won't forget your land." He wrote poetry in Arabic, which he published in a collection titled *Whispers in Exile*. He was committed to the Palestinian cause, but Odeh was a peaceful warrior, leading a cohort of speakers, filmmakers, and musicians into his Southern California community.

Odeh had spent the week of the hijacking doing damage control. He arranged an invitation to speak at a nearby synagogue that Friday evening for Sabbath services and offered to speak to reporters for CNN and on a local television station, KABC. He didn't seem worried about his safety, even though FBI Director William Webster had recently issued a warning that Arab Americans had entered a "zone of danger," referring to several attacks on Arabs by Jewish extremist groups that year, even before the *Achille Lauro* hijacking. A pipe bomb had exploded outside the Boston ADC office the previous month, critically injuring one of the bomb disposal experts trying to defuse it. Odeh dismissed suggestions that he might be in peril, even though the Santa Ana branch had received more harassing telephone calls and threats than any ADC location apart from the New York office.

On Thursday afternoon, October 10, Odeh taped both interviews and then met friends for dinner at a restaurant. He was in good spirits; he told the group the interviews had gone well. The KABC segment was aired throughout the Los Angeles metropolitan area on the eleven o'clock news report that evening, just after the hijackers were taken off the EgyptAir Boeing by the Italian police in Sigonella, where it was already early Friday morning.

Odeh said he condemned the hijacking but defended Yasser Arafat and the PLO, echoing media reports that credited Arafat and the PLO for helping force the hijackers to surrender. While the Israeli government insisted that Arafat was behind the hijacking, this was not the official position of either the U.S. or Italian authorities.

The broadcast included only Odeh's defense of Arafat. "The media ought to give the PLO and Arafat recognition, inform the public about the PLO as a political organization and Arafat in particular as the chairman of the PLO, who is a man of peace," he said.

Another sister, Angela Odeh, lived nearby. After watching her brother on television, she telephoned to tell him she was worried. "Why are you worried?" Alex asked her, a question that revealed how fully Americanized he had become. He took non-Arab friends to Middle Eastern places to introduce them to his culture, but he also ate lunch at the Roy Rogers fast food restaurant near his office. He believed that free speech existed in the United States and felt secure that in America it was possible to state your beliefs without concern that you would be locked up or harmed in any way. Despite threats he'd received in the past at the ADC, he had acquired an American veneer of invulnerability. He had confidence that the kinds of things that happened to Palestinians living in Israel, in the area now called the West Bank, as well as in most Arab countries at the time, didn't happen here.

The following morning, Friday, October 11, Odeh went to his office earlier than usual. He was preparing for the talk he was giving at a synagogue that evening. His administrative assistant hadn't arrived yet; she was doing an errand for Odeh before she came to work.

Shortly after nine, Alex Odeh stood in front of the ADC's offices on the second floor of a three-story stucco building on a palm-lined street. It was a clear and sunny morning; the smog level was low. As Odeh opened the door something exploded, shattering more than a dozen of the building's floor-to-ceiling windows. The street outside filled with fragments of glass, concrete, and cloth from tattered drapes.

Two hours later, the surgeons at Western Medical Hospital's trauma center admitted defeat. Alex Odeh was pronounced dead.

Washington, D.C.

FOURTEEN MINUTES after the bomb exploded in Odeh's office, President Ronald Reagan began speaking to the reporters gathered in the briefing room at the White House. It was 12:25 on the East Coast. As he often did, the president opened with a joke about a serious subject—that Friday it was the patch he was wearing on his nose. He'd had a basal cell carcinoma removed from his nose in July and had a follow-up visit the previous day, after he flew back to Washington from the visit to the Sara Lee factory. A biopsy revealed some additional cancer cells, which had been removed. "Now I have a verdict of…" The Great Communicator paused.

"My nose is clean," he said with a smile.

Having warmed up the audience, he turned to the latest development in the *Achille Lauro* saga—the capture of the hijackers. Offering no hint of the behind-the-scenes diplomatic whipsawing, the president praised the governments of Italy and Egypt (although his gratitude toward Egypt was tempered: "I disagreed with their disposition of the terrorists"). He thanked Tunisian President Habib Bourguiba for refusing to let the fugitives land in his country.

It was time to begin the oratorical crescendo that his speechwriter, Pat Buchanan, had crafted to galvanize a doubting public. Leon Klinghoffer's murder could have seemed like another example of America's vulnerability, one in a series of U.S. losses in the Middle East. The intercept was the president's victory.

"I am proud to be the Commander in Chief of the soldiers, sailors, airmen, and marines who deployed, supported, and played the crucial role in the delivery of these terrorists to Italian authorities," Reagan said. "They and the men and women of our foreign service and intelligence community performed flawlessly in this most difficult and delicate operation. They have my gratitude and, I'm sure, the gratitude of all of their countrymen. These young Americans sent a message to terrorists everywhere."

And then the president delivered a headline-grabbing punch line, a catchphrase that would stick. He did everything for the journalists but scribble it down in their notebooks. "The message," he said, was "You can run but you can't hide."

It was brilliantly plainspoken, if unoriginal. Heavyweight boxing champion Joe Louis is credited for delivering the taunt to his opponent Billy Conn, when Louis was defending his title in 1946. It was such a good line that Reagan had used it before, three years earlier, almost to the day—same script, different enemy. The first time he was sitting on the patio at Camp David with his wife, Nancy—they had matching red sweaters, hers tied pertly around her neck. Reagan reported that, with drug-related arrests up over 40 percent, drug traffickers were on the run, delivering this exaggerated claim with reassuring certainty. "To paraphrase Joe Louis, they can run, but they can't hide," said the president.

When the president opened the press conference up to questions, reporters probed the purported seamlessness of the operation. They asked about Mubarak's lies and Prime Minister Craxi's waffling. They wondered if Reagan felt the Italians would impose a harsh enough sentence. Would the United States demand extradition?

Andrea Mitchell of NBC News asked the toughest question of all: "Were you prepared to shoot that plane down?"

Reagan skillfully deflected. "This, again, is one of those questions, Andrea, that I'm not going to answer," he said. "That's for them to go to bed every night wondering."

He ignored the reporter who asked about the two additional Palestinians left on the airplane, choosing instead to end the news conference by responding to a more sympathetic question.

"Have you called the Klinghoffer family yet, sir?"

The president grabbed the opportunity to end the conversation. "That's what I'm going to the office to do, and you're making me late."

He returned to the Oval Office, ate lunch, and reviewed a memo prepared by Oliver North.

SUBJECT: Phone Call to Family of Leon Klinghoffer, American Murdered Aboard ACHILLE LAURO.

Attached at Tab I is a recommended Presidential telephone call memorandum. The memo suggests that a call be placed to the family and wife of Leon Klinghoffer, who was murdered by the terrorists responsible for hijacking ACHILLE LAURO.

The State Department task force has been in contact with the son-in-law of Mr. Klinghoffer, Jerry Arbittier, and concurs that a Presidential phone call would be appropriate. Mrs. Marilyn Klinghoffer was aboard the motor vessel with her deceased husband and is presently in Cairo (Nile Hilton Hotel). If successful, she will be returning to her home in New York today to be reunited with her family. Since the State task force is able to help relieve some of the family's immediate anxieties, it would benefit the families the most if the Presidential phone call could be placed upon their reunion.

Note: Cable News Network (CNN) has reported that Klinghoffer's family allegedly attempted to call the White House and was "hung-up on." A check with White House operators and signal board indicates that no such calls were received.

TOPICS OF DISCUSSION: I. Nancy and I were deeply grieved to learn that your father has been slain by terrorists. 2. I know that the operation last night aimed at bringing these brutal men to justice cannot relieve your anguish. 3. It is a sad fact that Americans cannot be safe from the scourge of terrorism unless we respond as we did last night. 4. I have been told about your father and you must be very proud of him. He was the kind of person who have [sic] made America a great nation of free enterprise opportunity. 5. I would appreciate it if you

pass along to your mother that Nancy and I have you all in our prayers. God Bless you and the rest of your family.

New York

JUST FIVE days earlier, a telephone call from the president of the United States would have seemed phenomenal, as far-fetched as winning the lottery—perhaps even more unlikely, since the Klinghoffers were solid Democrats.

But by that Friday, October 11, 1985, for Lisa and Ilsa Klinghoffer, all presuppositions were out the window. It was Alfonse D'Amato, New York's Republican senator, who helped the family make connections to the State Department, while calls to the office of New York Democratic senator Daniel Patrick Moynihan had been ignored. A family that had never tried to be newsworthy now had the *New York Times* reporter Sara Rimer embedded in their apartment. Except for excursions to television studios, they had been trapped there since Monday, shrouded in sorrow and fear, encircled by the media people who had set up camp outside their building. A police car remained parked nearby and another policeman guarded the door to the apartment. Would it ever feel safe again on the streets that, just five days ago, had seemed like an extension of home?

They had joined the ranks of public victims, accidental celebrities—another hostage story turned into an instantaneous made-for-television drama, played out on the evening news. That summer, during relentless coverage of the TWA hijacking, ABC commentator George Will criticized the networks for the endless footage of benumbed families and friends, calling the coverage "the pornography of grief," a glib analysis that captured the exploitation, yes, but not the underlying sense of helplessness that accompanied it.

The coverage positioned the Klinghoffers as avatars of loss. Leon's story—and theirs—became public property; after all those television interviews, their faces had been seen by millions of Americans. Letters and telegrams from strangers had been pouring in—some addressed to just "Klinghoffer Family, New York City."

Lisa and Ilsa couldn't read them yet, but they saw the postmarks—from across the United States and abroad, as well as from people in Greenwich Village they'd never met. The letters came from nuns, rabbis, schoolteachers, politicians, diplomats, and military people; typed neatly on nice stationery or scribbled on loose-leaf notebook paper. Those who reached out related in various ways, some obvious, others oblique: because they were sixty-nine years old like Leon, or nurses who had treated stroke victims, or Jews, Christians, Muslims, pacifists, veterans, kibbutzniks, patriots, skeptics, politicians, pet owners, daughters whose fathers had died. A few were anti-Semites.

The call from the president was anticlimactic because they'd received a far more important call the day before—from their mother. It was Thursday morning in New York when they'd received word from the State Department that Marilyn would be calling soon, so they should stay near the phone.

They heard her voice a few minutes later.

"Girls, I have something I have to tell you," Marilyn said, and then groped for words.

As Lisa and Ilsa heard their usually forceful mother stumble, they realized that she had no idea that the *Achille Lauro* had become an international cause célèbre.

"We know, Mom," they told her.

"You know?" she replied. "How could you know? What could you know?"

One of them said, "We know about Daddy."

Silence.

Then Marilyn spoke. Now she sounded like the fearless mother they knew. This was the mother who allowed Ilsa to take a city bus to school alone when she was eight, protected only by a little whistle on her key chain. This was the Marilyn who warned Lisa as a girl to remember to ask someone to cross with her when she got to the corner. "I will know because I have my people watching," Marilyn would threaten. For years Lisa looked around as she walked, wondering, Who are those people?

"Your father was a hero," Marilyn said. "Do your crying now because I've done mine and when I come home we've got a lot of work to do. And call my boss and tell him I'm not going to be into work for a few days."

Lisa said, "Milt is standing right here next to me, tell him yourself."

"What do you mean, Milt's there?" Marilyn asked.

"Mom, everybody knows," Lisa said. "The world knows what happened to Daddy."

Sigonella NATO Base

MARILYN HAD called her daughters from shore at Port Said, not long after she and the others met with Ambassador Veliotes on the *Achille Lauro*. She was wearing the flowered sundress the ambassador had admired, with a white sweater thrown over her shoulders. Her face was sunken. It had taken all her strength just to walk across the pontoon bridge connecting the ship to the dock at Port Said, supported by her friends Charlotte Spiegel and Neal Kantor, who had been on the Pyramids tour. When they arrived at the dock, Marilyn confronted hundreds of people jostling one another, pushing cameras into her face, calling her name. She tried to ignore them and then her inner Jersey girl broke through.

"Get away," she yelled.

She couldn't bear to speak to the press; there were plenty of others eager to tell their stories. For them, this nightmare had already become an exciting adventure they'd survived. Many former hostages spent the day sunbathing by the ship's swimming pool. The young British women singers who called their group Los Ferraros—who had entertained the passengers—were posing for photographers on the upper deck.

Marilyn just wanted to get home. After the phone call, she returned to the ship. Throughout the day, people from the embassy offered the American hostages options. Did they want to take a commercial flight or a military plane? Marilyn left the details to the others. The group decided to take a commercial flight to the United States, leaving from Cairo the next day. That evening, they were taken by bus to the Egyptian capital, 120 miles away.

They arrived at the Cairo Hilton at 11 p.m. Thursday night, where an American intelligence officer debriefed them. Seymour Meskin told the officer about Sylvia Sherman's sketches on the menu and about the coat jacket one of the terrorists had given him. Several of the hostages held an impromptu press conference; Marilyn stayed in her room as her friends and the other passengers had their moment in the glare.

In the middle of the night, the embassy staff woke the Cairo Hilton contingent up with electrifying news. An airplane carrying six passengers had been captured and was being held at a NATO base in Sicily; it was believed the four hijackers were among the six men. The U.S. government wanted to know: Would they go to Sicily to identify them, understanding the detour would delay their trip home? None of them hesitated, even though it meant waiting in Cairo until word came that it was time for them to fly across the Mediterranean.

They waited all day that Friday, as the hijacking of the *Achille Lauro* evolved into a legal battle over jurisdiction. Officials from the FBI and the Department of Justice were dispatched to Egypt and Italy, ready to conduct lineups and take depositions that would satisfy U.S. jurisprudence. Sicilian magistrates from Syracuse, the district covering Sigonella, argued with investigators from Genoa, the *Achille Lauro*'s home port, over who owned the investigation, assuming the cases would proceed in Italy.

Political pressures had escalated. There had been bloody demonstrations in both Italy and Egypt protesting the forced landing of the Egyptian plane. Israeli and Palestinian leaders didn't sidestep the opportunity for recriminations. At the U.N. Security Council session in New York the previous day, Benjamin Netanyahu repeated the assertion that Leon and Marilyn Klinghoffer had been singled out because they were Jewish; he also declared that Yasser Arafat had "full and prior knowledge" of the hijacking. After the meeting, a PLO leader named Farouk Kaddoumi told reporters that the killing of Leon Klinghoffer was "a big lie fabricated by the intelligence service of the United States."

Finally, as evening approached, the Italian magistrates had agreed to organize an American-style lineup, with U.S. Department of Justice officials watching. It was time for the former hostages to travel to Sigonella. After supper, a bus took the Americans and an Austrian couple to the Cairo airport. At 11:30 Friday evening., they boarded a C-141 military transport bound for Sigonella.

Seventeen passengers from the *Achille Lauro* emerged from the cargo jet, shivering from exhaustion and cold; the military plane was not outfitted for comfort. After a brief restroom stop and getting some coffee, they were taken by bus to a local police station near the NATO base.

General Stiner greeted Marilyn Klinghoffer and escorted her and two others into a room where the four hijackers were standing in a row next to a few local men enlisted for the lineup. None were handcuffed; the room was full of both American and Italian armed soldiers.

Stiner stayed by Marilyn's side as she walked along the row of men until she stopped directly in front of Molqi, with about four feet between them.

She took a closer look and then spit at him.

"Let me have your pistol," she said to the general in a steely voice. "I want to shoot him."

Stiner was over six feet tall. As he leaned down to hear Marilyn, whose head barely scraped the five-foot mark, he connected to her cold rage.

"I know how you feel," he said. "I'd want to do the same thing. But you have to understand that it would only further complicate matters. It's best to let the Italian courts handle this thing in the appropriate way."

She didn't argue. "It hurts," she said, "but I guess you are right."

Marilyn reverted to type, the well-brought-up person who reminded her daughters to send thank-you notes.

"Please pass my thanks to all your troops for what they have done for us," she said.

Stiner appreciated how calm she was, impressed at how quickly she was able to understand the protocol, to realize that it was out of her control and under theirs. This brief encounter filled him with emotion. The strength of this small woman fortified him in his mission to serve his nation.

When the taciturn general was called on to express his feelings about Marilyn, he declared, "She was a beautiful lady, a caring lady, trying to do what was right."

Less than two hours after they arrived, Marilyn and the others got back on the military transport. Finally, she was on her way home.

8

Machinations

Sigonella NATO Base

Abu al-Abbas spent Friday waiting, trapped inside the EgyptAir plane, as the Italian government decided his immediate fate.

For Bettino Craxi, the Italian prime minister, Abbas had become a time bomb, threatening to disrupt the Italian's grand foreign policy initiatives—his alliance with President Reagan in destroying Soviet influence and his efforts to broker a solution to the Palestinian-Israeli conflict.

Craxi was a wily operator, a tough Sicilian who dropped out of college and became a lifelong politician. By age forty-two he had achieved leadership of Italy's Socialist party and was elected prime minister before his fiftieth birthday. He was unabashedly manipulative, a useful quality in the roiling tumult of Italian politics; he was the twenty-fourth prime minister in the forty years following World War II. A prominent figure in Europe's anti-Soviet left, he substituted a rose for his Socialist party's hammer and sickle symbol and supported the U.S. initiative to station 112 cruise missiles at the NATO base in Sigonella. Although leader of the Socialists, he was also a defender and friend of Silvio Berlusconi, the crass media tycoon and right-leaning demagogue who would become prime minister within a decade. Craxi endorsed Palestinian aspirations while boasting that Italy had brought more terrorists to justice (often working with Israel) than any other country.

As the showdown at Sigonella intensified, Craxi was multitasking at full tilt, trying to placate the United States and Egypt (and every other moderate Arab country), uphold Italy's jurisdictional honor, and show deference to Yasser Arafat.

The U.S. government had become determined to take custody of Abbas, the suspected mastermind of the plot, although he was a man whose name nobody seemed to know just two days earlier. "Everything began to focus on Abu al-Abbas," said a U.S. official on the scene in Sicily that day. "The fact that we had the four hijackers was quickly forgotten."

Arafat sent Craxi a letter that expressed wounded outrage at "the American act of piracy" and warned that the failure to free the Egyptian plane and its passengers could unleash reactions "we fear we might not be able to control, not us, not you, not the Egyptians." Craxi, whose country had been ravaged by internal political terrorism for almost twenty years, was well aware of the menace that lay behind such words. Arafat reminded Craxi that the PLO intervened with the Egyptians to bring the *Achille Lauro* into Port Said peaceably and that "everything that occurred was with your knowledge, including the commitments made with the hijackers which allowed us to convince them to hand themselves over to the Egyptian authorities."

That Friday morning, Hussein al-Aflak, head of the PLO office in Rome, called the Italian foreign minister's office and left a message. "Mr. al-Aflak said he was interested in the fate of Hani-el-Hassan [sic], counselor to Arafat [believed to be on the plane with Abbas]," wrote the person taking the call. "The representative [al-Aflak] would like to go visit him as soon as possible, asking that the Italian government take all possible measures to protect him. Concerning the four hijackers, on the other hand, Mr. Al-Aflak stated: 'They do not interest us at all. Do with them what you see fit. If you want, you can even hand them over to the Americans.'"

Enter Antonio Badini, Craxi's top foreign policy aide, a behind-the-scenes adviser who wielded significant influence with his boss. Badini was a career diplomat, a member of the Christian Democrat party, the main rival of Craxi's Socialists. Badini was brought on board early in Craxi's tenure to acclimate the maverick politician to the nuances of being prime minister. Whatever their political differences, Craxi soon saw Badini's professional value and kept him by his side.

As for Badini, he had been dubious at first about Craxi, who spoke bluntly without regard for the protocol and procedures that were the diplomat's lifeblood. But Badini came to appreciate the authority the prime minister demanded and often achieved. He saw how Craxi won the admiration of President Reagan by working to discredit the Soviet Union. He was heartened to discover that the prime minister seemed to care sincerely about peace in the Middle East. Badini had been with the prime minister during the secret talks in Tunis with Arafat the previous December and on another occasion had watched him negotiate with Shimon Peres of Israel and King Hussein of Jordan, hoping to find a crack in the historic intransigence that marked the relationship between the two countries.

Craxi told Badini to go to Sigonella, to see whether he could find out who Abbas really was. Was he the neutral party described by Arafat or was he the scoundrel depicted by the United States and Israel? Craxi had been receiving Israeli intelligence reports from the Americans all day, detailing Abbas's history of violent attacks. But nothing he'd seen so far made a direct link to the *Achille Lauro*.

In Tunis, Badini had heard Arafat mention Abu al-Abbas as a dissident, a possible danger to the peace process, nothing more. In the West, Abbas hadn't been considered a major player—or even known—until the *Achille Lauro* affair, when he appeared in Port Said as the PLO point man negotiating with the hijackers. The transcripts of those negotiations that Israeli and Italian intelligence provided showed Abbas attempting to persuade the young Palestinians to surrender but did not implicate Abbas in the hijacking or the murder of Leon Klinghoffer.

Badini decided to bring along Hussein al-Aflak, the PLO representative in Rome who had called earlier to inquire about Hani al-Hassan. The Egyptian ambassador had assured Badini that he could trust the

PLO diplomat. They were accompanied by Admiral Fulvio Martini, chief of Italian military security and intelligence.

Badini spent the short flight from Rome to Sigonella—less than one hour—debriefing Aflak about Abbas. Aflak warned Badini to be careful when questioning Abbas, who Aflak felt had made many attempts to weaken Arafat. He is not a friend, warned Aflak. He should not be considered an ally.

They arrived at the NATO base at three that Friday afternoon, October 11, landing not far from the EgyptAir plane. Admiral Martini left his companions standing next to their small executive jet and walked over to Carl Stiner, the American general, in the impromptu command post he had set up on the runway. Martini and Stiner had faced off the night before during the intercept and had reached an understanding, between military men. Now Martini explained why they were there and Stiner gave them permission to board but kept his distance from the civilians in suits. Badini felt uneasy; he was in Italy yet there were American soldiers milling around. He had the surreal feeling of being under surveillance.

Having taken Aflak's warning to heart, Badini wanted to consult with Renato Ruggiero, secretary general of the Foreign Ministry, in Rome before he talked to Abbas. He asked a colonel helping him to take him to a private telephone.

When Badini placed the call, he heard an American voice saying, "Who are you?"

Badini was shaken. This was proof that his sense of being under surveillance was not imaginary.

"Why is there interference by an American?" he asked the colonel. "How come?"

The colonel smiled and said, "They are everywhere," as if he were saying "The sky is blue."

Badini hadn't trained as a spy, but suddenly he found himself talking in code. "The sky is getting cloudy, threatening strong rains," he told Ruggiero, hoping he would understand his meaning, that the situation with Abbas might require swift action.

By the time Badini and Aflak climbed aboard the Egyptian aircraft, the Italian diplomat's nerves were fraying. He hadn't slept for two days and was exhausted. He couldn't believe that he was unable to find a secure telephone line on a base located on Italian soil. It was infuriating!

Badini forced himself to focus on his urgent task. Would he be able to extract a confession from Abbas that would explain the contradiction between what Aflak had said and the evidence in the transcripts? Was Abbas a terrorist aimed at disrupting Arafat's peace initiatives, or was he a crucial emissary in bringing the *Achille Lauro* episode to a close? The international tug-of-war didn't allow for the third possibility, that Abbas could be both.

Badini and Aflak were greeted by a man who introduced himself as an official envoy of Egypt. Before introducing them to Abu al-Abbas, he made sure they understood that the plane should be considered Egyptian territory and Abbas was there as a guest of the Egyptian government.

Abu al-Abbas did not make a good first impression on Badini. The Palestinian was rumpled after spending a full day and night in the airplane with stale air; the Americans had turned the power off hours before. Badini was dressed formally, in suit and tie; he expected a show of respect but didn't see any from Abbas.

Aflak saw the second Palestinian was not Hani al-Hassan and asked who he was. Abbas waved dismissively at his friend and good luck charm Badratkan. "He's just a bodyguard," he said.

The absence of niceties foreshadowed a conversation that began badly from Badini's point of view. Speaking in Arabic to Aflak, who translated, Abbas said the Egyptians and Arafat knew what had happened on the ship and there was nothing more to say.

When Badini explained that he had the power to recommend whether to allow Abbas to go free or not, the Palestinian smiled slightly and began to talk. Abbas rarely raised his voice or let his nerves show, and he didn't now—not even lighting his habitual cigarette. He spoke calmly and with intelligence, demonstrating that he could dissemble with the aplomb of a practiced politician.

Badini was listening for contradictions between what Abbas said and what Badini knew. The wiretaps from Israeli and Italian intelligence indicated that Abbas was a legitimate broker who had helped bring the hijackers into custody. Aflak—agreeing with the Americans—argued that he was a dangerous dissident bent on disrupting Arafat's peace efforts, with a connection to the hijacking that was far from neutral.

Abbas presented himself to Badini as an emissary of Yasser Arafat, nothing more. Arafat sent him to Port Said to act as a mediator, Abbas said, because of his prestige among the hijackers as an "ex-leader" of the PLF, to which they belonged. His instructions had come from Hani al-Hassan, Arafat's political counselor, who told Abbas that Arafat "was very irritated and worried about the hijacking, which he considered to be an act of sabotage against his peacemaking efforts."

Abbas said he was happy to accept the assignment because he, too, had been "surprised" by the hijacking and wanted to do all he could to bring the ship and hostages to safety. Abbas couldn't understand why he was being held on Italian territory because, he said, "his role was decisive for the release of the passengers and their safety and that he was able to cooperate with great effectiveness together with Egyptian authorities to get the four hijackers to desist from pursuing the crime."

Abbas acknowledged that he knew the hijackers while disavowing any direct relationship. He reassured Badini that he was "not informed of this operation they were carrying out."

He explained that he accompanied the hijackers on the plane because the PLO wanted to bring them to justice in Tunis, where there would be an investigation and a trial, held by the PLO. Abbas acknowledged that the PLO was in a "difficult phase" that made it hard to "maintain constant and complete control on all its groups and factions."

Abbas expressed his hopes that Italy would continue helping peacemaking efforts in the Middle East and repeated that the "PLO is not a terrorist organization but rather of liberation." He indirectly scolded the United States for putting Egyptian President Hosni Mubarak in a "difficult position" with the intercept and reminded Badini that "many uncertainties within the behavior of the PLO have stemmed from the harsh Israeli action taken against its headquarters in Tunis."

Abbas held his ground, even when Aflak began badgering him in Arabic. Badini didn't know what Aflak said, but it sounded like a reproach.

The encounter lasted less than an hour. Badini listened with a diplomat's ears and he wasn't hearing evidence to make a legal case against Abbas.

At age forty-five, after years in the foreign service dealing with politicians, Badini was practiced at quickly digesting complex and contradictory information. These were the considerations: Whatever Abbas's true relationship to the hijackers, Arafat had chosen him to bring the hijacking to a close without further injury to the hostages. That had been accomplished. Wherever the truth lay, Badini felt there was enough uncertainty to justify getting Abbas away from the Americans at the NATO base while the Italian government decided what to do. After all, Badini had entered the Boeing with intelligence reports that Hassan was on the plane. That information had turned out to be false. The Israelis said that Abbas was connected to the hijacking. Could that be wrong as well?

After leaving the plane, Badini debriefed with a prosecutor from Syracuse who had come to Sigonella. The prosecutor agreed that no further investigation was necessary, and that Abbas should be allowed to leave. Badini called Rome and reported his conclusion to Secretary General Ruggiero.

Ten minutes later Badini received a call from Craxi. "*Ciampino, Badini, mi raccomando!* (To Ciampino, Badini, I'm counting on you!)" Before Badini could reply, the prime minister had hung up.

Badini told both Admiral Martini and the Egyptian pilot to get ready to take off for Rome's Ciampino Airport, which was part military, part civilian. There the Americans couldn't touch Abbas, while the Italians decided their next move.

When Badini told Aflak the plan, the Palestinian was disappointed. As an Arafat loyalist, he would have been happy to see Abbas disappear. "Why don't you send it to Tunis?" he asked, referring to the Egyptian plane. "So the Americans will shoot down the plane and kill them."

Badini understood Aflak's words were a bleak joke, but perhaps also a wish.

At 11 p.m., the EgyptAir Boeing 737 left Sigonella for Rome, escorted by four Italian jet planes.

When General Stiner learned that the EgyptAir plane had been cleared to leave Sigonella, he ordered a U.S. Navy jet fighter to follow it—without permission from airport authorities. The American T-39 took off, despite the efforts of Italian troops to block it by putting machinery on the runway. The Italians immediately launched four additional jet interceptors from another base to protect the EgyptAir 737 from interference. Once again, a high-altitude chase was on, between purported allies.

The pilots cursed at one another all the way to Rome.

"Shithead! You're nothing but an ugly shit!" an Italian pilot screamed. "Get out of here before you bang into us. You're dangerous for us and for yourself."

"Sons of bitches," replied an American. "Goddamn sons of bitches. That plane is mine, understand. It's mine."

Yet for all the American bluster, the plane carrying Abu al-Abbas and Badratkan landed safely at Ciampino. Stiner heard various stories about what happened next, but only one thing was certain. Abu al-Abbas had vanished, and the Italians helped make that happen.

Stiner took this defeat philosophically. Overall, he felt things had gone well; Abbas had slipped away, but the hijackers had been captured. He'd been on missions that had gone worse—much worse.

Rome

ABU AL-ABBAS was accustomed to being on the run, but this time was different. Now he was wanted by the most powerful country on earth and the whole world was watching.

When the plane carrying him and Badratkan landed at Ciampino, several cars sent by the American embassy were waiting outside. The drivers in those cars watched as two men who appeared to be the Palestinians emerged from the airport and were hustled into a waiting police vehicle, part of a convoy. A chase began. The police cars, with sirens wailing, flew through the streets of Rome, followed by the American cars until they reached the Egyptian Art Academy, which was under Egyptian sovereignty. The police escorted the two men inside, where the Americans couldn't get to them.

The cat-and-mouse escapade continued through the night. An American federal judge in Washington, D.C., issued warrants for the arrest of the four hijackers and Abu al-Abbas; the FBI and Department of State sent U.S. Ambassador to Italy Maxwell Rabb additional information from Israel that indicated Abbas knew more about the hijacking than he was saying, though most of the "evidence" was a rehash of Abbas's previous operations. At 5:30 a.m. Rome time on Saturday, October 12, Ambassador Rabb personally delivered a request to the Foreign Ministry that Abbas be arrested and extradited to the United States.

Within Italy there was dissent, as legal authorities offered different views on what should happen to Abbas. That whole morning, while the Palestinians remained in hiding, Prime Minister Craxi was inundated with opinions, pleas, and warnings from Egypt, the PLO, and the United States, including a direct message from President Reagan that ended on a threatening note: "I would not want a precipitous decision to become such a great problem between our two countries."

Craxi was squeezed on all sides, including by opponents in his own governing coalition who wanted Abbas turned over to the Americans and others who did not. His defense minister, Giovanni Spadolini, strongly supported the U.S. backing of Israel and felt that Craxi was too conciliatory to Arafat and the PLO. The minister had already been upset by Craxi's sharp criticism of Israel for bombing PLO headquarters in Tunisia; for Spadolini, the release of Abu al-Abbas was a further outrage, another concession to people the defense minister saw as terrorists.

In the midst of these fulminations, Antonio Badini and Admiral Martini were arranging Abbas's escape—not from the Egyptian Art Academy, however, but from Italy. The PLF leader and Badratkan had never left the plane. They'd spent the night at Ciampino. The elaborate escape the night before had been a ruse, complete with decoys, designed to distract the Americans.

For Badini, the deception was painful but necessary. His uneasiness about the entire *Achille Lauro* affair was heightened because he loved the United States. As a young boy, he had spent time in an orphanage after World War II, placed there by his mother while waiting for his father to be released from an Allied POW camp. The young Badini survived thanks to canned meat, jam, and other food sent by the Americans; he never forgot the largesse shown by Italy's conquerors. He still had fond memories of the American soldiers who taught him and the other children how to play baseball—and the chocolate and chewing gum the GIs handed out to the winning team. After that he always thought of the States as "a dream place."

Badini believed Abbas could destroy everything Craxi had done to bring the PLO toward peace and would have been happy to put him on trial or extradite him. But justice moved slowly in Italy and it could take days, even weeks, for an investigation to decide whether there was enough evidence to charge him. Abbas was there under diplomatic immunity from Egypt. To hold him would be disastrous for Italian relations with the Arabs, even more dangerous than incurring the displeasure of the United States.

Admiral Martini investigated flights to countries friendly to the PLO and found three possibilities, all leaving from Fiumicino, Rome's main international airport, that Saturday afternoon. Badini called

Aflak, now his accomplice, and asked which country he recommended. Aflak chose Yugoslavia and offered to arrange safe haven there for Abbas while Martini created tickets for Abbas and Badratkan, complete with fake personal details.

Once Badini got the go-ahead from Craxi, word was sent to Ciampino that the Egyptian airplane should make the short hop to Fiumicino.

There was one problem: the Egyptian pilot wasn't there. He had gone into Rome to go shopping.

Martini called air traffic control at Fiumicino and told them to delay the Yugoslav flight. In a scenario more Pink Panther than James Bond, Badini learned that a Roman prosecutor was on his way to Fiumicino, determined to stop Abbas from leaving the country until more questions could be asked.

The EgyptAir 737 landed at Fiumicino as the prosecutor was driving to the airport from the Egyptian Art Academy, where he thought he would find Abbas. The Palestinians were shuttled on foot from the Egyptian to the Yugoslav aircraft, while Martini called the director of the airport to give the green light to the Yugoslav pilot. Just as the prosecutor arrived at Fiumicino, the plane carrying Abu al-Abbas and Ozzudin Badratkan lifted off, taking them to their next destination.

Belgrade

ABBAS DISCOVERED after landing in Yugoslavia that the media was creating a legend out of the *Achille Lauro* and had appointed him the story's most colorful villain. His face was about to appear on every American television network and in every leading U.S. publication. White House spokesman Larry Speakes called him "one of the most notorious Palestinian terrorists." U.S. Attorney General Edwin Meese made threats on television. "We'll pursue Mr. al-Abbas as we would any other fugitive," he said. "There is no safe haven as far as we're concerned."

The international press had been riveted by the hijacking, Kling-hoffer's murder, the American intercept, and now Abbas's escape. In the United States, the reaction to the Reagan administration's response was overwhelmingly positive; even the *New York Times*, usually critical of the president, ran an enthusiastic editorial under the headline "Jubilant Justice."

The reaction elsewhere was far more condemnatory. Italian head-lines reflected the anti-American outrage that had erupted there, un-paralleled since the height of the Vietnam War. The United States became "the American Enemy," "Rambo," and "Big Brother." A mag-azine cover showed President Reagan as a cartoon cowboy spanking a tiny Prime Minister Craxi, bent over the American president's knee.

In Saudi Arabia, Bahrain, Kuwait, Jordan, and Syria, the American intercept of the Egyptian airplane was called "Piracy," "A Terrorist Ac-tion," and "Cowboy Diplomacy."

The official Yugoslav press agency praised Abu al-Abbas for nego-tiating the surrender of the four *Achille Lauro* hijackers and scolded the United States for being a hijacker.

In Egypt, student protesters marched in the streets. "For the first time [these] featured anti-Mubarak slogans, as well as those against the U.S. and Israel," Ambassador Nicholas Veliotes wrote in an urgent cable to the White House on October 12. "Mubarak delivered an impassioned defense of the Egyptian role in saving 400 passengers' lives on the hijacked ship," the ambassador reported. "After explaining the background of Egypt's successful efforts to rescue the passengers, Mubarak repeatedly and emotionally, bordering on outrage, expressed incredulity that a friendly state like the U.S. could have sent military aircraft to intercept an Egyptian civilian airliner....Mubarak stated with obvious anger that there is great propaganda being made about the American operation in intercepting the plane, but in his opinion the real heroism was that of Egypt in rescuing more than 400 people."

Veliotes requested that all administration participants on Sunday TV appearances should be briefed carefully on the issue. "Take the high road," he advised. "Accentuate the positive on the Egyptian role in saving human lives and downplay differences in the context of stressing our basic mutuality of interests."

In Jerusalem, Israel's military intelligence chief, Major General Ehud Barak, told reporters there was abundant evidence linking Abbas to the hijacking, but most of it was "too sensitive" to be divulged. These two men had a long history by then. This was the same Ehud Barak who led the retaliatory raid in 1972 to kill Kamal Nasser, the relative of Samia Costandi, Abu al-Abbas's first wife.

"Al-Abbas is not a marginal figure in the PLO," Barak said. "He is one of the closest to Yasser Arafat. His own headquarters in Tunisia is a hundred yards from Arafat's headquarters which are in ruins following our [October 1] bombing."

Barak played excerpts from the tape recording of a conversation between Abbas and Majid al-Molqi on October 9, the day after Klinghoffer was killed. The Israelis said the tape proved that Abu al-Abbas wasn't an impartial mediator, as the Palestinians claimed, but an active participant, who knew the hijackers by their first names and gave them pointed instructions about what to do and what to say.

Abu al-Abbas was learning that some battles were fought with words and perception. Emulating the Israelis and Yasser Arafat, he began his own spin campaign on Monday, October 14, two days after he was spirited out of Italy. Reporters began receiving calls from PLO officials arranging telephone interviews with him from Yugoslavia, where Abbas was the guest of Nemer Hammad, the PLO representative about to replace Aflak in Rome.

Abu al-Abbas told Egypt's Middle East News Agency that the four Palestinians who took command of the ship didn't intend to hijack it. "Their destination was the Israeli port of Ashdod for the purpose of carrying out a suicide mission," he said. In an interview with the Kuwaiti press service, Abbas expressed his gratitude to Italy for allowing him to leave, even though the United States wanted to have him extradited to America.

When he spoke by telephone with a *New York Times* reporter in Tunis, Abbas became statesmanlike. "My plans are to keep resisting, fighting and asking for the peace process and our sovereign rights," he said. He assured the *Times* reporter, Edward Schumacher-Matos, that he never "arranged any operations outside Israel," but warned that he was "proud to arrange operations against military and economic targets inside the occupied territories in Palestine." His goal, he said, was "to do his best" to send the hijackers "to a Palestinian court."

Asked whether he was worried about being extradited to the United States, Abbas said, "There are millions of people saying, 'Welcome, Abu al-Abbas,' and I am proud of it."

Schumacher-Matos was based in Madrid, but his coverage area included the entire Maghreb region. He'd been invited by the PLO to headquarters in the Tunisian capital, to talk to Abbas on speakerphone while someone in the office there translated.

The reporter had interviewed many PLO officials, but until the *Achille Lauro*, he had never heard of Abbas. Now an interview with him was a coup.

Schumacher-Matos was scrambling to assemble the details he needed to produce an authoritative-sounding report. In his dispatch, he tossed in a random bit of color: "Mr. al-Abbas's wife, Rim [sic], 30 years old, stood by in Tunis during the half-hour interview."

In this brief encounter, Reem al-Nimer made an impression on the journalist as an attractive woman who was smart and sophisticated. There was no time to chat, however. He had to file his story, and then move on to the next one.

Reem (who was actually thirty-three) had been unable to talk to her husband for more than a week. But she had been watching the news and saw the American anger against him building with frightening force. Having spent so much of her adult life on the run, she recognized the danger signs. PLO officials had told her it was too risky to speak by telephone; she decided to leave for Belgrade, to find out directly from her husband what she needed to do for the safety of her sons. Reem left the boys behind, feeling it was too dangerous to take them until she knew more. Their housekeeper was trustworthy. Moreover, in El Menzah, the middle-class enclave where many PLO families lived, Reem had relatives and friends whom she trusted to look in on the children.

She moved quickly, but not quick enough. By the time she reached Yugoslavia, her husband was gone. But Nemer Hammad reassured her that Abbas was safe in the Iraqi capital of Baghdad, and that the PLO would arrange for her to join him in a few days. The days stretched out to a week for a prosaic reason: a dense fog settled over Belgrade, closing the airport for four days.

Reem controlled her rising sense of panic by reminding herself that she had been moving from place to place since she was a teenager, absorbing the tension and insecurity that came with the life she had chosen—"chosen" being the operative word. Unlike so many other Palestinians, she had made a choice, knowing she had a prosperous family who could take her in, knowing she could have pulled out anytime she wanted. But she wouldn't abandon Abu al-Abbas. This was her decision, and it was made not just out of duty or love. In moments of reflection, she admitted to herself that she had tied herself to Abbas for many reasons—the cause, yes, but also the adventure, even knowing how hard it was on her boys.

When the fog lifted in Belgrade, Reem followed her husband to Baghdad.

9
Corpora Delicti

Santa Ana, California, October 15, 1985

She was told not to look: his abdomen had been destroyed, his hands were missing. But Norma Odeh insisted on viewing her husband's remains because she could not believe the horror was real. Then she saw Alex's face, and it was him, marred only by blisters from the explosion.

"Let him wake up!" she cried out to the counselor who met with her at the hospital. Over and over she repeated, "I don't care what anybody tells me, he is not gone."

Even when the terrible truth sank in, she didn't stop dreaming, night after night, that when she woke up Alex would come home.

She kept thinking, "This could not happen in America," as if that belief would bring Alex back to life.

Yet political violence and racism were embedded in the American landscape, as endemic to Southern California as sunshine and palm trees. Local targets of arson and firebombings in recent years had included women's health centers, a Planned Parenthood clinic, and the campaign office of Jesse Jackson, the African American candidate for the Democratic presidential nomination in 1984. Orange County was infamous for its right-wing extremists; the state's attorney general told an Anti-Defamation League gathering in Santa Ana that many of the country's twenty-three known terrorist groups had a "strong California tinge, more specifically Southern California."

The Jewish Defense League (JDL) was one of the extremist groups under investigation by an FBI antiterrorism task force. This radical far-right group had been established by Meir Kahane, a Brooklyn rabbi who advocated violence and whose founding premise was that "the image of the Jew as a weakling, as one who is easily stepped upon and who does not fight back is an image that must be changed."

The JDL did not take responsibility for the bombing that killed Alex Odeh but did endorse it. "I have no tears for Mr. Odeh," said JDL leader Irv Rubin. "He got exactly what he deserves."

Norma had been constantly frightened ever since Alex took the job with the American Arab Anti-Discrimination Committee (ADC). After he began appearing in public as a representative of the Arab community, they began receiving threatening phone calls at home, from people who identified themselves as from the JDL. They would find their car covered with splattered eggs.

"What if they do something worse?" Norma asked her husband. "What if they kill you, what am I going to do?"

His answer was not reassuring. "It would be an honor for me to die for my country," Alex told her. "God will take care of you and the girls." When he spoke of "my country," Alex was referring to Palestine, which didn't conflict with his loyalty to his adopted home, or the gratification he took from carrying an American passport. Palestine represented his heritage; the United States had become his home. When asked where he was from, he would say, "I am from the Middle East, but I am Arab American."

President Reagan called the bombing "heinous" and ordered FBI agents to join the investigation. But there was no presidential telephone call to Norma or her little girls—just a statement issued by the deputy press secretary, saying that Reagan "extends his sincere condolences to Mr. Odeh's widow Norma and his three small daughters, as well as to other members of the family."

The family read about it in the newspapers. Since the message was not delivered to them personally, it was rendered meaningless, almost an insult. The presidential snub cut especially deep because Norma and Alex Odeh had done their part to contribute to the American mythology of the great melting pot. They were part of a prosperous Arab American community in Orange County, educated and upwardly mobile.

One of the friends who had dinner with Alex the night before his death had established the Arab-American Republican Club of Orange County, which claimed to be the biggest ethnic volunteer organization in the county's 1984 Reagan-Bush campaign.

Alex was a Democrat but had contributed to the GOP. The summer before he was killed, Alex had received a gold "medal of merit" from Ronald Reagan, delivered in a blue velvet case. Along with the president's signature, it carried the inscription "Presented in appreciation for your support as a member of the Republican Presidential Task Force."

The medal now seemed like a mockery, a false source of pride. "If he [Reagan] thought so much of Alex, why doesn't he say something to us?" Norma asked.

Alex's funeral took place on October 15, four days after he was murdered, at St. Norbert's, a large, modern Catholic church almost directly across the street from the Odeh home. Sorrow was permeated with anger and dread, sharpened by the presence of the helmeted police officers taking the license number of each car as it entered the parking lot. The church had received two bomb threats the previous night. Other officers stood on the roof of the rectory, keeping watch through binoculars.

Despite the uneasiness in the air, heightened by the security measures, the mourners reflected Odeh's idealistic hope that tolerance was possible. There were people wearing yarmulkes as well as kaffiyehs, rabbis who had worked with Odeh as well as the Jordanian ambassador to the United States and the Egyptian consul general in Los Angeles. The sanctuary overflowed, with more than fifteen hundred people in attendance.

American and Palestinian flags draped the casket; the service was spoken in Arabic and English, with an elegy played on a shepherd's flute. "It is rare today that someone speaks the truth without violence," the priest told the mourners. "It seems Alex could not do otherwise." Sami Odeh, one of Alex's brothers, asked that there be "no banners, no slogans, no undignified conduct."

Four hundred people made the fifteen-minute drive to the Cemetery of the Holy Sepulcher. Several Palestinian flags unfurled during the walking procession to the grave site, where a Palestinian anthem was sung under the bright California sun.

Ellen Nassab, Alex's sister, had brought the bottle of soil from Palestine that Alex had given her. She had been keeping it on her dresser with her cologne and perfume, as a constant, precious reminder of her heritage. She had asked the priest whether he could give her a minute to speak before the service concluded. When he agreed, she gathered courage she didn't know she had and explained to those gathered why she decided to return the gift to her brother. Just as his casket was draped with the flags representing Palestine and the United States, she explained, she was going to sprinkle the contents of the bottle on his grave, so he would be buried under Palestinian and American soil.

Norma Odeh stood by her husband's grave reeling in the heat from pain, anger, and confusion. For the past decade, her entire adult life, she had been dependent on Alex for everything. She was twenty-six years old and a widow. As her daughters clung to her black dress of mourning, she wondered how she would support them. They had lived comfortably enough on Alex's $30,000 annual income—Norma cared little for material things—but there had been no excess.

Her heart broke looking at her little girls. She had lost her own father at age three, and her mother had sent her and her three siblings to boarding school because she couldn't take care of them. Norma had cried herself to sleep every night for the twelve years she was there because she wanted to be with her mother.

When Alex had chosen her to be his wife—an arrangement he made with her mother—she had asked her mother, "Why are you making me get married when I have two older sisters?" Her mother said, "He wants you."

When Norma joined her new husband in America four months after their wedding, she was frightened. She had learned English in school yet was still scared to speak, no matter how much Alex reassured her. But there was a bigger fear. In their culture, if you didn't come back from your honeymoon pregnant, something was wrong with you. Norma had summoned the courage to inform Alex, this older man she barely knew, that she wanted to wait. "I want to finish high school, learn English, and get my driver's license, and then have a baby," she told him.

He didn't hesitate. "Take your time," he said. "Whenever you are ready, let me know."

That's when she fell in love. She saw he was a good man who had endless patience. He made her feel like a queen, always calling her *habibti*, "my love" or "sweetheart" in Arabic. Norma finished high school in California. That's when she began to lie about her age, adding a couple of years because friends asked her if Alex was her father when he picked her up from school. Three years after she moved to the United States, having earned her degree, and gotten her driver's license, Norma gave birth to their first child.

Norma was happy until Alex joined the ADC and became a public figure. When the hateful incidents began, Norma told him, "I don't want my kids to grow up without a father, to be like me, growing up in a boarding school." Alex always reassured her, saying, "That won't happen."

Now she wondered about everything they had come to believe about the United States. Did they not matter? Were they not Americans? She had seen the difference in the official reaction to her husband's murder and the killing of Leon Klinghoffer. Alex's death was treated as a local murder; Leon Klinghoffer's death had become an international incident, called an act of terrorism. The newspaper said that when Marilyn arrived at Newark Airport, she was greeted by a cadre of American dignitaries, the U.S. ambassador to the United Nations, and U.S. senators from New York and New Jersey.

Maybe it was unintended, but the message Norma Odeh received seemed clear. "It's as though her husband was something and mine wasn't."

That thought would never go away.

New York City, October 22, 1985

ON OCTOBER 16, the day after Alex Odeh was laid to rest, Leon Klinghoffer's body washed ashore on the coast of Syria.

Leon's miraculous reappearance changed the nature of the investigation. Now there was an actual corpus delicti, a body whose existence refuted claims by Yasser Arafat and Abu al-Abbas that Klinghoffer may have died of natural causes, since an examination revealed two gunshot wounds, one in the head and the other in the back. As a State Department spokesman drily noted, "Gunshot wounds are not exactly natural causes." The emergence of Klinghoffer's body was a political as well as an evidentiary rebuke. The Syrian government's decision to send the body to Rome for identification was a pointed slap at Arafat and the PLO. In the Byzantine logic of the Middle East, it was possible for Syria to condemn the hijacking, in apparent sympathy with the United States, while condemning Arafat for participating in U.S.-sponsored peace negotiations with Israel.

For the Klinghoffer family, there could be no joy in the recovery of Leon's corpse, but there was relief. There was symbolic force in the corporeal reality of bones, flesh, and muscle, even a body like Leon's, weakened by illness and then battered by force; even after death, when the tangible iterations of fathers, mothers, children, relatives, enemies, and friends become carcasses, no more, no less. Without his body, there was no proof that Leon was really gone, leaving the unsettling possibility that he was alive and suffering. Without his body, there was an inexplicable feeling of emptiness, of trying to embrace a ghost.

Like many religions, Orthodox Judaism provides a ritual for the psychological transition away from the physical being into spiritual existence. Between the time of death and burial, volunteers stay near to the deceased, reciting soothing psalms in the belief that the human soul continues to linger awhile near the body that held it, while awaiting passage to the next world. As Reform Jews, the Klinghoffers didn't know this practice, called *shemira*, meaning "watching" or "guarding," which is just as well. Leon had been thrown into the dangerous depths of the Mediterranean, where his body drifted for eight days without protection from the ravages of seawater and hungry fish. An autopsy performed in Rome, witnessed by a U.S. pathologist and FBI agents, provided a gruesome report. Leon's face was swollen and disfigured; his right arm, left leg, and the tips of several fingers were missing. With this ghastly evidence, what could possibly provide Leon's survivors the balm of *shemira*? What process would help ease their metamorphosis from wife and daughters of a living person to guardians of his memory?

Unexpectedly, a comforting rite of passage was provided by the United States government.

Leon's remains arrived at New York's Kennedy Airport at 3:30 p.m. on October 21 in a plain wooden coffin covered by an American flag, in deference to his military service. A seven-man military honor guard escorted the coffin off the Pan American World Airways jet and stopped in front of the widow and her daughters, who were flanked by relatives and a contingent of friends, politicians, and reporters.

The tarmac was transformed into holy ground. Lisa and Ilsa Klinghoffer couldn't remember what was said—including a message from the president, read by a State Department official, the former ambassador to Algeria—but the words provided solace nonetheless. A soldier began to fold the flag, one triangle after another, attending to this duty with such gravity and sincerity that the very act of lining up edges of cloth provided a hypnotic sense of order and calm.

When the flag had been folded thirteen times and was reduced to a compact bundle, the soldier walked up to Marilyn, who accepted the totem with regal dignity. Leon's widow showed no sign of the apprehension that had enveloped her daughters. Ilsa had become frightened to walk out the front door onto the streets that had been her domain for as long as she could remember. Lisa kept asking, *Why them? Why us? Why our family?*

The daughters had watched dumbfounded as their mother entered the scene at the airport as if she'd gone to boarding school with Jackie Kennedy and had been groomed in the art of public comportment. They were still acclimating to the spotlight, to having the doorbell ring to find Simon Wiesenthal, the celebrated Nazi hunter, or a congressman or senator or the mayor arriving to pay his respects. But Marilyn accepted this public role naturally. Within a day of coming home, she was receiving guests graciously but without deference to their titles. Not everyone was welcome; when a delegation from an Arab organization dropped by to pay respects, the doorman was told not to let them in.

The funeral took place on October 22, the day after Leon's body arrived. The contentious Klinghoffer relatives were not impressed with the celebrity status conferred on Leon's family or the solemnity of the occasion and carried on as they always did. Lisa had to separate two quarreling Klinghoffer cousins when the family gathered in the rabbi's study before the service. The quarrel had to do with who was riding in what limousine. When the two relatives continued to scream at each other across the long table, Lisa begged them to call a truce for this one day and they did. Lisa felt terrible for her father, who always tried to make everyone get along.

The funeral was of a scale and consequence that would have astonished Leon. To think he would be the center of all this attention, that his funeral would be covered by the *New York Times* and attract almost eight hundred mourners to Temple Shaaray Tefila, their Upper East Side synagogue! There were those who criticized Marilyn for taking too much care with her appearance, for being a little too decked out for this somber occasion. However, she dressed the way Leon would want her to look, giving her black dress some panache with a fur stole and several strings of pearls, her hair and makeup impeccable.

The ceremony was presided over by Rabbi Harvey Tattelbaum, who had been the family's rabbi for twenty years, from his days at the

Village Temple, the cozy Greenwich Village congregation where the Klinghoffers had been members until they followed Rabbi Tattelbaum uptown to Sharaay Tefila, a larger congregation in a tonier neighborhood.

Tattelbaum was an impassioned orator whose remarks were grounded in biblical text, empathy for this family he had known for years, and his own psychological acuity. He invoked Moses and Maimonides and the trials of Job but did not insult the Klinghoffers by finding theological justification for Leon's murder. "I cannot conceive of his brutal slaying as being God's will," he said.

The rabbi spoke tenderly of Leon the loving father and husband, his struggles with paralysis from the strokes, and his business successes. He deftly wove together personal and geopolitical references, even bringing on the ruin of Bettino Craxi's coalition government, which had fallen apart a few days after the prime minister's recent decision to let Abu al-Abbas flee Italy.

"Leon's mischievous, puckish sense of humor was well-known to all who knew him," said Rabbi Tattelbaum. "I have the feeling that he too would have burst into laughter a few days ago when, while watching the news of the fall of Italy's government, Ilsa exclaimed, 'Oh my, even the Italian government collapsed because of Leon Klinghoffer!'"

Then the tenor of the eulogy changed, as Tattelbaum turned political. On two occasions, the rabbi repeated an incendiary phrase, calling Leon's death a "holocaust of one." He invoked the suffering of the Jews and the miracle of the Israeli state, without acknowledging the concomitant suffering of the Palestinians.

"Who are those who murdered Leon?" he asked. "They are simply murderers, liars, and thugs. They kill for no legitimate cause. They destroy the process by which their people would find peace. Their circle invites psychotics and psychopaths, as do all terrorist enclaves—and they are the betrayed dupes of their own Arab brothers who will not resettle or repatriate them in their vast lands."

The rabbi said he would add to the $250,000 bounty the U.S. government had placed on the head of Abu al-Abbas. "I want cold fear to strike the hearts of these murderers, so they can find no rest and no one to trust," the rabbi thundered. "Let the arm of justice be strengthened and reach out wherever they are. Let Leon's brutal death not achieve revenge, but justice—justice for his life and for so many others...and, when someday justice is done, let there be peace."

Marilyn Klinghoffer listened intently to the rabbi's words, and vowed to God that she would find justice for Leon, little knowing what an elusive promise she had made.

PART TWO

Reckonings

1985–2009

10

Ilsa's Wedding

New York City, Autumn 1985–Spring 1986

When Ilsa and Lisa had met Marilyn at the airport on her arrival home in October, they were shocked by how drained she looked. But they were comforted when their mother held them close and then took charge. They were reassured that she hadn't been beaten down when she received a call from President Reagan that same day and told him, "I spit in his face," and he said, "God bless you."

Marilyn's presence reminded them that they were still a family, and they were going to survive this intact, even if they didn't yet know how. How many times had she yelled at them, as kids: "Knock it off! Don't be a wimp!" Before Leon's body washed ashore in Syria, she tried to prepare them for how they might feel. "This is going to be very hard, not to have a body," she said. "You're always going to think you see your father walking down the street, or in the distance."

When Ilsa wanted to postpone her wedding because of her father's death, Rabbi Tattelbaum told her and her fiancé, Paul Dworin, that they should proceed with their plans, and Marilyn agreed. She helped Ilsa understand that Leon would want the celebration to go on, to give everybody something to look forward to.

Despite her physical exhaustion, Marilyn rallied: first getting Leon's body home, then the funeral, dealing with the piles of mail that continued to pour in, and contending with reporters and the stream of visitors.

Theirs was a matriarchy, descended from Marilyn's mother, Rose, who owned a successful delicatessen in Newark, with her sisters. Rose had been the backbone of the Windwehr family, just as Marilyn became for the Klinghoffers. But Lisa and Ilsa soon recognized that the *Achille Lauro* disaster transformed the nature of their mother's authority and ambition. She had been overtaken by a sense of mission and was now eager to present her case to the world, to provide some meaning to Leon's death, just as she had struggled to infuse his life with purpose after he became an invalid. When Gerardo De Rosa, the ship's captain, told her Leon had been killed, something elemental had been unleashed, a ferocity that was more powerful than sorrow.

She was primed when, during Leon's shivah, the traditional seven-day period of mourning, the doorman called up sounding alarmed, to warn them that someone had asked for the apartment number, then kept going without stopping to be announced. The unexpected visitor was Benjamin Netanyahu, the Israeli ambassador to the United Nations. Glib and good-looking, the thirty-six-year-old Israeli had spent many years of his boyhood in the United States and spoke perfect English with an American inflection. Everyone in the room, including Marilyn, was aware of the Netanyahu family's chapter in Israel's national mythology: Benjamin's brother Yonathan was killed while leading Operation Entebbe, the legendary 1976 rescue by Israel Defense Force commandos of hostages held in Uganda by two members of the Popular Front for the Liberation of Palestine. At the time, Benjamin Netanyahu—a veteran of the Israel Defense Forces with degrees from MIT (undergraduate and graduate)—was working for the Boston Consulting Group, an ideal place to launch a lucrative financial career. There he became friends with Mitt Romney, the future governor of Massachusetts and U.S. presidential candidate.

Yonathan's death changed Netanyahu's course. In 1976 he helped establish the Jonathan Institute, named in honor of his brother, an organization devoted to counterterrorism research. Netanyahu returned to Israel in 1978 to run the institute, and then moved into government, where he quickly grasped the power that lies at the intersection of politics, money, and a tragic personal narrative. As U.N. ambassador, he moved fluidly among New York's circles of influence. He befriended Rabbi Menachem Schneerson, the leader of the Chabad Lubavitch messianic movement, who had a vast following, and he cultivated acquaintances with powerful businessmen, including Donald Trump.

It quickly became clear that Netanyahu's wasn't a mere condolence call. He knew the political potential in the Klinghoffer story, from his own family's experience and what he had learned from the telling of it. All kinds of dignitaries had stopped by to pay their respects, but none of them commanded center stage, instead speaking intimately with Marilyn and her daughters. Netanyahu, however, had come to make a speech.

Maura Spiegel, the college professor and daughter of Marilyn's friend Charlotte, watched the Israeli ambassador lay out an agenda for Marilyn, urging her to address Congress, to be a voice against Palestinian terrorism.

Like many visitors that day, Maura and her sister, Jill, the physician, knew the Netanyahu story and had watched and been affected by the 1976 TV movie *Victory at Entebbe*, packed with Hollywood stars. At first, as Netanyahu spoke, Maura was dazzled. Then the Israeli ambassador made an offhand racist generalization about Arabs that made the liberal New Yorker recoil.

"They are liars," he said coldly. "They don't tell the truth."

Maura thought to herself, "Wow, did you say that?"

Netanyahu's force of persuasion helped focus Marilyn's fury. "She prided herself on her toughness and not taking shit—that was a big part of her character," Maura said. "That toughness was often presented in a humorous way, getting people to do things they wouldn't normally do. In terms of how to wear this experience, who am I in this crazy role I've been thrust into, Netanyahu gave her a way that really fit with who she was."

Soon Marilyn was invited to testify before the House Foreign Affairs Subcommittee on International Operations in Washington, D.C., on October 30, specifically to endorse an antiterrorism resolution introduced by her own congressman, Ted Weiss, a Jewish Democrat. Marilyn sent a message to the White House that she would be interested in meeting President Reagan while she was in town. Meanwhile, she established a foundation called the Leon Klinghoffer Memorial Fund to Combat Terrorism, with seed money provided by her boss at Gralla Publications.

Her campaign for Leon's legacy became paramount, conducted between the constant interruptions by visitors. Guiding her through this unfamiliar terrain was a self-styled kitchen cabinet, led by Charlotte Spiegel, who had been a constant presence since she and Marilyn were reunited in Port Said, where Charlotte had waited after returning from the Pyramids tour. Charlotte's daughter Jill had been assigned medical tasks, like getting Leon's records from the Veterans Administration to identify the body. Maura was enlisted to take notes as Charlotte helped Marilyn create a compelling narrative for her House testimony and for the press conference Letty Simon arranged, Marilyn's first public appearance since returning to the States. Maura recorded both possible questions and suggested answers in neat longhand on yellow legal paper.

How do you feel now?
Grateful my husband's body is home. I want to see justice done.

Would you go to Italy?
I will go to testify and help in any way I can.

Abbas — How do you feel about his release?
I am outraged that he was allowed to escape and if he had anything to do with it I want him brought to justice.

Do you feel the U.S. acted quickly enough?
I am grateful that they acted for the first time — Hope it will not be necessary again — but if it is, I hope they will do so again.

Israel's decision not to release 50 prisoners?
I agree with them. As a nation most victimized by terrorism on a daily basis, the position they have taken is more difficult than for anyone else.

How was your trip to Washington arranged?
Going at invitation of Committee extended to me through Cong. Weiss.

Killing of Calif Arab anti-defamation member?
I don't condone violence or terrorism in any form.

Do you think Leon provoked them? Was capable of fighting?
Didn't provoke—he would have fought back if he could've gotten out of chair.

Plans for the future?
Planning to resume our lives—a close family.

In Washington, the president's advisers had also been analyzing how best to capitalize on the attractive Klinghoffer family, who provided a compelling, human endorsement of the aggressive strategy promoted by Robert McFarlane and Oliver North's counterterrorism group. They decided the best time for Reagan to meet Mrs. Klinghoffer would be in New York, on October 25, 1985, the day after his address before the General Assembly of the United Nations, part of a fortieth-anniversary celebration of the organization's founding.

North prepared a memo for National Security Adviser McFarlane, his boss, with background information on Marilyn and Leon, their daughters, and Jerry and Paul, as well as talking points for the president and a plan for photographs during and after the fifteen-minute meeting, scheduled for 11:45 a.m., in a suite at the Waldorf-Astoria Hotel, right after presidential meet and greets with Prime Minister Yasuhiro Nakasone of Japan and another with Chancellor Helmut Kohl of the Federal Republic of Germany.

TALKING POINTS FOR MEETING WITH MRS. KLINGHOFFER

—Having talked to you on the phone, I am glad to have the opportunity to meet you in person.

—I was told of the session you had in Sicily with the Italian authorities and your bravery in identifying the terrorists. I am told that your husband, Leon, was similarly courageous.

—Please know that Nancy and I were deeply grieved over the murder of your husband by those four brutal men.

—I want you to know that we will also pursue the terrorists' leader (Abbas) until he, too, is brought to justice.

—You should also be aware that your husband's tragic death could well be a turning point in this terrorist "war without borders." If this is indeed the case, as I believe it to be, terrorist crimes will become more costly to the perpetrators, and therefore, more difficult. Thus, Leon Klinghoffer did not die in vain. Even in death, he was a man whose bravery served his nation and his people.

Marilyn wore an elegant purple suit with black trim and open-toed high-heeled pumps to the presidential photo op at the Waldorf. She brought a preapproved entourage—her daughters and their husband and fiancé; her mother, Rose; and Letty Simon, the family friend who had been helping them deal with the press since the hijacking. Marilyn's purpose was to explain that Leon was not a legal abstraction or political symbol or rallying cry, though he was becoming all of those. He was her husband of thirty-six years, the father of their daughters. She looked regal, sitting across from the president. Reagan said very little as he, his wife, Nancy, and Secretary of State George Shultz listened to Marilyn's story—the story she hadn't stopped telling for two weeks. Nancy Reagan rather than her husband did most of the talking, uttering appropriate responses of sympathy and dismay at the Klinghoffers' travails.

At the end, Marilyn shook the president's hand and told him, "I'm proud of you."

*   *   *

For the Reagan administration, the visit with the Klinghoffer family culminated a week of diplomatic meetings that dealt with the *Achille Lauro*—meetings that involved cementing the U.S. bond with Israel and fence-mending with Egypt and Italy. On Thursday, October 17, President Reagan met Israeli Prime Minister Shimon Peres in the Oval Office. In his remarks following a private discussion, Reagan affirmed the American commitment to Israel's security and well-being and "a shared desire to move forward together toward a just and lasting peace between Israel and all its Arab neighbors."

The president's words had been chosen carefully, to give the appearance of shared regional goals. "We also discussed the evil scourge of terrorism which has claimed so many Israeli, American and Arab victims and has brought tragedy to many others," Reagan said. "Terrorism is the cynical, remorseless enemy of peace, and it strikes most viciously whenever real progress seems possible. We need no further proof of this than the events of the last few weeks. The Prime Minister and I share a determination to see that terrorists are denied sanctuary and are justly punished. Furthermore, and just as important, Prime Minister Peres and I agreed that terrorism must not blunt our efforts to achieve peace in the Middle East."

A memo signed by Robert McFarlane before the meeting was far less sanguine, offering indications of what the two leaders discussed in private. "The Tunis raid and the *Achille Lauro* episode have buffeted the peace process—how severely, it is too soon to tell," the memo said. "Where Peres has in the past tried not to 'slam the door' on an eventual PLO role in the process, you can expect him now to be very critical."

The memo continued: "The Tunis raid raised the same problems we have always had with Israeli responses to terrorism: proportionality of the response to the incidents that preceded it and linkage of the perpetrators with those against whom the retaliation is directed," it said. "U.S. and Israeli standards for retaliation almost never coincide."

The pessimistic vein ran throughout the McFarlane memo: "While Peres will try to contain domestic Israeli appetites for further attacks, his room for maneuver may already be shrinking; since Larnaca [Cyprus, where the three Israeli tourists were killed, resulting in the retaliatory raid in Tunisia] and Tunis, there have been fresh terrorist kills in both Israel and in Barcelona. Israelis have also taken to heart that the only casualty of the *Achille Lauro* was a Jew. If another 'spectacular' success occurs even partially, we should expect another major Israeli response."

On Sunday, October 20, Deputy Secretary of State John C. Whitehead had been dispatched to Tunisia and Cairo—Tunisia, to deal with the fallout from the U.S.'s endorsement of the Israeli bombing at Hamman Chott; Egypt, to soothe Egyptian outrage over the American intercept of the Egyptian airplane carrying the *Achille Lauro* hijackers. Reagan had sent the State Department a handwritten note of advice regarding Mubarak: "I believe we can construct a reply that does not apologize but that indicates we had information different from his, etc. And that cools him down."

Reagan dealt personally with Italy. Prime Minister Bettino Craxi was in New York for the U.N. summit; the two heads of state met on October 24, the day before Reagan's meeting with the Klinghoffers. Craxi appeared remarkably robust and relaxed for a man who had just survived the collapse and revival of his five-party government coalition, all within the two weeks that had elapsed since the *Achille Lauro* hijacking.

"The government crisis was the fruit of the garden of Italian political life, and not the fault of the Americans," Craxi said at a press conference after he arrived in New York. He described the tension that led to the dissolution of the coalition government as "a little incident, a little incomprehensible turn of events that has been set right."

The "little incident" was Craxi's decision to let Abu al-Abbas leave Italy for Yugoslavia.

Craxi told reporters he couldn't believe his actions had been criticized rather than praised by the U.S. government and the American press. "I don't know what the Americans were thinking," he said. "What should have been important to everyone was that the passengers were freed after forty-eight hours. What should have been important is that we prevented an enormous disaster."

He also assured American journalists that Italian-U.S. relations were "as good as ever—the climate is as it was before."

A *New York Times* reporter noted: "Mr. Craxi's attitude toward the United States was markedly different from just a week ago, when he expressed 'the most profound regret' and 'bitterness' over American criticism of the way his government handled the Achille Lauro crisis."

And at the New York press conference, the Italian prime minister continued to voice Italy's support for the PLO and described the Israeli raid in Tunisia—in which about seventy people were killed—as "more serious" than the *Achille Lauro*.

Still, Antonio Badini, who had played a central role in shuttling Abbas out of Italy, assured reporters that "Mr. Craxi's participation in the summit shows how much importance he attaches to relations with the United States." Badini added, "Everything is behind us."

Yet a White House report written the previous day offered a far more disquieting prognosis. In "Post Mortem on the *Achille Lauro* Hijacking," a memorandum prepared for the deputy secretary of defense on October 23, 1985, an analyst predicted, "The *Achille Lauro* affair will serve to accelerate the prospects for Middle Eastern terrorism." In addition to damaging the peace process by destroying Yasser Arafat's credibility, the report said, Palestinians would "be incensed by what they perceive as a closer alignment, if not outright cooperation, on counterterrorism policies between the U.S. and Israel."

Furthermore, the report continued, "the simple fact that the U.S. has taken its first military step in combatting international terrorism will also intensify the prospects for terrorism."

Marilyn's embrace of the political represented a complete about-face from the position her daughters had taken, at Letty Simon's advice, when they had gone public to plead for their parents' lives. As Sara

Rimer of the *Times* reported, "At news conferences, they declined to answer such questions as: 'What do you think of Israel?' 'Should Israel give up its hostages?' 'What do you think of the PLO?' 'What is your position on how to stop terrorism?' 'Should the hijackers be put to death?'"

Marilyn's combative approach unnerved Lisa and Ilsa, who had been aching for ordinary life to resume, a fantasy dispelled the day they found Marilyn sitting at the dining room table with Jay Fischer, a lawyer Charlotte Spiegel introduced to the family. He did the legal work for the Klinghoffer Foundation and had become an adviser to Marilyn.

Quite casually, as if announcing plans for a family outing, Marilyn told her daughters what she had been discussing with the lawyer. "Girls, I am suing the PLO," she said. "You are either with me or you are not. I hope you are with me." After Marilyn made this declaration, she pushed herself away from the table and walked out of the room.

Ilsa and Lisa stared at each other, unable to respond. "We were petrified," said Lisa.

The sisters shared similar fears in the aftermath of the hijacking. These fears were triggered specifically by the occasional hateful, anti-Semitic letters and the nasty calls that led Marilyn to unlist their telephone number; more generally, they were enhanced by a feeling of alienation, even from well-meaning friends and family, who didn't know what it meant to be assaulted, who couldn't understand what it was like to have your reality upended. Lisa and Ilsa worried about retribution when Jay Fischer filed the lawsuit against the PLO on November 27, 1985, as well as another against the owners of the *Achille Lauro*. They were skeptical of and uncomfortable with Fischer's ambitions: he asked for $1.5 billion in damages.

Ilsa and Lisa manifested their concerns differently from each other, however, which was not surprising for sisters with such divergent personalities. Though Ilsa felt anxious every time she left the apartment building, she soon went back to work. *Keep busy* was her mantra. She loved her job as an administrator at the NYU College of Dentistry, working with the director of patient services, operating clinics where dental students provided affordable dental care.

But, each time she stepped out the door of her building, getting to the office proved to be a psychological test. The short distance now seemed filled with danger. She stopped walking to work and began taking cabs, making sure there was someone to meet her at the door when she arrived. Marilyn told her that was the right thing to do, insisted on it, even though she felt cabs were a waste of money. Indeed Marilyn, too, had gone back to work and still took the subway, even when her daughters begged her not to.

Lisa became immobilized after Ilsa and her mother returned to work. She had no job to return to. The question that plagued most artists at one time or another was harder to avoid in an existential moment like this: Did anyone care if she produced yet another painting? Lisa had always feared being regarded as a dilettante. She had made a commitment to herself that she had to work every day, which she did, nine to five. She continued this pattern, year in and year out, producing dozens of paintings that she didn't try to sell. The problem was twofold: she had no business savvy and she couldn't handle rejection. Now she was immobilized, unable to lift a brush. She wouldn't go to her studio; she could barely leave her mother's apartment, where her husband, Jerry Arbittier, picked her up at the end of every day.

Marilyn had always been Lisa's coach, but even she was at a loss. Although Marilyn scoffed at psychotherapy, she contacted a therapist who was a trauma expert and took Ilsa and Lisa to meet him. Ilsa went for one session, while Lisa continued on her own, week after week, beginning a long process that would eventually lead her back to the studio.

Lisa began thinking of all the choices she had made—or not made. She was thirty-four years old and had been married for twelve years, yet she and Jerry hadn't seriously considered having children. Thinking they had all the time in the world, they hadn't even discussed it, even though they were now in their midthirties. Her parents never pushed them except once, in the gentlest way: Leon had asked Marilyn if she thought Jerry and Lisa would ever have kids and Marilyn responded, "If they want to have kids, they'll have kids."

Without consulting Jerry, Lisa decided to stop taking birth control pills, but wondered if she was just doing so because her father died.

"Is that a good reason to have a child?" she asked her gynecologist. "To have a child because you lost a member of your family?"

"It's normal," the doctor told her. "It's not a good or a bad reason, but it's normal to think these things."

But the hijacking wasn't the only source of disquietude. Marilyn had resumed cancer treatments. Her bursts of energy were offset by an ever greater need for rest. The zaftig beauty who spent her life dieting now struggled not to become too thin. Lisa and Ilsa told themselves that Marilyn had been in treatment before the cruise and was still able to hoist Leon's heavy wheelchair into the trunk of the car. The cancer had gone into remission before; why couldn't that happen again?

The sisters didn't know that after Marilyn returned from Europe, Charlotte Spiegel had taken her friend to a famous oncologist for a consultation. The doctor misread Marilyn, confusing her impressive fortitude with realism. "I'm going to help you die," he told her. Marilyn rejected the doctor and the diagnosis. She returned to her own physician.

Marilyn continued to receive guests in their apartment, propped up with pillows on a blue divan, her makeup in place, her gift for engagement running at full throttle. Then she would collapse.

On the car trip to Washington, on October 30, to testify before the congressional subcommittee, Marilyn lay down in the backseat, wrung out, while Jerry drove. But when they arrived in D.C., Marilyn checked her hair and makeup and performed her now routine metamorphosis, from invalid to warrior. "I believe that my husband's death has made a difference in the way that people now perceive their vulnerability," she told the House Foreign Affairs Subcommittee on International Operations. "I believe that what happened to the passengers on the *Achille Lauro*, and to my family, can happen to anyone, at any time, at any place."

Six weeks later, on December 5, Marilyn was the guest of honor at a posh fund-raising dinner, held at Manhattan's Pierre Hotel, for Rambam Hospital in Haifa, celebrating the new pediatric wing's Leon Klinghoffer Garden. Both U.S. senators from New York were there, as was Israeli U.N. Ambassador Netanyahu.

Marilyn's talk was brief but ferocious. "We would like to believe that the forfeiture of [Leon's] life was not merely a mindless act of barbarians; but, that it will serve to foster the realization that terrorism is an unacceptable extension of war, undeclared war, waged against innocent civilians; that his death will reinforce our rejection of the inevitability of terrorism as a fact of our lives, or of our deaths; and that all people will dedicate themselves to the concept that hands must be joined across the dark and vast abyss of ideological differences, in order to forever shut every door, cut off every escape, and eliminate every rat hole, so the perpetrators of terrorism will have no place to run, no place to go, and no place to hide."

Shortly after the Rambam dinner, Marilyn reminded Ilsa that it was time to seriously focus on buying a wedding dress. Ilsa had once been chubby and though she was now slender, she remained hypercritical of how she looked. She quickly rejected department store dresses—too predictable—and couldn't find anything she liked in more offbeat boutiques in SoHo and Greenwich Village. Finally, in early January, she found the dress she'd been looking for and wanted Marilyn's approval.

By then, Marilyn was unavoidably frail. Jerry drove his mother-in-law to the boutique on the Upper West Side. As she walked inside, her head was hanging down, as though holding it up was too much effort.

Ilsa was waiting for her, already wearing the tea-length dress of champagne-colored satin and crinoline that reminded her of the ballerinas in paintings by Degas. Marilyn's face lit with maternal pride. "You're going to be a beautiful bride," she told Ilsa, with an approving smile.

Ilsa was so happy and relieved that she barely registered how sick her mother looked. When the thought flickered through her mind, she told herself, "It's the medication. We'll just push the wedding back if we have to until she gets better."

In two weeks, Marilyn collapsed at work and was in the hospital.

For a week after that, Lisa and Ilsa were still able to convince themselves she would recover. Marilyn managed to sneak a smoke out in the waiting room of the hospital every evening. She continued to dispense opinions and advice, and her daughters continued to seek her counsel. She continued to hide her illness from their Grandma Rose, her own mother.

Standing at Marilyn's hospital bed, Lisa asked, "Do you think I'd be a good mother?" Marilyn didn't hesitate. "You'd be the best!" she said and then dropped her head onto the pillow.

This time, however, she wasn't resting. She had fallen into a coma, where she remained until her death, on February 9, 1986, in the company of her family and friends, four months and a day after Leon was murdered.

Her death was front-page news. "Hijack Widow's Secret Agony: Marilyn Klinghoffer Dies of Cancer," read the *New York Post* headline. She was eulogized by the *New York Times* as "a voice of defiance against international terrorism."

Marilyn's daughters laid her to rest dressed in the purple suit she wore to meet the Reagans at the Waldorf.

Once again Paul and Ilsa asked Rabbi Tattelbaum whether they should postpone their wedding. Once again, he said no. On April 6, 1986, two months after Marilyn's death, Ilsa walked down the aisle, arm in arm with her brother-in-law, Jerry, with her grandmother and sister looking on, along with 150 other guests. Maura and Jill Spiegel were bridesmaids, wearing pink dresses as Ilsa had requested. A three-piece jazz band played.

Everything looked just as Ilsa had planned, but the sorrow was palpable. It rained that day—signifying good luck, people told the bride, though it felt to her as if even the sky was weeping.

Paul and Ilsa left for their honeymoon, hoping to put the horror of the past six months on hold. They had chosen the Caribbean island of

Saint Martin as their destination, someplace where there wasn't much to do but relax on the beach.

At the hotel, they unpacked their bags and gazed out at the magnificent view of the harbor. Immediately, they realized the island paradise had been a terrible miscalculation.

Everywhere they looked, there were cruise ships. They couldn't escape.

II

Trials

New York City, May 5, 1986

A month after Ilsa and Paul's wedding, the newlyweds sat with Jerry and Lisa and watched Abu al-Abbas look out from their television set and declare that the United States might be the target of an attack by Palestinians.

"In the beginning, our operations were only targeted at the Israeli enemy, inside Israel," Abbas said, speaking on the *NBC Nightly News*, while a disembodied voice translated his words into English. "The United States is now conducting the war on behalf of Israel. We therefore have to respond against America in America itself."

They watched in disbelief as Abbas brazenly challenged Ronald Reagan, saying, "I used to think our greatest enemy was some Israeli person, but now Reagan has placed himself as enemy number one."

Talking to NBC correspondent Henry Champ from an undisclosed location "in an Arab-speaking country," Abbas spoke with a calm, thoughtful air, as if engaged in a dispassionate debate, not making a declaration of war. Wearing a nicely tailored gray suit, with a sober necktie and white shirt, his demeanor was that of a poised politician or academic. The only signs of stress were a few beads of sweat on his forehead and the cigarette he kept lit throughout the interview.

Champ provided viewers with a recap of the *Achille Lauro* hijacking, as well as a history of other killings believed to be the work of the Palestinian Liberation Front, including the 1979 raid in Na-hariyya that resulted in the death of four Israelis, two of them young children.

"[Abbas] freely claims responsibility for the hijacking of the Italian cruise ship the *Achille Lauro*," said Champ, "but says evidence that his men killed wheelchair-bound Leon Klinghoffer was fabricated by the U.S. and Syria."

Abbas defended his men, who were imprisoned in Italy while await-ing trial, scheduled to begin the following month. "What is the use of killing an old man?" he asked. "Why, after all, he is old, and so he will be dead anyway soon without killing. I do not believe our comrades on the boat carried out any killing."

The NBC correspondent explained that Italy had allowed Abbas to flee to Yugoslavia, over the protests of the U.S. government. "Like so many battling in the Middle East," said Champ, "he does not see him-self as a terrorist."

Abbas spoke quietly. "The Palestinian is accused everywhere, is hunted everywhere and is a terrorist everywhere," he said. "This is the picture that Americans have. In fact, the Palestinian is a homeless refugee without the right to a passport, without the right to visit his village or birthplace, or even his father's grave. The Palestinian has lived in a state of oppression and subjugation for forty years. Is he now a terrorist?"

The segment lasted less than four minutes, long enough to fan the outrage that had been building since Leon and Marilyn's family noticed promotional spots for the interview. As they saw it, NBC was collabo-rating with the terrorists, giving Abbas the platform he wanted.

They had already grown accustomed to feeling angry. Jerry had first noticed it on the final day of shivah for Leon. He and Lisa were taking a walk around the block after sunset, respecting a Jewish custom that advises mourners to physically mark the separation between grieving and resumption of ordinary life. As they were crossing Fourth Avenue, a young man coming toward them didn't move out of the way, as if he didn't see them right in front of him.

His inattention felt like a provocation. Without thinking, Jerry shoved him aside.

Nothing happened. The man continued to go his way and so did they.

Under normal circumstances, the incident would have passed unnoticed, a minor annoyance in the catalogue of everyday urban grievances that were part of life in New York City. But for the Klinghoffer family, nothing was normal anymore. Jerry felt his hands clenching, as he realized something fundamental had changed inside of him. A month earlier, before the *Achille Lauro*, he would have just walked around the guy. He would have never pushed someone intentionally, inviting a fight. He was a liberal; not just politically, he was the kind of person who was willing to get along, to let someone else have something he wanted rather than create disruption.

His immediate impulse on watching the Abbas interview was to strike back. With the help of someone from the Anti-Defamation League (ADL), a contact Marilyn had made before she died, Jerry wrote a letter to Lawrence Grossman, the president of NBC News, asking for airtime to make a rebuttal.

After receiving a polite kiss-off from an NBC vice president, Jerry wrote the editor of the *New York Times*, identifying himself as chairman of the Leon and Marilyn Klinghoffer Memorial Foundation (the organization was renamed after Marilyn died).

In the letter, which was published by the *Times* on May 18, Jerry accused NBC of providing Abbas an "unchallenged forum to threaten to kill Americans on their own shores." He said the network had "consorted with a known felon" by not revealing his location to authorities and urged the State Department and the Justice Department to investigate possible criminal implications in "aiding and abetting a known and wanted international criminal."

Grossman responded with his own letter to the *Times* a week later. "I hope Jerry Arbittier shows more common sense and respect for facts as chairman of the Klinghoffer Foundation than as a letter writer," Grossman began. The network president challenged Jerry's complaint that

NBC News didn't help arrest Abbas, noting that a news organization doesn't have "the authority or the ability" to arrest fugitives.

Grossman compared the segment with Edward R. Murrow's television interviews with China's Zhou Enlai and Yugoslavia's Marshal Tito, which elicited "similar cries of outrage…from those with little respect for the American public's ability to sort right from wrong."

Various columnists and advocates joined the battle, denouncing or defending NBC. The contretemps provided free promotion for the network's June 17 edition of *1986*, NBC's struggling newsmagazine show. The ads for the episode, "The *Achille Lauro*: A Study in Terror," promised unaired portions of the Abbas interview and the revelation of new information. The show was timed to air the night before the hijacking trial began in Italy, on June 18.

Terrorism had become an even hotter topic in the eight months since the *Achille Lauro* hijacking. In November, six weeks after Klinghoffer's murder, the most violently militant Palestinian faction, led by Abu Nidal, hijacked an Egyptian airplane and forced it to land on Malta. The hijackers killed three passengers; fifty-seven more died in a failed rescue attempt by Egyptian commandos. The next month Abu Nidal's group attacked ticket counters for El Al, the Israeli airline, at the Rome and Vienna airports, killing twenty people, including five Americans.

Jerry himself had worked for a while at NBC, in the research department. He understood the reasoning that news organizations had a duty to see all sides of an issue. But wasn't there a line? he wondered. Isn't there a point at which journalists who publicize terrorist acts become complicit, legitimizing the people who commit them?

What really bothered him, though, was Grossman's opening salvo, implying that Jerry wouldn't do a good job as the chairman of the Klinghoffer Foundation. This hit a nerve, even though it was already becoming a moot point. Before Marilyn died, they'd all agreed to transfer the assets of the foundation—less than $30,000—to the ADL. The family realized they didn't have the resources to carry out the foundation's lofty goals—"to combat or eliminate terrorism through education, publicity and support of groups or organizations devoted to

eliminating international terrorism; to promote a public awareness...;
to provide recognition to those who take conspicuous personal action
against terrorism, and to assist in the strengthening of cooperation
among nations in combatting terrorism."

Jerry knew it was hard for other people—even his own brother,
who warned him not to let what had happened to Leon dominate
his life—to grasp how he felt. ("Jerry, don't get consumed by the
Achille Lauro," the brother said.) People didn't understand that Leon and
Marilyn didn't feel like in-laws. They had been his best friends. He and
Lisa had friends who were contemporaries, but they didn't see them as
often, or care about them as much.

For Jerry, Leon and Marilyn had been the core of the family, the
centrifugal force of everything they did. Now he felt the burden was
on him and it was heavy.

Genoa, June 18, 1986

EVEN BEFORE Gianfranco Pagano entered the Palazzo di Giustizia, the
courthouse where the *Achille Lauro* hijackers were about to be tried,
the thirty-five-year-old defense attorney was vividly reminded of the
case's magnitude. Since daybreak, police helicopters had been buzzing
over Genoa, the *Signora del Mare*, the "Lady of the Sea," as Petrarch, the
fourteenth-century poet, romantically referred to the Mediterranean
port. Streets around the courthouse had been sealed off from traffic.
Once inside the courtyard leading into the palazzo, Pagano encountered the security system the government had just installed: six metal
detectors, two X-ray scanners, and four video cameras. The building
was crawling, inside and outside, with more than six hundred local
police and *carabinieri*, Italy's paramilitary police force, as well as with
journalists, most of them foreign. He'd read in the newspaper that
121 reporters and photographers—predominantly American, only
one Arab—had received press credentials to cover the trial.

In the seven years that Pagano had been practicing law, he had never been exposed to a proceeding of extreme gravitas presented like a circus. Most of his previous clients had been accused of the commonplace thuggery endemic to the urban underbelly—theft, drug dealing, the occasional murder. Now he was defending three of the five men being tried for their part in a violent terrorist episode with weighty implications.

His *Achille Lauro* clients were Issa Abbas (who claimed to be a distant cousin of Abu al-Abbas), accused of transporting the weapons used in the hijacking, and two of the four assailants who carried it out—Abdellatif Fataier, the twenty-year-old Palestinian the passengers called Rambo; and Majid al-Molqi, twenty-three, the man accused of murdering Leon Klinghoffer. Bassam al-Ashker, who was seventeen at the time of the hijacking, was being tried separately as a juvenile. The remaining hijacker, twenty-four-year old Omar al-Assadi, had been assigned a lawyer known for representing *penitenti* (the repented), those who cooperated with the authorities in exchange for a lower sentence and the chance to assume a new identity on release. Another lawyer represented the fifth defendant in custody, Gandura Said, a minor player arrested for his association with the PLO and for possessing false passports. (When Pagano's client Abbas heard this charge, he commented, "There is not a Palestinian alive who travels the world with a legitimate passport.")

Given the odds against his clients and his own lack of experience in this arena, it wasn't a stretch for Pagano to imagine himself as David battling Goliath—the latter presenting himself in the form of Luigi Carli, the lead prosecutor for the government. Carli had the professional swagger of someone accustomed to the spotlight. He had investigated the Red Brigades and was responsible for other terrorism prosecutions, including a hijacking attempt on a Lufthansa flight. Furthermore, Carli had been involved in the *Achille Lauro* case from the beginning; he was one of two magistrates who had flown to Syracuse immediately after the hijacking to interview the Palestinians in captivity there, as well as dozens of witnesses from the ship's passengers and crew. Those interrogations and testimonies, along with secret reports provided by U.S., Israeli, and Italian intelligence services, became part of the 115-page indictment—the *requisatoria*—that laid out the prosecution's case.

For Carli, this case was merely a job, and not a particularly taxing one. He was not impressed with the caliber of the defendants. "Very succinctly, in my opinion, the hijacking of the *Achille Lauro* was an action taken without much care and fanciful goals," he said.

Pagano brought to the table liberal idealism and a sense of duty instilled in him by a stern father, the director of a military hospital who had discretion to exempt people from military duty. (He did not exempt his son.) The defense attorney sympathized with the Palestinian cause. "They were the poorest, the most disenfranchised, the most marginalized, the ones with the most difficulty," he recalled. "In comparison with the military, political power of Israel, well, there's no comparison."

Pagano spoke French and Spanish in addition to his native Italian, as well as some English and German. Early in his career he began defending foreigners who had been arrested for various crimes. In Genoa, that meant his clients tended to be Arabs, especially Moroccans and Tunisians. Through a jailhouse network, his name had been brought to the attention of Issa Abbas, who had been captured shortly after the hijacking and was imprisoned in Spoleto, a town in Umbria 250 miles from Genoa. His court-appointed lawyer was happy to relinquish the case to Pagano.

Issa Abbas introduced Pagano to Molqi and Fataier, who were imprisoned in separate cities as a security measure. They were already represented by a lawyer from Rome, but they didn't feel he was simpatico toward them and their cause the way Pagano seemed to be. They didn't fire the first lawyer but added Pagano to the defense.

Getting to know these clients was not easy. Pagano's English was broken, theirs was almost nonexistent, and that was the only language they had in common. Pagano enlisted some of his Arab-speaking clients to act as interpreters, but it was difficult to elicit information.

In Pagano's view, of the two hijackers, Fataier was more open and his story more consistent. Though he wasn't rude and always thanked Pagano, Molqi never let down his guard. With Molqi, the lawyer came up against a wall every time they met. Their relationship stayed focused on Molqi's claim: "I am a combatant for Palestine, we merely wanted to go to Ashdod and die for our homeland."

Well before the trial began, Pagano understood the hopelessness of the case, if he had ever dared to dream that the goal was to achieve a not guilty verdict. He had read interrogations conducted by the Italian prosecutors and the U.S. FBI agents. Both Fataier and Molqi admitted they had hijacked the ship and denied killing Klinghoffer.

Pagano knew that in Molqi's case, this claim was absurd. He had read Molqi's contradictory statements. The Palestinian denied on several occasions that he had killed Klinghoffer, and then, in one interrogation, claimed that he had deliberately chosen Klinghoffer because he was disabled, "to show that we had no pity for anyone, just like the Americans, by arming Israel, don't realize that Israel has no pity for anyone and that it kills, without discriminating, women, children and the disabled among our people."

On another occasion, Molqi said he was provoked by Klinghoffer, who tried to hit him with his cane. Nonetheless, the Palestinian denied a suggestion that Klinghoffer was killed because he bit Molqi (Molqi even urged the interrogators to examine him for tooth marks). Then before the trial began, Molqi reverted to his initial claim, that he had not killed Klinghoffer

Pagano didn't believe his client. How could he? The lawyer had read the eyewitness accounts in the prosecutor's report. The deposition of Manuel De Souza, the Portuguese crew member who also identified Molqi in photographs, was vivid and specific. "I saw a terrorist who with a machine gun in hand asked me to follow him," the waiter told investigators. "He ordered me to push a wheelchair on which sat an elderly man, rather corpulent, with glasses." De Souza recounted being forced to push the wheelchair to the stern and then wait out of eyeshot for a couple of minutes. He heard two blasts of gunfire. "I saw the terrorist come toward me and he called me and made me exit the walkway," De Souza continued. "When I got a bit farther ahead I saw the elderly man turned upside down in the wheelchair with a hole in the middle of his chest and covered in blood. I saw a lot of blood on his chest. The person was certainly dead."

The waiter described how the man he identified as Molqi ordered him to throw the body into the sea. De Souza couldn't manage the task. "I was beside myself," he said. "I let him fall to the ground."

Molqi left, first warning the waiter not to move under threat of death. The hijacker returned with Ferruccio Alberti, the hairdresser. "Under the threats of the terrorist Ferruccio and I were forced to throw the body into the sea and the wheelchair, too," De Souza said.

The evidence seemed irrefutable. Why would the waiter and hairdresser lie about seeing the dead American, or about Molqi's orders to throw Klinghoffer overboard?

Pagano could hope only to mitigate the consequences by emphasizing the circumstances that led to the hijacking and the killing of Klinghoffer. His primary aim was to refute the most serious accusation, the charge of *delitto di banda armata*, "the crime of an armed gang" or "conspiracy to commit terrorism." This classification had been created in 1978, as part of an antiterrorism law passed to address terrorist kidnappings, making them a crime against the state. The maximum penalty of a life sentence could be imposed if the kidnapping resulted in the death of at least one person.

Even though his clients had recanted previous versions they'd given of events, changed their positions, and told investigators versions of events that were unbelievable, there had been one constant: all of them categorically rejected the charge of *delitto di banda armata*. When Molqi was notified of the charge, he refused to accept a warrant for his arrest, saying that from his point of view, "armed gangs are like those of Abu Nidal." Fataier and Issa Abbas were equally vehement. Fataier declared, "We are not terrorists; I prefer death than to hear these accusations." Similarly, Issa Abbas said, "I prefer death than to be accused of terrorism."

Whatever lies had been told or stories had been changed, Pagano believed his clients were sincere about this point. "It was about being soldiers, fighters, people who were combatants in defending their nation," he said. That would be his defense.

He admired what he considered their idealism, if not their competence. He saw them as young men who didn't know what they were doing. The more he had read and heard about the hijacking, the more convinced he became that the ill-fated mission had been poorly planned. In this instance, Pagano agreed with Carli, the prosecutor. "They behaved like people who were unprepared, not like people who were sure of themselves," Carli said. "They made a lot of mistakes."

As he entered the courtroom, Pagano felt he was embarked on a worthwhile cause, something he hadn't felt with previous clients. "They weren't thieves, killers, or drug dealers," Pagano said. "I am convinced that what they did, wrong or not wrong, they did it for the freedom of their country."

It had already been made clear by the prosecutor's report that this was a political as well as a legal trial. The report had specifically absolved the Syrian government and Yasser Arafat of complicity in the hijacking and avoided criticism of the Italian government for allowing Abu al-Abbas to leave Italy, allowing that there were "political reasons" for the decision. However, the prosecutors made a forceful indictment of Abu al-Abbas, a defendant who would not be appearing in court. "[He] conceived the action, selected its actors, trained them for the specific enterprise, financed them, had them conducted to Italy. Provided them with the means to conduct the action, intervened during the hijack making them return the ship to Port Said, rescued the members of the commando and tried to lead them unpunished to their base of departure." The charges against Abu al-Abbas, concluded the prosecutors, "are many, unequivocal and overwhelming."

Most damning, the prosecutors rejected the prevailing story about the hijackers' goal. The indictment explained that "two currents of thought [had] hovered" over the investigation. The story the hijackers told, and which had been widely reported, could, according to the prosecutors, "be defined as 'heroic,' which presupposed not the hijacking-kidnapping of the ship and its passengers but only its use as a vehicle to reach Ashdod in Israel, where the command would have sacrificed itself by dying on its native soil…after having attempted a carnage of Israelis. This plan also called for the possibility of a failed/missed 'suicide' and the return to the ship (still without hijacking/kidnapping of the ship) to obtain an exchange between the passengers on the ship and the prisoners in Israel."

But, the prosecutors said, there was an alternative theory, one that was "much less heroic." In this scenario, the view the prosecutors endorsed, the hijacking itself was the mission, "with the goal of pursuing the exchange between passengers and prisoners, an exchange that would have had a wide propagandistic effect, whose measure is easily intuited if compared to the world clamor that followed what happened."

However, the indictment said, whether Ashdod or the hijacking itself was the mission, "it is beyond doubt" that the events that took place on the *Achille Lauro* "cannot eschew the terrorism definition, according to the applicable laws and their most faithful interpretation."

Although the power of the Red Brigades had waned throughout the 1980s, Italy still suffered aftershocks from the organization's reign of terror, which had lasted almost twenty years. Born out of the student and worker protests of 1968, the founders' decision to take up arms was traced to a meeting held in Chiavari, a small city located twenty-three miles down the coast from Genoa. First the group attacked property, then people, with primary targets being symbols of capitalism, especially politicians affiliated with the center-right Christian Democrat party. These attacks led to the kidnapping and murder of Italian Prime Minister Aldo Moro in 1978.

This violent backdrop as well as more ancient histories were reflected in the trial's physical setting. The Palazzo di Giustizia, the Palace of Justice, a dark and forbidding fortresslike structure made of concrete, glass, and steel, was constructed in the 1960s on the grounds of Genoa's historic Pammatone Hospital, built in the fifteenth century. The original building had been heavily damaged during World War II and then demolished to make way for the new courthouse. The palazzo contained an homage to the past in the reconstructed colonnades of the interior courtyard, now outfitted with brand-new security equipment.

On Wednesday, June 18, 1986, the trial opened in a large underground chamber, resembling a war bunker. Fifteen men had been charged, including Abu al-Abbas and his loyal sidekick Badratkan, who had been on the plane with him at Sigonella. Only five of the defendants had been captured; with Ashker being tried separately, the other four appeared in court handcuffed, locked in black cages made of metal and Plexiglas, surrounded by *carabinieri*. The cages had long been used in Mafia criminal proceedings and then for Red Brigades prosecutions beginning in the late 1970s because of violent outbreaks during those trials.

A large cadre of attorneys was assembled for the trial: Pagano and four others for the defense; two prosecutors; and three additional private attorneys, one representing the Klinghoffer family and two others arguing on behalf of the company that owned the *Achille Lauro* (Italian law allowed injured parties to take part in the prosecution). Arabic- and English-language interpreters were available to translate when needed.

Dozens of reporters packed the press section, though the general viewing area was sparsely occupied. No sooner had opening formalities gotten under way than two young women and two men in the spectator area stood and raised their arms in a clenched-fist salute. One of the women began to read aloud in German-accented English from a piece of paper. "Companions/friends, we are here to show our solidarity with the Palestinian revolution," she said.

Her speech was cut short by security guards and police, who jumped on her and her companions, hauling them out of the room yelling and punching. As the protesters were dragged up the stairs, their voices could be heard screaming: *"Viva la Palestina, viva la Palestina!"*

After the young Germans were removed and the courtroom settled, Pagano made a motion to dismiss all charges against his clients. He argued the evidence was tainted by the act of "aerial piracy" committed by the United States at Sigonella. The lawyer representing Abu al-Abbas in absentia asked the court to call Foreign Minister Giulio Andreotti as a witness, presumably to align the Palestinian cause with Italian diplomacy. Both motions were denied.

The following day, June 19, the presiding judge, Lino Monteverde, read the confession Molqi had made to prosecutors and reminded the jury of the many witnesses who had confirmed it. But when Molqi testified that day, he rejected his own confession.

"I have not killed," Molqi testified, denying that Klinghoffer even existed, at least not on the *Achille Lauro*. "This is not true. This person was never on the ship. He was never seen by me or my comrades. It was a scheme created by the United States and Syria."

As if everyone wasn't jittery enough, a bomb exploded at the Italian Chamber of Commerce in Athens that day, and an unexploded bomb was found at the Italian consulate. Both incidents were linked to the *Achille Lauro* trial.

By the third day, June 20, the pressure on the accused had grown almost unbearable. Fear and the strain of months of imprisonment made them look even younger than they were. The prosecutor called Ahmad Maruf "Omar" al-Assadi, the *penitenti* who had cut a deal, to the stand.

Assadi had a slight build and small face obscured by his arching eyebrows, large drooping mustache, and longish black curly hair. He looked like a side man in a rock group, perhaps because he resembled George Harrison of the Beatles, when he was that age.

Assadi provided the first direct testimony asserting that Abu al-Abbas was the commander in charge of the hijacking. Then he pinpointed Molqi as Leon Klinghoffer's murderer. Assadi said that Molqi came to him on the *Achille Lauro*, his clothes splattered with blood, and declared, "I have killed the American."

The accusation acted as a trip wire for Molqi and Fataier. The courtroom erupted with shouts coming from the cages, as Assadi's former comrades rattled their cages and screamed insults in Arabic while journalists implored, "Speak Italian!"

The Arabic interpreter turned pale and refused to translate the defendants' words.

The prosecutor tried to cut through the din by speaking into the microphone. "I would like to know what is being said," he commanded.

Judge Monteverde cleared the courtroom, and the *carabinieri* backed him up with a show of muscle. The trial was suspended for a few hours. When court reconvened that afternoon, the Arabic interpreter had been replaced by someone willing to reconstruct the morning's events, which had been recorded on tape. According to this new interpreter, Molqi had yelled, "Long live the Palestinian revolution! Abu al-Abbas is an honest man."

Molqi added, "This man [Assadi] is a liar. Carli is a liar, too, and this is all an American-Syrian ploy. You murdered the murdered." Molqi threatened to shoot Carli between the eyes and called him a son of a bitch.

Carli played it cool. He said he was not perturbed by the outbreak, adding it was not the first or last time he had been threatened.

Molqi and Fataier had become furious with Carli earlier, when they realized Assadi was likely to turn on them. They were convinced the prosecutor was playing dirty and had bribed Assadi to lie.

Molqi had already accused Assadi of being a traitor. "You cannot be a supporter of our cause," he had said to him on the first day of the trial. "The fact I am here does not mean that Palestine will always belong to Israel. I will be condemned but we will prevail."

The afternoon session wasn't much calmer. Pagano's clients became enraged again, pounding their fists against the metal bars so hard their Plexiglas cages shook. They hurled insults and accusations in Arabic at Assadi.

"You say you are against Abbas, but then why did you go to him?" Molqi asked.

"Because Abbas was not like this before," replied Assadi. "I was not in agreement with him anymore after the *Achille Lauro*."

Though Fataier and Molqi were partners in fury against Assadi, they were not allies. Fataier had already told investigators about his frustration with both Molqi and Assadi. He said that he had yelled at Molqi for killing Klinghoffer without consulting the rest of them. He reprimanded Assadi for not paying attention when Molqi spirited the man in the wheelchair away from the others. Fataier had confirmed that Assadi cried when he learned what Molqi had done. Fataier, too, was demoralized by the killing. This hadn't been the plan, he told investigators.

Antonio Badini, Prime Minister Craxi's diplomatic adviser, was caught off guard when the prosecutor summoned him to testify at the hijacking trial. He had already submitted to a lengthy deposition about his conversations with Abu al-Abbas on board the Egyptian airliner at Sigonella. It was unusual for a diplomat to discuss government action in the context of a criminal trial, but legal consultants in the prime minister's office reassured him that the request was legitimate.

Badini was glad to be escorted from Rome to Genoa by Admiral Martini. The chief of Italian military security and intelligence had ably guided Badini through the crisis at Sigonella and his companionship helped calm Badini's nerves. Although he had traveled extensively with Craxi, meeting heads of state and engaging in the most sensitive discussions, the prospect of the appearance in court had shaken him. The trial revived all the anxiety surrounding the *Achille Lauro*, and the tensions it had created between Craxi and the United States, while fracturing the prime minister's fragile governing coalition. Even though Craxi had survived the crisis, the trial was a reminder of lingering sensitivities.

As Baldini walked through the courtroom on Tuesday, June 24, 1986, the fifth day of the proceeding, he barely noticed Molqi, Assadi, and Fataier in their cages, though he felt the eyes of the reporters and other people scrutinizing him. As Craxi's representative, he felt as though he was on trial for the decisions they'd made about Abu al-Abbas, rather than a witness.

The ninety minutes he was on the stand felt interminable. Badini relaxed somewhat as Carli politely questioned him about what happened at Ciampino Airport, and how Abbas managed to transfer to Fiumicino and board the Yugoslav aircraft going to Belgrade, just as the general prosecutor in Rome was approaching the airport to arrest him. Badini explained that the Italian government saw Abbas as an intermediary who had helped encourage the hijackers to surrender. It was only later that investigators charged Abbas with masterminding the hijacking and by then he was long gone.

Even though this could be seen as an obstruction of justice on the part of the government, Carli didn't press Badini further. The prosecutor agreed that there hadn't been sufficient proof to hold Abbas at Sigonella and didn't see the need to keep Badini any longer.

Badini's relief was brief. Then he was approached by another attorney, Alfredo Biondi, who was representing the Klinghoffer family. Badini became apprehensive. Craxi's adviser knew that Biondi was close to Israel and aligned with the U.S. position regarding Abu al-Abbas. The lawyer belonged to the Liberal party, which had opposed Craxi's decision to let Abu al-Abbas leave the country. As a member of the Chamber of Deputies, Biondi was part of the vote that created the crisis that rattled the governing coalition.

It was clear to Badini that Biondi wanted to drag politics into the trial with questions aimed at illustrating what a serious mistake the Craxi government had made. This was exactly what Badini feared when he had been summoned for the trial. Still, Badini held his ground while Biondi hammered away. Finally, Carli intervened and told Badini he could go.

Badini left the courtroom and was encircled by journalists, who asked him to answer the accusations made by Biondi. Admiral Martini, who was expert at maneuvering his way out of uncomfortable situations, told the reporters Badini had "important business" back in Rome and they made a quick exit.

Badini's appearance was overshadowed by the star witness that day, Gerardo De Rosa, captain of the *Achille Lauro*. Speaking with pained sobriety, he provided damning evidence, though nothing he said was new to Pagano. The captain had been interviewed numerous times over the past few months by the Italian and foreign press, including people from NBC in the United States for "The *Achille Lauro*: A Study in Terror," the same episode of the documentary series *1986* that featured Abu al-Abbas. Stung by accusations that he had tried to cover up the killing of Leon Klinghoffer, De Rosa felt compelled whenever possible to explain what happened (he also had a memoir about the hijacking in the works).

The captain was impressive, a solid witness. He told the jury he had been on the bridge when Bassam al-Ashker appeared with Molqi, who had bloodstains on his pants. "I hoped it was just from a scratch," said De Rosa, adding that he had little hope left after Ashker held up one finger and gave the captain a passport with the name Leon Klinghoffer written on it.

"Then [Ashker] showed me the second passport—it was that of Mildred Hodes—and said, 'This will be the second one.'"

The captain spoke of his fear that more people were going to be killed. "I said that instead of killing everybody, they could kill just one person—the commander of the ship," he said.

De Rosa defended his early report to Prime Minister Craxi, saying that Klinghoffer was missing rather than dead. "I did not see the body," he said. "I did not hear the shots. I hoped desperately that the hijackers were lying."

The story became more coherent every day, as a stream of witnesses filled gaps in the narrative. On June 25, Bassam al-Ashker, the fourth hijacker, made an appearance. His own trial, as a juvenile, would take place later, out of the public eye.

Like his fellow hijackers, Ashker had given varying accounts to authorities.

Right after the hijacking, in November, he had told investigators his role was to stay with the captain while Fataier and Assadi guarded the hostages. He said his understanding of the mission—which wasn't all that clear—was that they were to attack the port in Ashdod, kill the greatest possible number of Israelis, and then somehow capture the American, British, and Israeli passengers to facilitate their getaway. But Ashker said he had his own plan. "I had decided I was going to die at Ashdod," he said. "I would not get back on the ship after I had gotten off. I considered it a great honor to irrigate my homeland with my blood and to die on the soil of my homeland."

He described confronting Molqi after learning that Klinghoffer had been killed. Ashker said he remembered the American well. "I had helped him earlier, covering him with a blanket and giving him a cigarette," Ashker said. "His wife had been so grateful that she had hugged me and kissed me."

He told the investigators that Molqi had offered several explanations. "First, he said the killing had been accidental, then he said he had killed him because he had bothered him, and then because he had not answered him when he asked a question," Ashker said.

A month later, in December 1985, Ashker offered a somewhat amended account. He told investigators he became suspicious about the true goals of their mission. He questioned whether Abu al-Abbas was involved at all.

Now on the witness stand he completely recanted, aligning himself with Molqi and Fataier, denying the killing of Klinghoffer. "Our plan did not call for any hijacking or for the killing of any American or English," he testified. "We are Palestinian fighters and in our laws we do not talk about killing."

Prosecutors introduced a report by Captain Antonio Marzo, who took the defendants' statements when they were first arrested at Sigonella. According to Marzo's report, Bassam al-Ashker confirmed Fataier and Molqi's story, that the intention was to reach Ashdod and the plan had been foiled when a crew member entered their cabin. Ashker gave the policeman a cuff link—a gift from De Rosa, the ship's captain—to prove that he had been there.

When asked in court whether Abu al-Abbas had organized the whole thing, Ashker punted. "I am merely a soldier," he said. "I receive orders and I carry them out. I am not interested in the provenance of the orders. I belong to the Palestinian revolution....I don't see any difference between the PLO and the PLF. It is you who wishes to divide these. It is American politics that divides the two."

That same day, the jurors received testimony from Marilyn Klinghoffer, who before she died had made sure her voice would be heard at the trial.

In a letter read aloud by prosecutor Carli, she wrote about her experience. She told of being separated from her wheelchair-bound husband and spending hours on a deck holding two drums of gasoline. The hijackers threatened to ignite these and blow up the hostages if "there were any surprises."

The letter described how she was unable to find her husband after being reunited with the other passengers. When she asked one of the hijackers about her husband, he didn't answer her. "He was moved and kissed me," she wrote. "He was crying."

From an evidentiary point of view, Mrs. Klinghoffer's letter was not important. But it had an emotional effect, erasing some sympathy that might have been aroused by Ashker's youth and eloquent affirmation of his belief in the cause he was fighting for, regardless of the disastrous outcome of the mission.

The trial wound down on July 5, a Saturday, three weeks after it began. Throughout the arduous proceedings, Pagano carried opposing thoughts in his head. He deplored what happened to Leon Klinghoffer. "The killing of a paralytic man is an inexcusable error, surely, a killing that is indefensible," Pagano believed. "The only excuse is the fear of the moment and having lost one's head. The killing though was only on al-Molqi; the others never knew and never condoned in any case this terrible mistake of killing this man and throwing his body in the sea. It is a matter of indefensible gravity. I am the first to condemn this."

Yet he also believed that his clients were not terrorists, that they genuinely believed they were fighting a war. He observed that they hadn't hung their heads like hooligans during the trial, but stayed upright, like military men.

As Pagano rose to make his final argument, his goal remained the same as it had been when the trial began. He hoped to avoid the conviction for terrorism and the life sentence it carried. There was only one card to play—so he played it. Call it the Pisacane defense.

Carlo Pisacane, Duke of San Giovanni, was a nineteenth-century Italian quixote who believed in promoting his socialist cause through memorable acts of violence, including the hijacking of the *Cagliari*, a passenger ship, off the coast of Sardinia in 1857. Pisacane was considered a patriot, a romantic hero killed after sailing from Genoa on an ill-fated mission to enlist followers in the Neapolitan kingdom, three years before Garibaldi's more successful embarkation from Quarto near Genoa to Sicily, which led to the unification of Italy. Streets throughout Italy are named for the martyred Pisacane.

Invoking the Pisacane legend, Pagano asked the jury to think of the hijackers as modern-day patriots engaged in a similar quest for a homeland. Playing to the sympathy he knew many Italians felt toward the Palestinian cause, Pagano recalled the Israeli attack on PLO headquarters in Tunisia, in which many civilians were killed. He sensed that even the presiding judge shared his feeling of "*simpatia*"; during the proceedings, Monteverde had asked each of the five defendants on trial whether they had lived in refugee camps, and if any of their relatives had died in combat or as bystanders.

Prosecutor Luigi Carli was arch in his rebuttal. "Some of the defense arguments were interesting, others were simply in bad taste for people with a knowledge of the law," Carli told the eight-person jury, composed of two male judges and six ordinary citizens, three men and three women.

He said he was "astonished" at the comparison to Carlo Pisacane. "Nobody knows whether any passengers were killed on the ship Pisacane seized," the prosecutor said.

Carli went on to remind the jurors of Leon Klinghoffer's death and the violent circumstances that led to it. "There were 385 pairs of eyes aboard the ship that saw the weapons and the bombs," he said. "You are not here to judge the struggle for the liberation of Palestine, the Palestine Liberation Organization, or even the Palestinian Liberation Front. You are concerned with the crude facts and the criminal actions."

Carli asked for life sentences for seven of the defendants, including the hijackers and the three fugitives: Abu al-Abbas and his lieutenants, Ozzudin Badratkan and Omar el-Ziad, the treasurer of the PLF.

After the closing arguments, Judge Monteverde explained the complex assortment of charges involving numerous defendants, the majority of whom had not been in the courtroom. The charges ranged from the relatively minor infraction of using a false passport to far more serious crimes, including weapons possession, hijacking, murder, and "private violence" against De Souza and Alberti by making them dump Klinghoffer's body. Most serious was the charge of *banda armata*, the constitution of an armed gang for the commission of a crime against the state. In other words, were they terrorists as defined by Italian law, or were they—as they claimed—soldiers fighting for a cause?

This philosophical question had been resonating throughout the trial. The lawyers were asking the jury to parse a difficult distinction between unlawful terrorism and legitimate acts of war—a distinction whose logic becomes harder to maintain when distilled to its essence. Terrorism is violence committed against the state in the furtherance of political aims of groups not recognized as nations; these acts usually involve the deliberate targeting of civilians. "Legitimate" warfare is violence committed in the furtherance of political aims pursued by nation-states, involving the targeting of enemy military personnel, often knowing there is an extremely high likelihood that civilians will be killed. And then there is the even murkier territory covered by "counterterrorism," the reprisals committed by nation-states in the pursuit of terrorists.

The jurors had Sunday off and on Monday met in a secret location somewhere in Genoa to deliberate. For three days they sorted through the mass of testimony, trying to match the events with the legal instructions they'd been given. Unlike their American counterparts, Italian juries were empowered to issue sentences as well as the determination of guilt or innocence.

On July 10, 1986, the judge read the verdict. There was enormous disagreement as to whether the outcome was just or a travesty, but legal experts generally agreed that the jury made legal and political judgments that were unprecedented.

Six of the fifteen defendants were convicted of "kidnapping with the goal of terrorism, with the aggravating factor of the death of one of the kidnapped people." These were the three hijackers who had appeared in court—Majid al-Molqi, Abdellatif Ibrahim Fataier, and Ahmad Maruf "Omar" al-Assadi—and the PLF officials not in custody, Abu al-Abbas, Omar el-Ziad, and Ozzudin Badratkan.

For this crime, they were each sentenced to life in prison. However, Presiding Judge Lino Monteverde said that, because of "attenuating circumstances," the jury had lowered the sentences for the hijackers. "They have grown up in the tragic conditions that the Palestinian people live through," said the judge. Assadi's sentence was lowered to fifteen years, for cooperating with the prosecution—and for showing compassion to the hostages on the *Achille Lauro*; Judge Monteverde noted that "he cried, when he learned of the killing of Klinghoffer," referring to Marilyn Klinghoffer's letter. Fataier received a sentence of twenty-four years and two months in prison. Molqi was sentenced to thirty years "because he was the head of the group, he knew about the goal of the operation and he killed Klinghoffer on his own decision."

However, the jury found no extenuating circumstances for the PLF leaders. They were given the full sentence, Judge Monteverde told reporters, because they conceived of the hijacking as "a selfish political act" designed "to weaken the leadership of Yasser Arafat." The judge said the jury accepted the view of the Italian government and the prosecution, that Arafat knew nothing about the hijacking.

Still, even the top PLF leaders were not convicted under the *banda armata* charge. The judge explained that the PLF didn't exist solely to commit terrorist acts. Its aim, he said, was "the restoration of a homeland for the Palestinian people."

As for the other two defendants who were in the courtroom, Issa Abbas was sentenced to six months in prison and Gandura Said to eight months but released for time served. Four of the fifteen defendants were acquitted outright, and the rest received lesser sentences and fines.

The jury also ordered each hijacker and the PLF leaders to pay $20,000 apiece to Ilsa and Lisa Klinghoffer and $6,000 to the *Achille Lauro*'s owners in compensation and legal fees.

For Pagano, the verdict was a victory, the best he could have hoped for. None of the defendants were convicted of the *banda armata* charge, and his clients avoided life imprisonment. Pagano was already planning an appeal aimed at reducing their time in prison.

The prosecutors disputed the court's findings, most vehemently around the decision to forgo the *banda armata* charge. The prosecution's petition for appeal was a dense exploration of Italy's antiterrorism statute, filled with legalistic minutiae. But the indignation underlying the document was clear enough. The group behind the hijacking of the *Achille Lauro* was indeed a *banda armata*, the prosecutors asserted, writing that the point "does not seem to be contestable" even using the "minimal" standard required for proof.

Once news of the trial's outcome reached New York, the Klinghoffer family was asked to respond. At a press conference, Ilsa and Lisa summoned Marilyn's ferocity together with her sense of style, appearing in pearls, with hair and makeup carefully arranged. "My mother would be outraged," said Ilsa. "An opportunity has been lost to deliver a clear message to terrorists everywhere that barbaric, criminal acts in the guise of political activism will no longer be tolerated."

Lisa vowed that she and Ilsa would lead a campaign to extradite the Palestinians for trial in the United States. This wasn't an empty threat:

under U.S. treaties with Italy, extradition was a possibility after all Italian legal proceedings were complete, including appeals.

"Someone will pay," Lisa said.

The someone she had in mind was Abu al-Abbas, the specter hanging over the trial. His motivation, his leadership—indeed, the legitimacy of his cause—had become the central question overshadowing the guilt or innocence of the men who had done his bidding. He and his top lieutenants had received the harshest sentence, confirming his status as an international fugitive—a terrorist—in the eyes of the United States and its allies, while adding to his legend as a heroic, uncompromising opponent of Israel and America among Palestinians.

But where was he? As the Italian judge pronounced the verdict against him, not even his wife, Reem al-Nimer, knew the answer, and she was a month away from giving birth to their child.

Baghdad

THE PREVIOUS December, after the end of the fall school semester, Reem al-Nimer had moved with her sons to Baghdad, to join Abu al-Abbas. She loved Tunisia but after the *Achille Lauro*, her husband had been banned by the Tunisian government, in deference to American demands. In Baghdad, the Abbas family settled into a white villa in the bustling Karrada Dakhil neighborhood, just across the Tigris from the government palaces in the Green Zone. Iraqi officials had made the arrangements; the house had belonged to an Iranian politician who was evicted when President Saddam Hussein's Baathists came to power in 1968. There was a small yard filled with fruit trees; next door was an excellent bakery that sold baklava, *man al salway, basma,* and other treats. Reem and Abbas liked to stroll down Abu Nawas Street, stopping for dinner at a favorite restaurant that served traditional Iraqi food.

Reem had survived her chaotic life through adaptation; she had become expert at creating an illusion of normalcy. When she and her first husband, Mohammad, were exiled in Algeria and Libya, and later when she lived in Tunisia with Abu al-Abbas, she became an experimental cook, incorporating North African cuisine into the dishes she had learned at home in Beirut. In Baghdad, she added the Turkish, Persian, and Indian influences she found there into the mix. The revolutionary would have been content to be a homebody for a while.

She had enrolled Reef and Loaye, her sons from Mohammad al-Ghadban, in the local French lycée; this was a relatively easy move for them—academically if not otherwise—since they had studied in a similar program in Tunis. She had deliberately chosen French schools because of her peripatetic life. She wanted the boys to be able to pick up and change schools wherever they had to live, whether it was Tunis, Beirut, or Baghdad.

Though she tried to protect them and to give them the best education that she could, there was constant fear of attack from the Israelis and other enemies no matter where they were. They had experienced a life of wandering and disruption from the time they were toddlers, when she and their biological father, Mohammad, had been constantly on the run. Right before the hijacking, Mohammad, now a noncombatant who worked as a PLF information officer for Abu al-Abbas, had been arrested in France. Reef and Loaye, nine and ten years old when the hijacking took place, were old enough to be aware of what was going on with their father and stepfather and to feel anxious.

Saddam had welcomed them in Baghdad; Iraq had been one of the better destinations for Palestinian refugees since 1948. Unlike other Arab countries, Iraq gave Palestinians the right to work and full access to health, education, and other government services. But, Reem wondered, would that hospitality last? The Iraqi leader supported the Palestinian cause, but he also courted favor with the United States, so Abu al-Abbas was an unofficial "guest," meaning he could be expelled—or worse—at any time. After breaking ties in 1969 because of America's close relations with Saudi Arabia and Israel, Iraq had restored full diplomatic relations with the United States in 1984, two years after the Reagan administration removed Iraq from a State

Department list of "state sponsors of terrorism." On the other hand, the Iraqis were bitter over reports that America had been selling arms to Iran in exchange for hostages, in violation of purported U.S. neutrality in the Iraq-Iran war, which had been slogging on since 1980 and would continue until 1988, at the cost of roughly a half million casualties. In fact, the Iranian arms deal actually made for a kind of perverse neutrality: the United States had been providing technological support to Iraq for several years and in 1985 the Reagan administration also approved the export of biological cultures that could be used to develop bioweapons, including anthrax and botulism.

After news of the Iranian arms deal emerged publicly the previous autumn, President Reagan had written a conciliatory letter to Saddam Hussein, trying to put a positive spin on the weapons sale to Iran. Two days later, Saddam replied, "Iraq, Mr. President, understands in principle your endeavor to establish normal relations with Iran, now or in the future, regardless of whether we agree with your justifications and goals or not. What concerns Iraq, in this matter, is that such relations do not involve a threat to its security, sovereignty and legitimate interests. I believe that you share with me the view that this criterion is essential and legitimate in relations between peace-loving States which have established relations based on mutual respect and non-interference in internal affairs."

He continued, "What has shocked us and caused our great surprise—and frankly, even aroused our suspicions—is that the process of your rapprochement with Iran has involved supplying that country with quantities of U.S. military equipment, and that the contacts have been undertaken in the manner uncovered recently...."

These larger forces—and his own impetuosity—made Abu al-Abbas's standing with the Iraqi government much more tenuous—especially after his spring 1986 interview on NBC. That April, Abbas was in Algeria, meeting with allies sympathetic to the PLF. This was the "undisclosed location," where he was filmed with the NBC reporter for the interview that aired on the nightly news in May, and again in an expanded version before the hijacking trial in June.

Asked during that interview whether he was daunted by the $250,000 bounty the U.S. government put on his head, Abbas responded with bravado. "Here comes again the American way of thinking which does not understand the nature of the East," he said. "A quarter of a million dollars may have an effect on American citizens. In the Middle East this aspect is worthless. I will offer to you $1 million to whoever hands President Reagan to us, to the Palestinian revolution, to be tried. I guarantee this sum."

After the interview first aired on American television, Abbas received a call from Tariq Aziz, Iraq's foreign minister and a trusted adviser to Saddam. Aziz told Abbas that the American ambassador to Iraq was not amused by the interview and informed Aziz that if Abbas was allowed to stay in Iraq, the United States might reconsider how much aid Iraq would receive. A similar warning was given to the Algerians.

Abu al-Abbas left Iraq shortly after Tariq's warning, leaving Reem and the boys behind, not knowing his destination. He couldn't even call; they knew the villa was bugged with hidden microphones. Reem joked that the bugs were part of the family—"a demure and silent cousin who always listened but never had the impulse to speak."

Occasionally Reem received word from a trusted contact that Abbas was safe, though the notion of safety felt more ephemeral every day. A few months earlier, in March 1986, Reem was told that her uncle Zafer al-Masri had been murdered in the West Bank by the radical Popular Front for the Liberation of Palestine (PFLP). Masri, her mother's brother, was forty-four years old, described as "a quiet, gentle man" by an American journalist. He had been appointed the mayor of Nablus by the Israeli government, as part of Prime Minister Shimon Peres's effort to give Palestinians in the occupied territories more responsibility over their daily lives. Both Abu Nidal's violent branch of Fatah and the PFLP, which was based in Damascus, Syria, claimed responsibility for the killing, the latter explaining that a death sentence had been levied on Masri for his part in "the Zionist-Jordanian plan aimed at liquidating the Palestinian cause."

Extremists on all sides of the conflict exulted. In the *New York Times*, Benny Katzover, a leader of Jewish settlers in the West Bank, said, "Whoever amuses himself with illusions is inviting murder. The Hussein-Peres coalition to develop independent elements in the area failed. The assassination puts an end to the development of local Arab leadership. In the long run, it's good for us."

Masri wasn't naïve. He believed Israel had appointed him mayor as a public relations move, but still felt the effort was worthwhile for the Palestinians. "It is a tactical and cosmetic move for them," he said, "but we are getting much more than that by getting some authority."

Reem felt that her uncle's murder made her husband more valuable to Yasser Arafat, whose peacemaking efforts had made many Arafat supporters question whether he was too conciliatory toward the United States. "If Arafat could still respond to Israeli attacks via the PLF, then he could maintain his profile as a freedom fighter," she would write.

The tactical analysis was small comfort. Reem grieved for her uncle, even though grieving was a luxury she didn't have time for. She was five months pregnant and had two young boys to take care of, and she had no idea where her husband was and when—or if—he would return to Baghdad.

As soon as her sons finished school in June, she packed their bags and moved back to Tunis, where the lease on her apartment still had several months left. Even before Abu al-Abbas had been forced to flee Baghdad, Reem had decided she did not want to give birth there. The Iraqi hospitals were teeming with wounded soldiers from the war with Iran. She didn't want her baby to enter the world in those conditions.

Her entire family came from Beirut to join her and the boys in Tunis: her parents, her sister and her daughters, and her brother, who brought his own wife and daughter. In some ways, she would remember that summer as a happy one. The beaches in Tunis were idyllic; she was reconciled with her family.

Toward the end of July, she finally heard from Abu al-Abbas. Tariq Aziz found a way to spirit him back into Baghdad without alerting the U.S. ambassador and soon Abbas called Reem to see how she was doing—and to let her know that Omar and Khaled, his sons from his first marriage, were coming for their customary vacation visit. However, he told her, their mother wouldn't let the boys travel with one of his men, as they usually did. Did she mind if Samia came to Baghdad with them?

Reem said, "OK, I have no problem," but that wasn't true. When their son, Ali, was born on August 16, 1986, his father wasn't there. "I was very sad I didn't have him around, especially during the delivery time," said Reem. "He didn't enjoy the first hours, minutes of our son. He couldn't even call to say congratulations because Tariq Aziz asked him not even to make telephone calls. I couldn't even hear his voice."

In the days after the hijacking, Samia Costandi had gone to her teaching job at a university in Beirut every day. She pretended that everything was normal, concealing the information from anyone who didn't already know that the father of her children was the man at the center of the *Achille Lauro* maelstrom. Fear for her family's safety escalated as she and her sons followed the hijacking on television and radio. Her older child, seven-year-old Khaled, told her, "I want to go to the North Pole and hide."

They had heard from Abu al-Abbas just once after it happened, when he called from Yugoslavia and little Omar had forgotten to pretend that he was talking to his uncle, not his father. Later they found out that Abbas was safe in Baghdad.

There had been no further communication with him until the day he was sentenced to life imprisonment in Italy. "I think this was implemented to satisfy America's desire, for sure," he wrote to her. "Anyway, the journey is still long, we will see what happens." Explaining that he could not travel to see them in Beirut—due to "unusual circumstances that are very exhausting"—he said the only option was for her to send their "two beautiful children" to Baghdad. "I really need them to be with me," he said. "You have to trust how much I appreciate and value you, and how much I care about Khaled and Omar as a father and as a human."

The request set off alarms, reawakening Samia's old anxieties, the worries that kept her in a state of depression throughout their marriage. Though the distance from Beirut to Baghdad wasn't huge, just over five hundred miles, it was a dangerous journey. Samia feared someone would kidnap the children, or they would be harmed by the war between Iraq and Iran.

Still, the boys wanted to see their father. They looked forward to summers with him and she didn't want to deprive them of that important connection. She didn't want to deprive him, either, still grateful that he'd given her custody, unusual for an Arab man. The letter reminded her of the dichotomy in her ex-husband that she was never able to explain, even to herself. She had seen his gentle side and believed in his idealism. "He definitely had a yearning for the normal life, which he was not able to have," she said.

Yet Samia still felt the double betrayal she had experienced when Abu al-Abbas left her in 1981 for Reem, who had been her friend. For the first two years after their divorce, Samia wouldn't speak to Reem. They had been so close; how could Reem do this?

Abu al-Abbas may have been a warrior, ruthless when he felt it was necessary, but he couldn't tolerate the animosity between the women he loved. He kept asking Samia when she was going to start speaking to Reem again. The rift was finally healed when Omar got sick during a visit to Tunisia. Reem called to talk to Samia about the medication he needed and Samia realized the grudge had to end because of the boys.

"The thing that brought us together were the kids," said Samia. "We both raised our kids to love each other. They call each other brothers, not stepbrothers. We both were keen on developing this relationship, so the kids will always love each other, which is very important."

Now Samia decided to take the boys to Baghdad herself, ostensibly to allay her fears, but also to settle some matters with her ex-husband.

"Why did you marry Reem?" Samia asked him after she arrived in Baghdad. "She was my friend!"

He answered with the flirtatious humor she knew well. "Because she reminds me of you!"

During her brief visit, Abu al-Abbas regaled her with stories about the *Achille Lauro*, stories in which he always emerged the hero.

"He described it as he used to describe some of the stories in his life, with a sense of heroism, of how he got away, how he challenged the United States of America," she remembered. "He had an ego, Abu Khaled. He described it as a miraculous escape, almost as a mythic story, he almost couldn't believe it himself how they were able to get out."

Her husband told her the four young hijackers said to him, "The most important thing is for *you* to escape, for *you* to fly again."

As they talked, she believed him when he said he felt sorry about what happened to those young men. "I rarely saw him cry, but I saw him cry once," she said. It was around the time they separated, but he wasn't crying about her. It was April 1981, when two teenagers he'd sent to fly across the Lebanese border into Israel in a hot-air balloon were shot down and killed by Israeli forces.

The story reminded her again of that dichotomy within him, that no matter how much he cared for her or for Reem or for his sons, the cause would always come first. "I could never figure it out, the hard part inside him," she said. "He was looking after his own interest in the end, not ours."

Samia came to understand this essential difference between her and Reem. "I was interested intellectually and morally, and in writing about the revolution," she said. "I was not interested in the military. Anything to do with killing and violence bothered me. She was tougher than me in that sense. She trained to fight, I never did."

Samia stayed in Baghdad for a few days and then left the children behind to spend the rest of the summer there. Abu al-Abbas assured her they would be well protected, and she decided to believe him, for her own peace of mind and for the sake of their sons.

12

Presenting...
The Death of Klinghoffer

Brooklyn, September 1991

In the six years that had passed since the *Achille Lauro* hijacking, Leon Klinghoffer had become, for most people, both larger and smaller than life, a representation more than a memory. Once the hijackers had been convicted, the story had run its course, replaced in the news cycle by fresh crops of civilian casualties. It became increasingly difficult, sometimes even for his own daughters, to distinguish the man from the symbol — *hero, martyr, victim.*

Ilsa and Lisa continued trying to fulfill the mandate their mother had given them, to keep their father's tragedy alive, to make sure that his life and death mattered. They became the poster children for a campaign by the Anti-Defamation League (ADL) to alert the public to the threat of terrorism, which still seemed remote to Americans in the days before 9/11. "The Klinghoffer sisters made the issue of terrorism a live issue, to make it human," said Kenneth Jacobson, then the ADL's director of Middle East affairs. "If you respond emotionally, you want to do something whether it's legislation, whether it's awareness. In Congress, you can have scholars talk about statistics on terrorism, OK. But when you have the Klinghoffers come in and talk about their loss, their family, that puts it up front again."

The ADL exerted influence on U.S. domestic policy through lobbying and via collaboration with the FBI and other government agencies investigating domestic hate crimes. In the 1980s, the ADL turned its focus on terrorism. Abraham Foxman, head of the organization's international affairs division before becoming ADL national director in 1987, embraced the Klinghoffer sisters, understanding their value to the ADL's efforts to protect Jewish interests, domestically and abroad, particularly in Israel. Foxman recognized the importance of the Klinghoffer story from the outset, dispatching a young lawyer from the ADL to Leon's shivah. The association began in earnest a few months later, after Marilyn's death. Letty Simon continued to help prepare the sisters for comment when acts of terrorism made headlines, but eventually the ADL took over, vetting and often writing every op-ed piece carrying the Klinghoffer name, managing media requests and public appearances, including on occasions when the sisters themselves testified before Congress. The ADL also managed strategy for the lawsuit Marilyn had filed, before her death, against the PLO as it continued to trudge through the legal system.

"Almost everything public they did with us," Foxman said. "Guidance, preparation, with intervention. We grafted them onto the ADL mission. How many times they testified, my god! There's no question that we used them, and they used us. Whenever there was an issue of terrorism anywhere, they were ready to put their face on it to remind people these aren't anonymous people. There is a Klinghoffer out there."

The organization, which was now operating the Klinghoffer Foundation as well, decided how best to deploy the appealing sisters in service of the ADL cause. The foundation began to sponsor luncheons to honor leaders designated by the ADL as supporters of its antiterrorism mission. The recipients thus far had been British Prime Minister Margaret Thatcher in 1987, for breaking diplomatic relations with Syria because of its involvement in a plot to blow up an El Al airliner, and George Shultz, the former secretary of state, in 1989, for his support of Israel as well as his efforts to initiate dialogue between the United States and the PLO. By then, George H. W. Bush, Reagan's vice president, had moved into the Oval Office. ("Oy, do we miss you," said Joel Sprayregen, chairman of the ADL's international division, at the

Shultz event. Bush's portfolio as vice president had not included the *Achille Lauro* hijacking, even though he was a former head of the CIA.)

Crucial players of the Reagan team involved in the U.S. response to terrorism had ended their White House careers in disgrace, brought low by the Iran-Contra scandal. Oliver North was convicted and then vindicated for his role in the illegal arms sale; in subsequent years he became a prominent figure in the conservative movement—as author, speaker, and television host—and in 2018 became president of the National Rifle Association. His former boss, Robert McFarlane, who pleaded guilty to four misdemeanor charges, attempted suicide in 1987 because he believed he had failed his country, and was pardoned by President Bush in 1992. President Reagan was legally exonerated by an investigating commission, chided only for having "a lax managerial style and aloofness from policy detail."

While these events filled headlines and were then forgotten, Klinghoffer's daughters felt little release from sorrow and frustration, no matter how hard they tried to discharge their duty. Lisa especially felt a nagging uncertainty, the hollow feeling of not belonging. Her friends and relatives, except for her sister and maybe their husbands, didn't feel the existential threat of terrorism the way she did. Despite their valiant efforts to follow their mother's orders, she felt a void, an inability to calibrate the balance between moving on and preserving the past. Ilsa seemed better equipped for the struggle. With her inbred determination and drive, helped by the structure provided by her work and a more natural affinity with public speaking, she was the arranger and organizer. For Lisa, every appearance brought on a siege of anxiety; though she was the older one, she relied on Ilsa (and the occasional pill) to steady her when she faltered, to fill in the blanks when a word or phrase eluded her.

When Lisa finally resumed going to her studio, she forced herself to show up every day, even during a long period of creative stagnation, as she waited for a revelation that would help her translate their family tragedy into art. The epiphany didn't arrive. She resorted to mechanical creation and began producing small pieces that contained writing about the *Achille Lauro*. The experiment felt fake, like she was trying to be someone she wasn't. She threw the pieces away.

She and Ilsa tried to replicate the world their mother had created. They hosted Passover seder gatherings and New Year's Eve parties and helped take care of their grandmother Rose in New Jersey. Yet for Lisa, everything seemed stalled. She and Jerry tried to have a baby without success. She felt out of sync with her friends, even Ilsa, who was ready to sell Marilyn and Leon's apartment, where she and Paul still lived, while Lisa couldn't bear to part with the space that had become an emotional shrine to their parents. The shrine needed repairs and the maintenance was expensive, more than the newlyweds could afford, but the family knew better than to try to force Lisa to budge. Rather than confront her sister, Ilsa accommodated while Jerry subsidized the monthly payments on the apartment for three years until finally, with continued therapy and the passage of time, Lisa was ready to let it go. Ilsa and Paul moved and Ilsa became pregnant. Max Klinghoffer Dworin was born on January 16, 1989.

Later that year, in November, Lisa and Ilsa heard that the San Francisco Opera had announced it was commissioning a work called *The Death of Klinghoffer*, based on the *Achille Lauro* hijacking, in collaboration with the Los Angeles Festival, the Théâtre Royal de la Monnaie in Brussels, the Opéra de Lyon in France, the Brooklyn Academy of Music, and the Glyndebourne Festival in England.

This wouldn't be the first attempt to resurrect Leon by means of fiction. There had been two disposable made-for-television movies, in which he had been portrayed by distinguished actors (Karl Malden and Burt Lancaster) in the waning days of their careers. Philip Roth had begun writing *Operation Shylock*, a novel he would describe as resonant with "Jewish menaces and ghosts and phantoms and memories," in which Leon's unsought celebrity would play a minor but critical role.

The sisters were thrilled when they heard about the opera. As culturally attuned Manhattanites, they appreciated opera's aesthetic distinction: the medium was of a higher grade in their minds than made-for-TV movies. They were also delighted to hear about the creative team involved—director Peter Sellars, composer John Adams, and choreographer Mark Morris—names certain to stir people like them, devotees of the *New York Times* arts section. They weren't as familiar with the librettist, Alice Goodman, but assumed she must be important when they saw that she had written the text for *Nixon in China*, a cheeky take on Richard Nixon's famous meeting with Chairman Mao, in collaboration with Sellars, Adams, and Morris. Lisa had seen and admired that opera's absurdist sensibility. She didn't fully understand it, but she thought it was hip. She liked it.

Lisa was impressed by the group's credentials. She felt an opera by them could enhance interest in her father and possibly ensure a kind of posterity. She was surprised as well. "I thought it was a little weird they would do this," she said. "I thought, 'That's a weird subject for them to undertake. It's too real.'"

Sellars was the most exciting component. He had become a noted figure in the theater world while still in his twenties, known as an exuberant enfant terrible, a clever showman who liked to startle. His hair was spiky; he wore colorful beads around his neck; his clothing was designed for effect, whether he was wearing one of his large collection of brightly patterned polyester shirts, a purple jacket, or the occasional kimono. He had become a public character who might have been dismissed as a poseur if he wasn't so brilliant. In 1984, at age twenty-six, Sellars had been hired by the Kennedy Center for the Performing Arts in Washington, D.C., to create the American National Theater; eighteen months later, after a short string of productions that lost money and affronted critics, that widely publicized experiment was abruptly terminated. But Sellars quickly recovered. While *Nixon in China* wasn't uniformly embraced when it premiered in Houston in the fall of 1987—reviews ran the critical gamut, vociferous on both ends—the heat generated proved that Sellars hadn't lost his touch.

After they heard the news, Lisa and Ilsa just assumed that Sellars and his colleagues would want to talk to them, to hear what they had to say about their father and mother. After all, the proposed opera's title was *The Death of Klinghoffer*.

They had been involved, to a greater or lesser degree, in both TV movies. Marilyn had sold rights to the producer of the first, *The Hijacking of the Achille Lauro*, starring Karl Malden and Lee Grant. As part of the deal, Marilyn asked if a family friend, an actress named Neva Small, who had played Tevye's youngest daughter in the 1971 screen version of *Fiddler on the Roof*, could have a part. She was cast as Lisa. Small, who had mourned with the family, invited the actual Lisa to come to the set in Australia (Ilsa was pregnant at the time and couldn't travel) and even offered to exchange her first-class ticket for two coach fares. Even though Lisa hated to fly, she couldn't resist, and then was offered the chance to appear in the film as an extra.

She and Ilsa had no official connection to the second movie, *Voyage of Terror: The Achille Lauro Affair*, an international coproduction, written and directed by Italians. The film was most notable for being filmed on the *Achille Lauro* itself. Before the film began shooting, the phone rang one day, Lisa picked it up, and a recognizable voice said, "This is Burt Lancaster. May I speak to Lisa Klinghoffer?"

She almost fell over. It was one thing to meet the president, something else to hear from a bona fide movie star! She swooned as she heard that familiar voice explain that he was playing her father in the movie and wanted to make sure he got Leon right. Could he come to New York and meet with her and Ilsa? How about lunch at Patsy's, the show business hangout on West Fifty-Sixth Street with bragging rights as the place "Frank Sinatra made famous"?

When the day arrived, the sisters were ushered to Lancaster's table. After greeting them warmly, he spent the meal gently grilling them about Leon. How did he move? How did he communicate? What did he do with his hand if he was just sitting there? Would he be like this? Or that?

They were enchanted.

Nothing like that happened with the opera people. In fact, nothing happened at all. There was no invitation to participate, not even a courtesy call. For Lisa, the silence reinforced the sense of alienation she was constantly struggling to keep at bay. The opera became a point of focus, even obsession, and she became determined to reach Sellars, finally tracking down his telephone number in California.

A machine answered. She left a brief message. "My name is Lisa Klinghoffer," she said. "I'd love to talk to you about the opera you are doing about my parents."

Sellars returned the call. "Nice to hear from you," he said evenly. "Yes, we're going to do an opera." When Lisa asked if he wanted her to tell him about their family, he said, "I don't think so."

"What do you mean?" she replied.

"Lisa, you're an artist," he said. "I'm sure you'll understand when you see it."

"You don't want to know anything?" she said, incredulous. "I'd like to give you some information."

When he declined, she made a final attempt.

"You can contact me any time," she said.

Though the exchange had been cordial, it was stilted. Regardless of the careful, diplomatic tone, Lisa understood the unstated message: "Why are you calling?" She felt embarrassed and confused. Why wouldn't Sellars want to know who her parents really were?

Then the opera fell off her radar for a happy reason. She'd been undergoing fertility treatments and she became pregnant. On September 26, 1990, she and Jerry welcomed their son, Michael Leon Klinghoffer Arbittier.

A year later, *The Death of Klinghoffer* came to Brooklyn. Lisa and Ilsa had bought tickets the instant they went on sale for the weeklong run at the Brooklyn Academy of Music (BAM)—not just for themselves and their husbands, but for the Beach People and many of their children. On Saturday night, September 7, 1991, two days after the opening, this large party met for dinner in a nearby restaurant and then walked to the theater, filling two rows of seats.

Both sisters were apprehensive. They had been following reviews of the opera since it premiered in Belgium, six months earlier, before going on to Lyon and Vienna.

The March opening in Brussels came soon after yet another flareup in the Middle East: American and NATO forces brought a quick end to the Persian Gulf War, the six-week battle to end Saddam Hussein's occupation of Kuwait. The estimated Iraqi death toll was as high as 100,000; the allies lost about 300 soldiers. The conflict became known as the first CNN war—televised in real time, from the dropping of the first bomb, presented to the public like a miniseries or sporting event, with catchy titles like "Showdown in the Gulf." Having learned its lesson from the messy TV images sent home from Vietnam, the U.S. Defense Department provided heroic video footage this time to offset independent reporting.

At a press conference aimed at reassuring reporters that the opera's libretto was not meant to take sides in the ongoing Palestinian-Israeli confrontation, composer John Adams invoked disturbing aspects of the Gulf War news coverage while explaining his aims for *Klinghoffer.* "I was reminded throughout the Gulf War that people are fed experiences in a totally pre-digested way and it particularly horrified me during the war because here was something absolutely cataclysmic," Adams told the reporters. "There were tens of thousands of people dying, suffering, their lives changed irrevocably, and yet it was presented to the American people like a soap opera. It was cleaned up, sanitized, turned into a patriotic rally."

He continued. "Why it pleases me so much to bring *Klinghoffer* to Europe at exactly this point is because we have the opportunity to address the exact same issues that Americans have chosen to go to sleep over or simply benumbed themselves over and bring it right down to the real human level. These people really are oppressed, these people really are being killed. The terrible, terrible tragedy comes about as the result of people hating and misunderstanding each other and oppressing each other. I don't take sides, each side does it to each other. The Jews do it, the Palestinians do it, the Arabs do it, the Iraqis do it. It's not a question of us against them."

The opera itself elicited a respectful, if muted, response on opening night, March 19, 1991, at the Théâtre Royal de la Monnaie, a rococo jewel box of a venue. Reviews were mixed, no surprise—works by Sellars rarely invited a uniform response. The critics who packed the house in Brussels did agree that *The Death of Klinghoffer* was staged to astound, with its huge cast of ninety singers and dancers, the high-tech set of giant steel scaffolding, and an onslaught of heavily amplified conventional and electronic music. The *Wall Street Journal* critic Manuela Hoelterhoff praised and denounced the opera with her characteristic acid wit: "*Klinghoffer* is not the opera it was meant to be, but a high-tech oratorio with ritualistic choruses and athletic dancers linking together a string of largely incomprehensible soliloquies delivered by inert characters wearing body mikes," she wrote. "There's much to admire in the often compelling score and the elaborate presentation, but neither can finally overcome the flabbergasting subject."

Hoelterhoff's mordant exposition invoked the foreword Sellars wrote for Goodman's libretto, in which he explained: "This is essentially a religious drama in the sense that Greek tragedy or the Bach Passions or the Persian Ta'ziyeh or the Javanese Wayang Wong are religious dramas."

Hoelterhoff dismissed the director's note as a "repulsively amoral and pretentious" justification of an opera which, in her view, "turns the sport killing of a frail old Jew in a wheelchair into a cool meditation on meaning and myth, life and death. And without a penny of subsidy from the PLO."

She singled out "an odd little prologue elliptically describing the banal world of the Klinghoffers," contrasted with the drama of "the chief terrorist, his face glistening on a huge screen, [who] tells us at great length about his lousy childhood."

John Rockwell in the *New York Times* was far kinder. While observing that the work "has problems that need refinement," he saw value and, with revisions, "the potential for eventual triumph." He ended his critique on an encouraging note: "Last night's premiere brought warm, friendly but curiously curtailed applause. In a more pointed production, that applause could turn into ovations."

Now, in Brooklyn, six months later, Lisa's trepidation was building throughout the opening "Chorus of Exiled Palestinians," as she listened to the performers lament what they had lost, sung to haunting music—"of that house, not a wall, not a wall / In which a bird might nest was left to stand. Israel laid all to waste."

Then the mood changed, becoming bright and snappy. She watched a family appear onstage, sitting in a facsimile of a suburban living room. They are the Rumors, fictional Jewish friends of the Klinghoffers, from New Jersey. As they kvetch, the music shifts, to the aggressive cheerfulness of a television sitcom theme song. The father sings, "Your mother haunts the markets when we go ashore, looking for some hideous relic to bring home." The son worries about taking the bar exam; the mother peers at the newspaper and says, after seeing an item about Yasser Arafat, "I'm sick to death of reading about misery. It's never ending."

After the mournful depiction of Palestinian suffering, the Rumors seemed callow, wrapped up in trivial concerns. Lisa felt overcome by embarrassment. What would her guests—her parents' friends, most of them from New Jersey, who had been on the *Achille Lauro* themselves—think of this caricature of them, or someone similar enough to them?

She could barely take in the rest of the first act, which contained the elegiac "Chorus of Exiled Jews," followed by the hijacking, as well as a scene showing Captain De Rosa exchange memories with one of the hijackers. Then came intermission. Thus far, there hadn't been a word from Leon and Marilyn.

Lisa and the others awkwardly trooped out to the lobby, not quite knowing what to say to one another. Someone from BAM approached the sisters and invited them to come meet John Adams and the others. "They'd love to meet you," the person said.

Lisa glanced over and saw photographers standing near the creative team. "I don't think so," she said brusquely, trying not to tremble. "We'd rather not." She was not in the mood to provide a photo op.

The second half of the opera turned to the Klinghoffers, whose characters had been given powerful, devastating arias. Lisa had to admit to herself that these scenes were arresting, even great. But as she left the theater and thought about it, she felt increasingly upset. She wanted to ask the creators, "Do you admire these people, or don't you? Do you feel for these people, or don't you?"

She kept replaying her brief conversation with Sellars. "He wanted to use what happened to my family as an instrument to make a point," she said. "If they really wanted to know, why didn't they call us? They didn't have to use it."

Not all the children of the Beach People had the same reaction. "We got kind of carried into the Klinghoffer girls' interpretation of everything," said Steven Hodes, a physician, son of Mildred and Frank. "There was a visceral reaction that this was wrong. How can you do an opera about this, that this is somehow sacrilegious." Yet on reflection he believed the fear that Leon would become a symbol rather than a human being was misplaced. "He did become a symbol," said Hodes. "That's what art does."

Kenneth Meskin, Seymour and Viola's son, an attorney, was offended by the scene in the Rumor household. "It was just gratuitous," he said. "You are just creating a negative light about these people that I thought was clearly politically driven." But he was moved by the rest. "John Adams does great music," he said. "I love his music."

The Rumor scene, the "odd little prologue" Hoelterhoff mentioned in passing, played quite differently in Brooklyn than in Brussels, and not just for the Klinghoffers and their friends. What was regarded as a minor artistic miscalculation in one venue became a firebomb in the other, prima facie evidence that *Klinghoffer*'s creators were anti-Semites. "Surely there is nothing in the libretto in an anti-Arab vein to match the repulsive anti-Semitism that drools from the mouth of a character called 'Rambo,'" wrote Raymond Sokolov, arts editor at the *Wall Street Jour-*

nal. In the *New York Times,* Edward Rothstein wrote that the opera gave "seemingly historical resonance to Palestinian wounds" while diminishing and even insulting the Klinghoffers and, by extension, the Jews.

Even Edward Said, a prominent Palestinian American scholar, a public intellectual whose purview included writing opera reviews in *The Nation,* felt the libretto's "easy satire" of the Rumor family tilted the balance. "In sticking to the American-Jewish, banal, middle-class aspect of the episode Goodman stacks the deck," wrote Said, "thereby letting the inherently more dramatic dimensions of the Palestinian tragedy take precedence over, and somewhat unfairly dominate, the senseless killing of the invalid tourist, whose only crime was that he happened to be on the *Achille Lauro* when the Palestinians boarded it."

Said found much he appreciated as well, and responded to the politically affronted, negative criticism with a pointed question for his fellow reviewers. "You need ask yourself how many times you have seen any substantial work of music or dramatic or literary or pictorial art that actually tries to treat the Palestinians as tragically aggrieved, albeit sometimes criminally intent, people. The answer is never, and you must go on to ask Messrs.-the-nonideological-music-and-culture-critics whether they ever complain about works that are skewed the other way, or whether for instance, in the flood of images and words that assert that Israel is a democracy, any of them note that 2 million Palestinians on the West Bank and Gaza have fewer rights than South African blacks had during the worst of apartheid, and that the paeans and the $77 billion sent to Israel from the United States were keeping the Palestinian people endlessly oppressed?"

For Peter Sellars, outrage and debate were encouraging measures of success—perhaps from the time he was a ten-year-old putting on puppet shows on the streets of Pittsburgh while absorbing the reality of his parents' divorce, a fracture that influenced the trajectory of his career. Though he preferred not to probe the connection, he acknowledged its existence. "My work does tend to gravitate toward areas of conflict and misunderstanding, where something's been suppressed," he said.

"What we can do as artists is make a space where there is a discussion. You can't leave the theater and say, 'That was nice.' You have to be in it and the person next to you is in it. At least you are creating something that will not allow silence around it. There will be talk."

He'd been an unusual child, raised by Christian Scientists who encouraged their son and daughter to read widely and listen to classical music instead of watching television. From an early age he was a whirligig of ideas, attuned to the hurts of the underdog, keeping snakes as pets because he felt reptiles got a bad rap. Shortly after entering Harvard in 1975, he began creating the legend that would cling, through outlandish works designed to thrill (or annoy), like his six-hour version of Wagner's Ring Cycle, "sung" by human-sized puppets. In 1983, at age twenty-six, Sellars became the youngest recipient of a John D. and Catherine T. MacArthur Foundation fellowship grant, known colloquially as the "genius" award, honoring "exceptionally creative people." The fearless provocateur came wrapped in a disarming package, a compact man with bright blue eyes, whose engaging sweetness included a habit of hugging people on meeting them, whether male or female, including interviewers.

Sellars had an infinite appetite for invention and ideas, ancient and contemporary. His bookshelves became packed with historic and philosophic works, as well as spiritual texts from Buddhism, Judaism, Hinduism, Islam, and Christianity. He was also absorbed by the news and the ways in which a flood of information distorted and obfuscated the reality being reported, always contemplating what corrective he could offer as an artist, his mind racing so continuously he barely could find time to sleep. "Our lifetime gets so reduced to a headline, to a screaming this, to an extreme photo," he said. "Massive conclusions have to be drawn immediately by reporters on the spot who don't have any idea of what the deep history of any of it would be."

While Sellars was working on *Nixon in China* with Alice Goodman and John Adams, between 1985 and 1987, he began thinking about the Klinghoffer story, and was struck by something the two had in common. "Both operas are about people who imagined they were far away from something winding up right in the middle of it," he said. "The boat is a strangely poetic image, all these people having this fight in international waters, not on anybody's land. Whose land is this? This strange floating vessel that contained this explosive conflict is such a metaphor for the world and how we're all on one planet and all in one boat."

Sometime before the premiere of *Nixon in China* in Houston, in the fall of 1987, Sellars suggested the *Klinghoffer* idea to Adams and Goodman. He wanted to create a kind of memorial service, something impressionistic that would capture the rapid-fire assault of images, myths, facts, and factoids that accompanied Leon Klinghoffer's murder. As the glimmer of an idea developed, he decided there would be dancers and video as well as music. Actors would wear street clothes, not costumes, and play multiple roles. If it was confusing, wasn't that part of the point?

Goodman and Adams were interested, despite their tetchy working relationship. The edginess that developed between them during the making of *Nixon in China* had not surprised Sellars, who had gone to Harvard with Goodman. In college, he recalled, "she was already prickly, difficult and impossible; I was one of the three people she deigned to speak to." Still, he said, "I loved her and thought her writing was wonderful. She was impossible but completely brilliant."

Adams, also Harvard-educated, was the oldest of the three, his musical and political education very much a product of the sixties. Born in 1947 into a music-minded New England family, he spent his formative creative years after college in San Francisco, submerged in the hothouse of alternative California culture without losing his East Coast drive and ambition. By the time he and Sellars met at a festival in 1983, Adams had achieved recognition in the mainstream music world, including a composing residency with the San Francisco Symphony. Adams was dazzled by Sellars's exhaustive intellect and inexhaustible energy. On that very first meeting Sellars suggested they collaborate on making an opera and even had the title, *Nixon in China*. Adams immediately said yes, even though he had never composed an opera. It took two years—encompassing an eighteen-month spell of writer's block that sank the composer into a deep funk—before the idea took hold. He wanted a poet to write the libretto and agreed when Sellars suggested his friend Alice Goodman.

It was never an easy collaboration. When work began on *Nixon in China*, Goodman had recently moved from Cambridge, Massachusetts, to Cambridge, England, with her husband, the British poet Gregory Hill and their newborn daughter. Adams lived in San Francisco with his wife and their two young children. Goodman was a night owl who worked in enthusiastic bursts; Adams described himself as a "plodding nine-to-fiver" who resented "even the slightest obstruction in the daily schedule." Goodman became a large obstruction; he couldn't compose without the libretto, so was often stuck waiting to receive new scenes, which she would fax to San Francisco from a local photocopy shop in Cambridge.

Adams, whose stress manifested in back and shoulder pain, dealt with his impatience by barraging the librettist with imploring letters. "More stuff!" he begged her. "I need the next act!"

Goodman, already resentful of the primacy of the composer, did not like to be pushed. "You could say all librettists are female even when they're male and all composers setting texts are male even when they are female," she said. "The music is the primary thing. The composer generally gets paid twice or one and a half times the librettist. The librettists are really, really not highly respected in the world of opera and only in the world of text setting only when they are already very famous poets. Nonetheless, the libretto and therefore the librettist's work is absolutely foundational to what happens to the music. So you're important whether anyone thinks so or not."

Yet with all the contentiousness, Adams and Goodman both recognized the value of what they created together and wanted to pursue the Klinghoffer project, especially after *Nixon in China* became a cause célèbre, shown on national television and winning a Grammy for Adams.

Of the three collaborators, Adams felt he knew the least about the Middle East, his knowledge of the Israeli-Palestinian conflict based almost entirely on what he read in liberal, mainstream outlets, including the *New York Times, The Atlantic, The New Yorker,* and what he watched on PBS. As a musician, many of his closest friends were Jewish and through them he had developed a sympathetic impression of the Jewish experience, dominated by histories of the Holocaust and the founding of Israel, stories he found moving, filled with "suffering, heroism, and redemption." He began to read more widely, reacquainting himself with the Old Testament, and then attempting to understand the Koran (finding it "difficult going") before immersing himself in the roots of the Israeli-Palestinian conflict. As he continued his research, he found a pro-Israel tilt in news reports that made him uncomfortable. In his memoir, he wrote, "journalists, lobbyists, and many intellectuals in the United States were too ready to invoke the Holocaust and charges of anti-Semitism to short-circuit the debate about the Palestinian question." Soon enough he learned firsthand that all parties to the conflict had thin skins. Shortly after the news that the opera would be produced was announced, he received a scathing letter from an Arab American in his hometown of Berkeley, who assumed the opera would be a blanket condemnation of the Palestinians.

It quickly became evident that the inherent tension in the material would be reflected in the creative process, and that whatever artistic friction had existed on *Nixon* would be magnified for *Klinghoffer.* As deadlines passed, Adams waited for the sections of the libretto to arrive from Goodman in England. "It was like water torture," he said. "It was not long before phone calls became heated and the whole process ground down to long periods of grim silences and anxious waiting."

Goodman wrote the opera mostly at night, between 8 p.m. and 2 a.m., when her now three-year-old was asleep. She exhibited little interest in the facts, ignoring the voluminous documentary material about the hijacking that Sellars kept sending her. The only source that fully engaged her was Captain De Rosa's memoir, which formed the basis of her exposition. She even kept the names he gave the hijackers, all fictive except for Molqi. ("Here I will call them the names I knew in the moment, because their real names do not stir up any memories or emotions for me," De Rosa explained in his book.)

As she was writing, she was filled with fervor. "I was thinking, 'I have never done anything as good as this!'" she told a reporter for *The Guardian*. "'By God, I can write! It's great! I'm going to be famous! I'll write another opera! And another! And another! That's what it felt like.'"

That surge of creative exhilaration was fueled by sleep deprivation and a heady personal transformation. Goodman, who had grown up in an observant Jewish home in Minnesota, had begun the process of converting to Christianity. Indeed, while writing *Klinghoffer* she was in the midst of a complete metamorphosis that involved exchanging an American accent for a British one, part of the journey that would lead a Jewish girl from Minnesota to become a Church of England parish priest.

"The Judaism I was raised in was strongly Zionist," she told the *Guardian* reporter. "It had two foci almost—the Shoah [the Holocaust] and the State of Israel, and they were related in the same way the crucifixion is related to the resurrection in Christianity. Even when I was a child, I didn't totally buy that. I didn't buy the State of Israel being the recompense for the murder of European Jewry, recompense not being quite the right word, of course. The word one wants would be more like apotheosis or elevation."

Reflecting on her disaffection with Judaism, she told the reporter about seeing a Holocaust documentary when she was eight years old. After it was over, a junior rabbi quoted from a song that begins "Cast out your wrath upon the goyim [a disparaging term for non-Jews]." She recalled thinking, "No, that's not the right answer.'"

"That thought is the thing that's brought me here," she continued— "here" being the church rectory where the interview took place. "And it has to do with Klinghoffer as well."

With the help of Alice Goodman's spiritual upheaval, Leon Klinghoffer became in 1991 a bellwether of Jewish angst, at least in New York, epicenter of the American Jewish world. When musicologist Robert Fink, professor at UCLA's Herb Alpert School of Music, evaluated wire service reports, newspaper articles, and classical music reviews written about the opera in 1991–1992, he concluded that "the

New York audience was uniquely hostile to the work." For Fink, the negative reaction to the opera wasn't so much about the Palestinians but the scene involving the Rumors, the fictional New Jersey friends created by Goodman. "It's about American Jews and the complexity of their identity," he said. "New York Jews were at a certain place vis-a-vis Israel and their own identities as Jews."

In a lengthy analysis written in 2005, Fink wrote, "Between the 1985 *Achille Lauro* hijacking and the premiere of *The Death of Klinghoffer*, almost every year brought a new attack on the integrity of American Jewish identity, and most of that pain was coming from the erstwhile source of comfort, the increasingly fractured and embattled State of Israel."

American Jews, the majority of whom thought of themselves as liberal minded, had begun to criticize Israel for a variety of reasons, including the rise in Israel of the ultra-Orthodox and the country's shift to the right. Perhaps most significant, however, was the first *intifada*, the "shaking off," a spontaneous outburst by Palestinians in the West Bank and Gaza that grew to last six years, ending with the Oslo Accords of 1993. This rebellion, which was initially led by coalitions of women group's, workers, academics—using Molotov cocktails and stones—transformed the image of the Palestinian struggle. Instead of being seen as a movement led by terrorists creating international havoc, Palestinians came to be regarded as the underdog, as they shifted tactics from hijacking to civil disobedience, boycotts, and sympathetic stone-throwing youths facing off against Israeli soldiers firing live rounds.

For Fink, *The Death of Klinghoffer*, especially the Rumor scene, became offensive and upsetting to New York Jewish audiences because "*it reflected perfectly their worst nightmares about their own conflicted identity as Jews back to them* [his emphasis]."

For Lisa and Ilsa, in September 1991, the wound was personal and ever present, not an expression of artistic or academic investigation. When a reporter asked Lisa and Ilsa to comment after they saw the opera at BAM, they released an angry statement: "We are outraged at the exploitation of our parents and the coldblooded murder of our father as the centerpiece of a production that appears to us to be anti-Semitic....While we understand artistic license, when it so clearly favors one point of view it is biased. Moreover, the juxtaposition of the plight of the Palestinian people with the coldblooded murder of an innocent disabled American Jew is both historically naïve and appalling."

Of the opera's three creators, only Alice Goodman chose to respond publicly, with words not designed for conciliation. "Anyone who attends this opera with an unprejudiced mind will perceive that it does honor to the destiny of the Jewish people and to the memory of Leon and Marilyn Klinghoffer," she said in a statement, released through a BAM publicity agent. "To those who come prepared to see and hear only what they want to see and hear, nothing one can say is of any use."

John Adams claimed his prerogative as composer and deleted the Rumor scene from the opera after the reception in Brooklyn. "In truth, I was glad to see it go," he wrote in his memoir. "The comedy of the Rumor family now seems in retrospect to be inappropriate and served only to obscure the seriousness of the rest of the opera." Soon enough, he and Peter Sellars went on to new projects with different emotional, historical, theatrical, musical, and intellectual conundrums to wrestle with. Alice Goodman, however, would never complete another published libretto. She told reporters she couldn't get work after *Klinghoffer*, although Adams and Sellars asked her to write libretti for two different pieces. She said she resigned from one of the projects "because of differences with the San Francisco Opera." Adams was surprised to read this in an article, after the former colleagues stopped speaking to each other. "My recollection is that she was unable to get liftoff, even after a year of waiting, and we finally had to go in another direction in order to make the deadline," he said. Goodman turned her attention to parish life, emerging occasionally to give pointed interviews. In 2017, when she published a collection of her libretti—a translation of *The Magic Flute* and the two Adams-Sellars collaborations—she reinstated the Rumor scene in *The Death of Klinghoffer.*

13

Finding Their Place
in the Story

Los Angeles, 1990

The hijacking of the *Achille Lauro* became, for Robert I. Friedman, another unsettling chapter in a decade-long campaign to discredit Rabbi Meir Kahane, founder of the Jewish Defense League (JDL). Friedman was a dedicated muckraker who frequently wrote for the left-leaning *Nation* and the *Village Voice* as well as liberal mainstream newspapers, including the *New York Times* and the *Los Angeles Times*. Friedman was described by his editors at *The Nation* as "the real thing: a courageous reporter who, operating freelance, made headlines exposing how the thuggish and the greedy, in all their guises as politicians, bankers, revolutionaries and mobsters, were preying on the weak." When other Jews called him self-hating, the journalist countered by saying it was his belief in humanistic Jewish values that motivated him to expose people like Kahane, whom he believed violated those principles.

For Friedman, Kahane's terrorist underground was a frightening manifestation of burgeoning Jewish fundamentalism in Israel, backed by right-wing politicians. In 1990, Friedman published his book *The False Prophet*, an exposé of Kahane's messianic journey from Brooklyn to Israel, a trail littered with victims of the JDL's racist vigilantism. One of those victims was Alex Odeh, whose murder was mired in a criminal investigation stymied by international politics.

Friedman met Kahane the first time in 1979, in his Jerusalem headquarters, an airless office that Kahane called the Museum of the

Potential Holocaust. The tiny space was crammed with Nazi flags and displays of anti-Semitic clippings from American hate groups. But for Kahane, the existential threat now came from Arabs. "As far as Kahane was concerned, no Jew in Israel, neither man, woman nor child, was safe as long as there was a single Arab in the country," wrote Friedman. Kahane publicly referred to Arabs as "dogs"; his professed goal, which he put in writing, was to remove all Arabs from Israel, calling them "a desecration of God's name."

Friedman wanted to know where this hatred came from. "People often ask me why I formed the JDL," Kahane told the journalist. "Was it personal trauma? No, I had an extremely pleasant life." He described his Brooklyn childhood fondly. "I loved my neighborhood, and my Jewish and Italian friends," he reminisced. Marty, as he was then known, was an athletic kid, good at Ping-Pong and basketball, but baseball was his passion—both playing and watching the Brooklyn Dodgers at Ebbets Field. Though he grew up during the Depression, deprivation wasn't part of his narrative. His father made a decent living as the rabbi in a large Orthodox congregation.

When Friedman scratched beneath the sentimental gloss, however, he found a family emotionally unhinged by its past. Kahane's parents, Charles and Sonia, had been protagonists in stories roiling with personal and historic trauma. Sonia grew up in Russia during the upheaval and starvation that accompanied the Bolshevik Revolution; her mother had been arrested and nearly executed for her involvement in student politics and taught her daughter not to take abuse from anyone. Charles came from a powerful Orthodox Hasidic family from Galicia, part of the Austro-Hungarian Empire. In the late 1800s Charles's father was sent by a rabbi to help rebuild Zefat, the ancient Kabbalist center whose population by then was largely Arab. Charles was born there, then sent at age thirteen to attend yeshiva in Oświęcim, Poland, which later would become infamous as the town closest to Auschwitz. After being ordained as a rabbi in 1922, at age seventeen, Charles moved to New York by himself, where he met Sonia.

Meir became the repository of their hopes for a Jewish future, which meant the bar for disappointment was set very low. "Maybe destiny sent him to bring redemption to his tortured people throughout the world," Charles once told a *New York Times* reporter, speaking about Meir with fatherly pride. But, Friedman observed, "if it ever seemed—as it often did—that young Meir was falling behind schedule in becoming the savior of his people, he was roundly ridiculed by his father."

Parental expectations and fears coalesced into a transformative moment in March 1938, when Meir Kahane was five years old. On the road between Haifa and Zefat, three Palestinian Arabs armed with machine guns ambushed a taxi carrying ten Jews home from a wedding party in Tel Aviv. "The massacre didn't take long," wrote Friedman. "Charles Kahane's sister-in-law Ziporah, who was thirty-seven, was shot twice in the chest and died instantly. Her seventy-one-year-old mother was shot three times in the head at point-blank range. In all, six people were murdered, including a young woman who survived the gunfire but was dragged to a stony slope, where she was gang-raped and hacked to death. One-year-old Rebecca, Ziporah's daughter, was found by police, buried alive under her mother's blood-soaked body."

Charles's brother Mordechai, who was in Tel Aviv when his wife and baby were murdered, soon moved into the Kahane home in Brooklyn, where he lived on and off for many years. Meir listened to his father and uncle discuss the massacre over Sabbath dinners, week after week, year after year. "The only antidote to Arab terror, the men declared, was Jewish counter-terror," Friedman wrote. "Even though Meir was then just a child, he was transfixed by his father's tales of Jewish heroism and Arab cruelty in Palestine." He became fascinated by strong biblical figures like King David, poet and warrior, remembered for his soulful Psalms and military exploits. Meir, whose adolescence overlapped with the Holocaust and its aftermath, became obsessed with the subject; in the seventh grade he invented a comic strip called "The Adventures of Bagelman," imagining Superman as a flying bagel that wore a cape, while saving Jews from Nazis.

Kahane and his followers became Nazi hunters, extortionists, and proponents of terrorist actions against those he considered PLO supporters, no matter where they lived. After immigrating to Israel in 1971, Kahane evolved from outsider lurking at the extreme fringe to part of the Israeli establishment, representing his party in the Knesset between 1984 and 1988. His acceptance in the mainstream—while still at the outer margins of legitimacy—reflected the change within Israel, away from the dominance of secular liberalism toward Jewish nationalism and religious rule. In the United States, according to an American Jewish Committee 1986 survey, 14 percent of American Jews expressed sympathy for Kahane, while 30 percent of Orthodox Jews supported him. Still, unfavorable views of Kahane outnumbered favorable impressions by a 7-to-1 margin—compared with a 10-to-1 margin favorable toward Labor party leader Shimon Peres.

Relying substantially on FBI sources, in his book Friedman describes a network of zealots who emigrated from America to Israel in the 1970s, drawn to Kahane and the JDL and its anti-Arab mission. At first, they kept their focus local, setting off bombs and killing Arabs who lived in Israel. In the 1980s, a group of these professional assassins turned their sights on targets in the United States. Senator James Abourezk of South Dakota, who founded the American-Arab Anti-Discrimination Committee (ADC), was a potential quarry; so was Alex Odeh, executive director of the ADC in Southern California. After the bombing that killed Odeh, the FBI tracked three suspects—Keith Fuchs, Andy Green, and Robert Manning, all followers of Meir Kahane—to the West Bank settlement of Kiryat Arba, described in a Justice Department document as "a haven for right-wing Jewish extremists."

A few months after Friedman's book was published, Kahane died as he lived—through political violence, assassinated in New York by an Egyptian-born American. The following year, in 1991, Robert Manning and his wife, Rochelle, were arrested in Israel on conspiracy charges related to a mail bomb explosion a decade earlier that had killed Patricia Wilkerson, a secretary in a computer company, for reasons that remained unexplained. (Robert Manning was extradited to the U.S. in 1993, where he was tried and convicted of murder, though he continued to deny any role in Odeh's death; Rochelle died in an Israeli prison in 1994.)

But there was no resolution in the Alex Odeh case. His killing remained an open investigation. An excerpt from Friedman's book, printed in the *Los Angeles Times*, only reminded Norma Odeh, Alex's widow, of the difference between her family and the Klinghoffers. In the five years that had passed since Alex's murder, the national media had devoted huge coverage to the trial of the hijackers. Then came the television movies. Now she heard that an opera was being made about Leon Klinghoffer. As the investigation into her husband's killers grew cold, Norma felt him disappearing altogether from the story of the *Achille Lauro*.

"If my husband was a Jew they would have hung those people who killed him," she said. "But he's a Palestinian. Who cares? Even though he's an American."

When she said "they," she clarified that she meant the government, not the many people she encountered in her daily life, including Jews, who showed unexpected kindness. The day Alex was killed, he was supposed to attend Friday night services at a synagogue, to light candles with the rabbi, who instead came to Alex's funeral. After Alex's death, because her face had been in the newspaper and on television, it felt to Norma that she was recognized everywhere she went. "They would approach me, and I would get so scared and they would say, 'We just want to give you our sympathy.' It didn't matter if we were Arab or a Jew, we were American. People made me feel better."

Norma stayed in touch with the Los Angeles Police Department and the FBI and made an annual trip to Washington, D.C., to meet with the ADC. However, the pursuit of justice was secondary to the more prosaic but overwhelming task of being head of her little household. Her family remained in Palestine and her relationship with her in-laws was complicated. When Alex was killed, she was twenty-six and didn't know how to shop, how to pump gas to fill up her car, how to write a check, how to deposit money in the bank. Alex had taken care of everything—to protect her, but his kindness left her vulnerable to living out her greatest fear, of being forced to repeat her mother's life. Just as Norma's father had when he died, her husband had left her a widow with three very young children. Even in the fog of sorrow she saw one thing clearly: she would not ever let her girls be separated from her the way she had been sent off.

Helena, the oldest, was hit the hardest by her father's death, even though she didn't immediately understand what had happened or why. When an aunt told her seven-year-old niece there was an accident and her daddy was in heaven, Helena realized her father was gone. In subsequent weeks she grew quiet and her long beautiful hair began to fall out. Norma saw that her daughter was depressed and asked what was wrong, but Helena said nothing

Norma and the girls moved to a new school district not long after Alex was killed. When she took the two older girls to the school, someone in the office asked Norma what language she spoke. "We can put your daughters into ESL classes," the woman said. Norma knew if she didn't stand up for her girls, no one would. "They were born here," she said. "They don't even speak Arabic, or just at home, a couple of words here or there." The girls were placed in regular classes. For the school administrators, the decision was simply clarification of a misunderstanding. But for Norma speaking up represented a small victory against rote assumptions about who her daughters were because their mother spoke English with an accent.

Norma wanted her daughters to fit in but also to be proud of who they were. "I explained their dad was a hero, a martyr, not just anybody," she said. This wasn't just a mother's desire to create a hallowed memory. Alex had shown Norma that his work was connected to the larger world. She wasn't shocked when bouquets of flowers started showing up at the house the day after Alex died; a new delivery arrived every day for five days, until the funeral. Nor was she surprised to see that they came from King Hussein of Jordan—or that a delegation from the Jordanian consul arrived at her home and gave Norma a watch, also a gift from the king. Alex's work had been important enough that when King Hussein used to visit Los Angeles with his wife, the American-born Queen Noor, they invited Norma and Alex to dinner. She kept the photographs taken of her standing next to the queen.

After Alex's death, when Queen Noor returned to Southern California, she invited Norma to meet with her at the Hotel Bel-Air a few more times. Norma remembered those get-togethers as fairy tale moments, suffused with the aura of loss. Queen Noor treated Norma like an intimate friend, shooing away the secret service agents following them when they took a walk through the hotel's luxurious gardens.

At first, Alex's income continued to provide for them, with the money from his worker's comp insurance. In addition, the ADC turned a fund-raising banquet Alex had arranged to take place in November, a month after his death, into a memorial for him, with all proceeds going to his widow and children. The family survived in this way until the youngest began school. Norma applied for a job as a bank teller and within a year became an operations officer. Eventually, her mother moved to the United States and stayed with the girls while Norma went to work. Norma got promoted again and found she loved making money and taking care of her family.

In 1989 she took the girls to the West Bank to visit their other grandmother, and then went back a year later because Norma's brother and his wife were having a baby. Her 1990 visit coincided with the fifth anniversary of Alex's death, October 11. When she walked out of her brother's house that morning, she was shocked. Alex's photograph was hanging from electricity lines all over Jifna. "Wherever you looked, there was Alex," she said. Her brother told her it was an annual tradition; Alex had become a martyr for the Palestinian cause.

Norma kept remembering the conversation she would have with Alex whenever he received threats. "What if they try to kill you?" she would ask. "It would be an honor to die for Palestine," he always replied. When Yasser Arafat invited her and her family to come to Tunisia, she declined. "I was scared to go for my girls," she said. "I didn't want us to go through this again."

On that same visit to Jifna, Norma had gone to nearby Ramallah on October 8, on an errand for her brother. As she walked down a street, someone pulled her inside a building and yelled at her, "Are you crazy? Don't you see the streets are empty?" Then she heard shots being fired by Israeli soldiers. Even when she saw they were shooting in the air, she was terrified. She didn't know that the police throughout the area were on high alert, following riots at the Temple Mount in Jerusalem, site of the Dome of the Rock and Al-Aqsa Mosque. A fringe Jewish group had come to the holy site to lay a cornerstone for the construction of a new temple, a deliberate violation of an Israeli government prohibition against the practice of any non-Muslim prayer there. In the third year of the first *intifada*, this provocation was explosive; two to three thousand Arabs threw rocks and metal tools at Israeli police; the police responded with gunfire. By the end of the day, at least 18 and possibly 23 Palestinians had been killed; 150 Palestinians were injured, along with 19 border policemen and 9 civilian Jews.

On the streets of Ramallah that day, Norma didn't need to know the source of the gunfire. To her, it didn't matter: one battle replaced the other, in an infinite continuum of violence. She knew the war would never end because both sides were fighting for land that represented a dream, not reality. Alex had that dangerous dream; she did not. "The shooting scared me to death," she said. "I just wanted to come home." When she said "home," she realized she was thinking of Southern California and the life she was building there for her children. That was her last trip back to her birthplace.

Montreal, 1991

In March 1991, as *Klinghoffer*'s creators were preparing for their opera's Belgian premiere, Samia Costandi was walking across the campus at McGill University. It was three o'clock in the afternoon. She felt peaceful, basking in the sense of tranquility she had just experienced during an afternoon stop in the small chapel at McGill's religious studies building.

As she headed home, she thought about the lucky break that had brought her and her sons to Montreal three years earlier. She had applied to the master's program at McGill—for a degree in teaching

English as a second language—and to escape the perpetual foreboding in Beirut. The day she received the acceptance letter was the happiest of her life. After arriving at McGill in 1988, she immediately changed her course of study to a more cerebral pursuit, philosophy of education. Her boys were enrolled in excellent schools, where they attended classes with children of all backgrounds. Even the Jewish kids didn't seem to care that they were Palestinian.

"Would I have imagined back in the early eighties when I was living in the Beirut inferno that I would end up in Montreal, Quebec, Canada?" she asked. "Could I have imagined that my children would also be going to school in a calm, friendly city and living a fairly secure and safe life?" Yet her serenity was shadowed by fear; no matter how peaceful things might seem, she was on constant alert, a habit that had become ingrained after living through years of civil war, after being the wife of Abu al-Abbas, who remained a part of her life and that of her children.

When she reached home, she offered a cheerful hello to the doorman and proceeded to her apartment on the seventh floor. She was preparing dinner for the boys when the doorbell rang.

"To say I was surprised would be an understatement," she would write about the incident. "No one could come to any apartment in our building without passing through the scrutiny of the security guard, and without calling us for permission to enter. Besides, we were not so familiar with the neighbors that any of them would knock at our door for a visit. Both my boys had keys; it was still early for them to arrive from school. Perhaps one of them forgot his keys, I speculated? Could a close friend be playing a joke on us—my good friends knew I was neurotic about security—but then the security guard would not have played along....I looked through the keyhole and saw a man and a woman. I opened the door, and looked at them apprehensively. 'Yes?'

"'We are from the RCMP [Royal Canadian Mounted Police].'"

Samia asked to see their ID cards. She had been anticipating this moment—or something like it—since she'd arrived in Canada as a single mother with two young boys. A ripple of fear went through her, recalling the terror she felt throughout her marriage to Abu al-Abbas. After the agents showed her their IDs, she stood there, debating with herself whether to invite them inside. What if they were Mossad agents disguised as RCMP? Or some other enemy? She'd lived through enough unexplained assassinations in Beirut to expect the worst.

To her relief, the government agents conformed to a Canadian cliché: they were low-key, courteous, literate. Assuring Samia that this was not an interrogation, they proceeded to ask her if she had any security concerns. Had she received suspicious calls, hate mail? They mentioned that they knew she had spoken at a forum at McGill called "Teach-in-Troops-Out" after the Gulf War ended. Yes, she said, inviting them to come hear her speak again, at a graduate school conference on "Language and War." The male agent scribbled the date in his notebook and said he would try to attend.

Then they zeroed in on what seemed to be the true purpose of the visit—to ask her about her marriage to Abu al-Abbas. When did they divorce? Did he remarry? Had her husband changed his views over the years? "Oh, immensely," she said. "He has mellowed much and has come to believe in the power of politics as a viable alternative to military struggle." She didn't go into the excruciating and alienating part of their marriage and divorce, focusing on the support he sent her for the boys, even telling the visitors about the painful history—the dislocation, the refugee camp upbringing—that led to her husband's political choices.

As visits from the government go, it was a pleasant encounter. She served the agents coffee, they told her they loved tabbouleh. The male officer told her, "I feel that there is a golden opportunity to make peace between the Arabs—namely the Palestinians—and the Israelis, today."

Samia was touched by the agent's quixotic hopefulness. He seemed genuinely sincere, but the experience was demeaning nonetheless. "The whole issue of having to prove my legitimacy as a human being weighed on me," she wrote later. "It seemed like a crime to simply be born a Palestinian and a greater crime not to hide it." (Samia didn't seem to consider that she was also the ex-wife of a fugitive still wanted for the *Achille Lauro* hijacking, and thus someone who might know something about his movements.)

How could she explain to strangers the intensity of feeling for Palestine, when she had spent her early years in Cyprus and England, most of her life in Beirut, and now lived in Montreal? Urbane and intellectual as her parents had been, they conveyed the sense to their children that their existence in all these places, including Lebanon, was transitory. Samia carried transcendent childhood memories of annual family reunions in Birzeit, the village twenty-five miles north of Jerusalem, in the West Bank, where her mother had grown up. She remembered her summer visits there as exhilarating, filled with enchanting hours spent dreaming under a large fig tree in her great-aunt's garden. Those Proustian imprints ended with the Six-Day War in 1967, when the West Bank fell under Israeli administration. Restrictions on travel became prohibitive. Israeli checkpoints were humiliating, and Lebanon refused to readmit residents with Israeli stamps on their passports.

Family conversations were filled with speculation about returning to their beloved Palestine. During car rides to the mountains, she saw tears streaming down her parents' faces whenever the radio played "Raji-oun" ("We Will Return"), an homage to Jerusalem sung to a haunting setting by the revered Lebanese vocalist known simply as Fairuz.

Now that Samia was living in Canada, experiencing a new kind of freedom for herself and her sons, she was determined to make her voice heard. This would be her life's work, her way of creating a better world for Khaled and Omar. Yet how would she shield her boys from danger? The long civil war in Lebanon had officially ended, but Beirut—where her parents still lived—was a scarred and broken city, its elegant streets filled with rubble from buildings gutted by bombs and gunfire. The fighting between the Maronite Christians and Muslims may have stopped, but in Lebanon, as elsewhere, Palestinians remained pawns of repressive Arab regimes—isolated in refugee camps, denied citizenship, barred from work outside the camps, denied due process. Wealthy Palestinians bought legitimacy, one way or the other. Her boys were now citizens of a Western democracy, yet every year she sent them back to the Middle East, to spend time with their father. Abu al-Abbas lived in Iraq, another war zone. She wanted to create a different world for her sons, even as she tried to convey love for Palestine dramatized by the tears of their grandparents. She wanted her boys to feel free, even though the *Achille Lauro* had made their father a pariah in the West. She wanted them to feel safe, while making sure they knew never to mention the name of Abu al-Abbas to anyone outside the closest family circle.

Samia heard the front door open. When she looked up and saw Khaled, her older son, who was thirteen years old, she rushed over to greet him. "We have two people from the secret service of the Canadian government visiting us," she whispered.

Khaled stopped in the living room to say a brief and quiet hello, then disappeared into his room. Samia worried about him. He was bright—he had skipped two grades and was already in high school—but he had suffered from the years of civil war in Beirut. Samia had been beset by depression throughout her life and recognized the symptoms. She knew Khaled was anxious about his father, though he kept his thoughts to himself.

A few minutes later there was another click of keys. Ten-year-old Omar swept into the room in a dramatic entrance that revealed a different personality from his brother's. His hair was tousled; he was complaining loudly about not wanting to study French, while managing to seem adorable. Samia could see he had charmed the visitors, as he did everyone. She told him to go play in his room. "These are people from the government and they are helping us."

He complied. Later, after the agents left, Samia felt spent from holding back her emotions during the polite exchange. She thought about how readily Omar accepted her explanation. "One would think that he would ask, 'Helping us with what?' But my children did not ask such questions. They knew that we needed a lot of help."

✳   ✳   ✳

Samia never stopped sending the boys to spend summers with Abu al-Abbas and Reem. Omar's strongest memories of his father were from Iraq, and the garden he planted. It was lush, not like the dry soil in Tunisia. Omar remembered a banana tree and date tree. Later there was a farm, where ostriches, peacocks, pigeons, and geese roamed; Saddam Hussein gave it to Abu al-Abbas and the other Palestinians living in Iraq to grow food.

In Omar's memory, the farm became nirvana, a chance to discover more about his father. "My fondest memories were just walking with him around the farm, and him telling me about his life," Omar recalled. "He always wanted to impart knowledge. He would ask me questions about geography and biology, history and the way the world works. He would tell me about the history of the Arab world. We would have debates with his friends about religion from an historical standpoint. He would talk about his travels around the world and how he learned Russian from a beautiful Russian girl he met while he was training there."

On the farm Omar saw relationships that made him feel as if he understood something primal about his father. He noticed that in the clusters of peacocks and ostriches, there was always a dominant male who ruled the others. "When you got close, you could see the male was always alert and the females were just chilling," he said. "One of the peacock males was the main guy—he made the other male just sit in the corner. Even the ostriches: I remember there was a dominant male who was the one always looking out for everyone. I remember my dad warned me, 'Watch out, don't get too close.'"

As he grew older and saw his father continue to be vilified in the Western press, Omar wondered what it would have been like if his father had been an American general who lived in Ohio, a general who had been in charge of military operations that resulted in civilian deaths. "People would say, 'Oh, you're a son of general whoever,'" he fantasized. "I would wear that as a badge of honor. And I do, in the Arab world."

14

Sidelined by History

Baghdad, 1986–2004

J ust as the Klinghoffer sisters saw Abu al-Abbas's freedom as a failure of justice, Abu al-Abbas began to resent the mere mention of
Leon Klinghoffer. To him, the sanctification of Klinghoffer above all
other victims sacrificed in the Middle East represented the unfairness
he had spent his life fighting against. It was as if this one American
were the only civilian who had ever been killed as part of the conflict.
"I wish the names of our victims and martyrs were as well known as the
name of Klinghoffer," he said. "Can you name ten Palestinians who
died from Israeli gas, or ten pregnant Palestinian women who were
crushed and killed?"

So long as people remembered Klinghoffer's name, Abbas would
not be able to shake the curse of the *Achille Lauro*. Nevertheless, at
times it seemed the PLF leader didn't want to do so, like when he
threatened to attack America on NBC less than a year after the hijacking. After that 1986 interview, Yasser Arafat distanced himself from
Abbas. In 1987, the PLF leader was dropped from the PLO's executive committee, the leadership body of the PLO's Palestine National
Council, which acted as a parliament in exile for the nonexistent state.
PLO officials told reporters that Abbas had become "too much of an
embarrassment and a political liability." However, Abbas attended the
meeting and told reporters that he had stepped down from the executive committee voluntarily.

In November 1988, just one year later, Abbas was back in the inner circle, appearing at the Palestine National Council in Algiers at the personal invitation of Arafat, accompanied by his wife, Reem, and Ali, their toddler. When the family arrived, Arafat himself was there to greet them, embracing Abbas in front of a crowd of reporters. Photographers snapped pictures of Abu al-Abbas picking up Ali, who had crawled out of the car and grabbed his father's knees.

Arafat was cagey as always when discussing Abbas's status. When a *Time* reporter asked why he endorsed a terrorist like Abu al-Abbas by keeping him on the executive committee, Arafat answered: "He was elected. I can't prevent that. [Israeli Prime Minister Yitzhak] Shamir, who was wanted by Interpol, was later elected and is the prime minister. This is democracy. I did not elect Abu al-Abbas. It was the Palestine National Council that elected him. And a part of the reason is this, that it was a matter of indignity, national indignity, when Reagan breached the agreement with President Mubarak and they hijacked the plane and tried to put him in jail, that caused a reaction of sympathy for him."

Abbas, tall and imposing in a businessman's suit, had a front-row seat at the meeting in Algiers. Arafat, his small and scruffy leader, marched into the hall wearing his usual military uniform with a pistol on his hip and made an astounding declaration. "The Palestine National Council announces in the name of God, in the name of the people, of the Arab Palestinian people, the establishment of the state of Palestine in our Palestinian nation, with holy Jerusalem as its capital." He did not call for the destruction of Israel. "Senior Palestinian leaders said the declaration, in calling for a two-state arrangement, implicitly recognizes the right of Israel to exist and that it had the support of the great majority of their followers," reported the *New York Times*. Abbas clapped and cheered along with everyone else in the room.

Abbas couldn't maintain the role of diplomat for long. A reporter's inquiry about Klinghoffer during the PLO gathering triggered a feeble joke that was guaranteed to sound cruel. "Maybe he was trying to swim for it," Abbas said, before giving a halfhearted apology. "We are sorry when innocent people are victims of the situation, but we are not sorry for the operation because the operation was against Israel."

Abbas's words had repercussions for Arafat. Two weeks after the Algiers conference, Secretary of State George Shultz denied Arafat's visa application, preventing him from attending the U.N. General Assembly in New York. "The most recent sign of Mr. Arafat's associations with terrorism," the official State Department statement read, "was the presence at the Algiers session of the Palestine National Council this month of [Abu al-Abbas], a member of the Executive Committee of the PLO who has been convicted by the Italian judicial system of the murder of an American citizen, Mr. Leon Klinghoffer." Shultz was particularly aggrieved by the "swim for it" remark.

The General Assembly voted to move its session to Geneva, so Arafat could attend, and Shultz relented, saying he would resume talks with Arafat if the Palestinian leader would renounce terrorism in Geneva. Arafat complied, renouncing terrorism and acknowledging the State of Israel.

Even as Arafat was making overtures toward peace, Abbas was about to meet with Libyan dictator Muammar el-Qaddafi—with the blessings of Arafat and Saddam Hussein, he assured his wife. It had been scary enough being under the protection of Saddam, but Reem al-Nimer was terrified of any association with Qaddafi, a man who eliminated his enemies in public executions. He supported the most violent terrorist groups, like Abu Nidal's, vicious combatants who openly and deliberately targeted civilians. What frightened Reem most was Qaddafi's theatrical craziness. He was bizarre, conducting meetings in a giant tent that traveled the world with him, dressing in flowing multicolored gowns, protected by female bodyguards outfitted in combat fatigues, red nail polish, and high-heeled sandals.

Crazy perhaps, but strategic. Born in a tent to illiterate Bedouin parents who devoted themselves to his education, Qaddafi had come to power almost twenty years earlier, at age twenty-seven, after a coup d'état. He idolized President Gamal Abdel Nasser of Egypt and his message of Arab unity and socialism, though Qaddafi's brand of socialism was dictatorial, anti-Western, and dangerously mystical. He bankrolled an array of violent groups, including the Irish Republican Army, the Italian Red Brigades, and various African organizations.

Abbas knew that becoming Qaddafi's ally was treacherous business, but they shared a common goal. The Palestinian cause was one of many Qaddafi supported in his quest to undermine Western dominance, though his ideology was difficult to pin down beyond a desire for permanent revolution. Abbas had one cause, and control of it was slipping away from him and the rest of the old guard; center stage of the Palestinian movement had been commandeered by the *intifada*'s young Palestinian stone-throwers within the occupied territories. Compared with unarmed teenagers putting their lives directly on the line, Abbas and even Arafat seemed distant and out of touch, spectators to the revolution from their comfortable exiles in Tunis and Baghdad. Abbas felt that staging a successful blow at Israel would put him back in the action. He recognized that his secular, left-wing brand of pan-Arab nationalism was losing ground, as the repressive regimes that had ruled Arab countries for decades were weakened. The future was becoming apparent with the ascendancy of Hamas, begun in Gaza as an offshoot of the Egyptian Muslim Brotherhood, cementing loyalty through ground-level charity coupled with a drumbeat of hatred. With fundamentalist Islamic religious fervor its core, Hamas was growing into a far more threatening form of opposition to Israel.

Abu al-Abbas traveled to Tripoli, Libya, on fake passports provided by the Iraqi government in July 1989, seven months after Libya was implicated in a horrific act of terrorism, the blowing up of Pam Am Flight 103, a regularly scheduled flight between Frankfurt and Detroit via London and New York. All of the 243 passengers and 16 crew members were killed; so were an additional 11 people on the ground, as debris fell onto the town of Lockerbie, Scotland. With 189 American victims, this was at the time the deadliest terrorist attack ever on American civilians. By aligning himself with Qaddafi, Abbas was ratifying his status as an enemy of the United States. Abbas convinced himself that he could accept financial support from Libya without being tainted by ties to its diabolical leader. Countries made deals with the devil all the time, he told himself. The United States had been allied with Stalin, numerous South American despots, and more recently Saddam. Israel built a huge armaments industry selling weapons to customers that included its own enemies, even Iran.

The meeting with Qaddafi was the first of many over a period of eighteen months. Once again, Abbas—the man who was afraid of water—was determined to invade Israel with yet another assault from the Mediterranean, with backing from Libya. When he described the improbable plan, Reem saw that he was happy for the first time since the *Achille Lauro.* "With the enthusiasm of a sixteen-year-old, he would sit with me during the night and tell me how his troops would impose a stunning defeat," she recalled.

Abbas was determined to get it right this time and Qaddafi spared no expense: He paid for seven hundred Palestinian fighters and staff people to fly in and out of Libya, and provided the PLF with villas, automobiles, military experts, passports, and military camps in the Libyan desert. Abbas spent entire days without sleep, training with his men. By Reem's count, her husband met with Qaddafi eleven times. Sometimes Reem flew to Tripoli with him, though she never met Qaddafi.

The closest she came was when she was asked to host a dinner for Qaddafi's brother-in-law at the home Qaddafi had provided Abbas during his visits to Libya. Reem took her cooking seriously, beginning the process hours ahead. While she was in the kitchen, Qaddafi sent a motorcade to bring Abu al-Abbas to his palace. Dinnertime came and went without word from Abbas. "Ugly thoughts began flowing through my head," Reem said. "I was certain that Abu al-Abbas had fallen into a trap and that Qaddafi had lured him into Libya to eliminate him." She sat on the porch of the house, and began to cry, as she had so many times during her marriage to Abbas.

Twenty-four hours after he left, he returned, annoyingly exhilarated. After calming Reem down, he told her of the strange journey he had been on—taken to see Qaddafi by means of train, helicopter, car, motorbike, and rubber boat. He sounded high, except she knew he didn't indulge in drugs; an occasional glass of wine and cigarettes were his modest vices. He told her that the trip ended up in the middle of the desert, where he encountered Qaddafi, dressed in bright orange, sitting on top of a mammoth, man-made stone. "He was meditating, Reem, and wanted me to meditate with him," Abbas told his wife.

Abbas was laughing in disbelief as he told his wife the story. Then he said, "He's crazy, Reem! Absolutely crazy!" Reem saw that her husband wasn't scared by the dangerous alliance. Rather, he was juiced. Qaddafi was giving the Palestinian leader the wherewithal for the grand play that would get the PLF back in the game. He told her the plan: four rubber boats, launched from Libya on the north coast of Africa, would travel through the Mediterranean to Nizanim beach, south of Tel Aviv, only twenty minutes from Ashdod. The PLF forces, young men recruited from refugee camps around Damascus, Beirut, and Amman—like the *Achille Lauro* hijackers—would disembark at the Israeli coastline and confront Israeli security forces.

The invasion, scheduled for May 30, 1990, was timed to coincide with an Arab League summit in Baghdad, hosted by Saddam. Reem was struck by the paradox that both Saddam and Qaddafi were endorsing the Abbas maneuver. "Qaddafi [was] making common cause with the Iranians at a time when Saddam was pummeling them with missiles," she wrote. But they had one overriding aim, in her view. "Both wanted to polish their credentials as Arab nationalists, and nothing would do that better than embracing the Palestinian cause."

The attack was another disaster for Abbas. The speedboats malfunctioned before they reached shore; Israeli security forces killed four of the Palestinian commandos and captured twelve others. There were no Israeli casualties.

For Abbas, the episode became a nightmarish repeat of the *Achille Lauro*. One of the captured PLF men said he believed that the goal of the operation was to kill civilians, though Abu al-Abbas insisted the targets were Israeli Army installations and the U.S. embassy in Tel Aviv. It didn't matter that Israeli military authorities backed Abu al-Abbas's claim. Just as before, Abbas's folly had repercussions for Arafat. Within a week of the foiled attack, the United States suspended talks with the PLO, demanding that the leadership punish Abbas or expel him from their umbrella organization. A PLO official told reporters Abu al-Abbas acted without authority and described the scheme as "a children's game." Within a year, Arafat once again dropped Abu al-Abbas from the executive committee.

Abbas didn't accept defeat. One of his sons said of him, "He was always positive; the world was going upside down, but he was always smiling." Less than four months after the failed mission, Abbas agreed to an interview with *Wall Street Journal* reporter Tony Horwitz. Their meeting took place in Baghdad shortly after Iraqi troops invaded Kuwait on August 2, 1990, igniting the Gulf War, which America and its allies would enter five months later.

Horwitz was strip-searched and driven to the meeting by guards who poked AK-47s in his nostrils. It was a harrowing ride; the Mercedes-Benz careened through back streets, finally stopping in front of a one-story building where young men holding machine guns lurked in the bushes.

Once inside, however, Horwitz felt the atmosphere change. Abu al-Abbas was disarming, greeting his guest with an apology. "I am sorry for the welcome," he said, with a nod at the guards standing by the window. "This is my life."

Over tea and Turkish coffee—while going through two packs of Marlboro cigarettes—Abbas, an engaging and observant storyteller, charmed the reporter. "Soft-voiced, his face wrinkles easily into laughter," Horwitz wrote of the PLF leader. "He speaks passable English and florid Arabic, filled with metaphor and rhythmic locutions. A graduate of Arabic literature from the University of Damascus, he also appears to be well-read. His favorite Western writer, he says, is William Shakespeare—'particularly the tragedies.' He says he was a school teacher in Syria before becoming a full-time 'freedom fighter.'"

In a markedly human portrait that didn't conform to terrorist stereotyping, Horwitz described a powerful man with an intellectual bent who once wanted to be a literature professor, sitting behind a messy desk. The reporter observed that the walls of Abbas's office were hung with photographs of his commandos in speedboats headed to attack Israel.

Abbas insisted on the distinction between acts of terrorism and acts of war, acknowledging that sometimes innocents got in the way. "Accidents happen," he told Horwitz. He showed the reporter his battle scars, though he sidestepped the question of whether he personally had killed anyone. "During the fight, you don't know what happens," he said. He asserted that he didn't regret the failed attack on Tel Aviv, even if it resulted in America's cutting off discussions with the PLO. "For two years we say yes, yes, yes to America, without results," he said in English. But he told Horwitz he wasn't against a negotiated settlement, if the terms were right.

It would strike Horwitz later how strangely comfortable it was to talk to Abu al-Abbas. "It felt odd to be calmly sipping tea and talking about Shakespeare with this wanted terrorist," he remembered. "I don't recall feeling alarmed or afraid, or any more so than I always did when reporting in Saddam's Iraq, by far the worst of many police states I visited. Being Jewish wasn't a big deal either, except when it came to getting visas to countries that technically didn't allow Jews in."

But a cold side emerged when Horwitz asked Abbas about Leon Klinghoffer. The PLF leader was unapologetic, even annoyed. "Klinghoffer, always I hear about this Klinghoffer," he said. "Nobody knows all the people who die in Palestine. But this Klinghoffer is like Jesus Christ."

As if to prove Abbas's point, less than two years later, Klinghoffer and the *Achille Lauro* were in the news again. In 1992, Abu al-Abbas's old friend Monzer al-Kassar was arrested in Madrid, charged with supplying the AK-47 assault rifles and hand grenades used in the hijacking. His accuser was Omar al-Assadi, the hijacker known as *il penitente*—the repented, a witness for the state—who from prison identified the arms dealer in a photograph.

Kassar, who was three years older than Abbas, met the future PLF leader casually when they were students in Damascus in the 1960s, taking part in street demonstrations for a variety of national and international causes. They became close later, in the late 1970s, after Kassar opened an office in Beirut on Hamra Street and started hearing about a prominent young Palestinian leader called Abu al-Abbas, and then discovered Abbas was the Mohammed Zaidan he'd known from their protest days in Damascus.

Kassar was of Arab Syrian descent, not Palestinian, but he sympathized with the cause and admired Abbas. A close bond wasn't formed, however, until Kassar came under scrutiny for smuggling weapons to the Muslim Brotherhood for use in an attack against the regime of Syrian dictator Hafez al-Assad (the father of the modern-day Syrian leader, Bashar al-Assad). Even though Kassar's father had been part of Assad's government, the Syrian leader's volatile brother Rifaat threatened to have Monzer hanged. Monzer's older brother Ghassan, his mentor in the arms trade, heard that Abu al-Abbas had PLF training camps in Syria and was then on good terms with the Assad regime (that would change). Ghassan met Abbas in Beirut and asked him to intervene. Abbas allowed Monzer to hide out in his apartment in Beirut for a month, while the PLF leader assured the Syrians that Kassar wasn't allied with Assad's enemies, it was just business. Assad agreed to absolve Monzer, cementing Kassar's loyalty to Abu al-Abbas.

"People would think a hundred times before going against his evil wishes," Kassar said, referring to Rifaat al-Assad, who some referred to as the Butcher of Hama for his role in a 1982 massacre that took the lives of an estimated twenty thousand Muslim Brotherhood rebels and destroyed large parts of that Syrian city. Yet even though he and Abbas were not yet close, said Kassar, "he opened his heart to me and saved my life."

Kassar's affection for Abu al-Abbas seemed genuine. He never forgot the intervention that kept him from the gallows. Years later, when asked to describe their relationship, Kassar translated an old Arabic saying, "In life, you can always find a brother who's not being born to your mother." Abbas was the only person, besides family, present at Kassar's marriage at age thirty-six to Raghdaa Habbal, the seventeen-year-old daughter of a prominent Syrian family in Beirut. When Abu al-Abbas decided to marry the second time, the ceremony—to the woman Kassar called "the amazing Mrs. Reem"—took place in Damascus, in Kassar's home, on February 4, 1982.

Reem did not return the compliment. "I was never comfortable sitting with Monzer," she said. "I don't remember that I had a lot of sympathy for him. I had a lot of sympathy for his wife. But he is not a real person. He is not genuine. He is a very smart man but at the same time—you know, not everybody can work in buying and selling arms or drugs. Maybe he really did like Abu al-Abbas and Abu al-Abbas did trust him in many things…but he was an arms dealer. An arms dealer would sell his mother if he had to."

Kassar spent more than a year in a Spanish jail after his arrest before posting bond of $15.5 million. His trial took place in Madrid during the winter of 1994–1995. The proceeding was a disaster for his accusers. Responding to charges that he had personally flown to Poland to pick up the weapons used in the hijacking, Kassar (a trained pilot) testified, "I am not sick or dumb enough to risk my plane, which is worth five million dollars, to go to Poland to pick up four Kalashnikovs." Many witnesses became unavailable due to circumstances a reporter referred to as "a string of misfortunes"—one fell from a fifth-story window, another's children were kidnapped, another kept changing his testimony. Kassar was acquitted on all counts.

While Monzer al-Kassar was awaiting trial in Spain for supplying arms to the *Achille Lauro*, Abu al-Abbas was being sidelined by history. On September 13, 1993, Yasser Arafat shook hands with Israeli Prime Minister Yitzhak Rabin on the White House lawn as President Bill Clinton looked on, confirming the principles of the Oslo Accords. The PLO's mantra now was the peaceful pursuit of Palestinian self-government in Israeli-occupied Gaza and the West Bank. Abbas was still responsible for the PLF, but the group's numbers had shrunk to a few hundred people in Iraq, Lebanon, and Tunisia. Abbas's attempts to create businesses for PLF members, with the permission of the Iraqi government, had failed in large part because Iraq's economy was a mess, stricken by sanctions after the invasion of Kuwait. Also, in his wife Reem's words, Abbas "didn't have a businessman character of mind." He was a military man.

The handshake between Arafat and Rabin—however reluctant— had been reported in the American press in emotional, mythological terms. The *New York Times* called the agreement between battle-scarred foes "a triumph of hope over history." Thomas Friedman, who had become a journalistic fixture in the Middle East scene, conveyed the intensity of the moment in the *Times*: "Mr. Rabin, whose face is etched with the memories of every Arab-Israeli war, captured in his remarks the exhaustion of all parties with the centuries-old conflict," wrote Friedman. "'We the soldiers who have returned from the battle stained with blood,' he said, 'we who have fought against you, the Palestinians, we say to you today in a loud and clear voice: 'Enough of blood and tears! Enough!'"

The story continued, "Mr. Arafat, relishing his moment of acceptance on the White House lawn, strove to give Mr. Rabin the appropriate response, declaring in Arabic: 'Our two peoples are awaiting today this historic hope, and they want to give peace a real chance.'"

However, foreshadowing the gloomy future, Friedman cautioned, "But much difficult work, many more compromises, will now have to be performed by these same two men to make it a lasting moment."

Optimism was the officially sanctioned mood. Not long after the White House rapprochement, back in Tunis, Arafat and his wife, Suha, invited Abbas and Reem to dinner. The Abbases often visited Tunisia, where the PLF maintained military camps; these and training grounds in Iraq kept alive the possibility that Abbas still had a purpose. After they ate, Arafat laid out his vision for the new Palestinian National Authority, using maps he spread across the dinner table to illustrate. "*This* is going to become ours once again!" he told his guests. "*That* is going to be given to us by the Israelis. See that point over there? *It*, too, will be with the Palestinians. All of this section will be ours."

Abu al-Abbas nodded but said nothing. Reem could see from the skeptical look in his eyes that he didn't believe a word of it. He didn't believe in the Palestinian National Authority, its toadying police, its truncated version of Palestine. That night, while they drove home, Abbas said to her, "Either he is lying, or the Americans and Israelis are lying to him."

She saw his distress and pitied him. "Can it be true, Reem?" he asked her. "Can it be true that they are going to be giving up all of that? I don't trust them. I never did."

Abbas had never been politically adept like Arafat, the guerrilla warrior who managed to transform himself from vilified terrorist to Nobel laureate when he shared the 1994 prize with Rabin and Israeli Foreign Affairs Minister Shimon Peres. The long, wary alliance of the two Palestinian leaders was built on a risky premise; while Arafat tried to convince Western leaders that he was serious about pursuing peace, he needed an ally like Abbas from among the militant Palestinian factions, to reassure Palestinians and Arab allies that the PLO had a military option in reserve.

Hamas and other extremist Islamic groups responded to the Rabin-Arafat effort by stepping up terrorist attacks within Israel, including suicide bombings that murdered Israeli civilians in Tel Aviv and Jerusalem; the casualty rate among Israelis between 1994 and 1996 soared to record levels. The Israelis hit back hard; Palestinian civilian casualties were double those of Israeli civilians in that period. In addition to the government response, the Israelis had their own extremist groups wreaking vengeance. On February 25, 1994, Baruch Goldstein, a fundamentalist Jewish immigrant from the United States and a follower of Meir Kahane, murdered twenty-nine Palestinians worshipping in the Cave of the Patriarchs in Hebron, a site sacred to both Jews and Muslims.

Arafat survived because he was a political animal, constantly pivoting between diplomatic and military maneuvering, whatever it took to achieve his goals, including changing them. Abbas was a purist, who stuck to an uncompromising dream of a Palestinian homeland. He didn't support Hamas and its charter proclaiming religious *jihad*. He told his sons that he didn't care if Israeli people stayed, but the government had to change, to give equal rights to everyone. But Abbas couldn't articulate how this could possibly be achieved.

The *Achille Lauro* remained a metaphor for Abbas's failure, even during the cruise ship's inglorious finale. On December 2, 1994, less than two months after the announcement of the Nobel Prize for Arafat, Rabin, and Peres, the ship sank into the Indian Ocean, off the coast of Somalia, after an explosion caused by a fire in the engine room. There were 979 passengers and crew on board; two of the passengers died, one of them, apparently, of a heart attack. Captain De Rosa had retired the previous year, apparently over frustration that the shipping company didn't maintain the ship adequately.

Less than a year later, on November 4, 1995, Yitzhak Rabin was assassinated in Tel Aviv by an ultra-Orthodox Jew, as a protest against the Oslo Accords. Arafat was living in Gaza by then and was urged by Israeli security not to attend Rabin's funeral. Later that week, however, the PLO leader flew to Tel Aviv to offer condolences to Rabin's widow, Leah; the visit was believed to be Arafat's first time in Israel. The already dim prospects for peace soon became dimmer. Within a year of the assassination Benjamin Netanyahu—the man accused by Leah Rabin of fueling the anger that led to her husband's murder—would become prime minister, effectively burying the hope for the wide-ranging peace promised by the Oslo Accords.

Age forty-seven as the calendar turned to 1996, Abu al-Abbas felt prematurely old, already a relic. The desk in his office was still piled with papers, which he needed glasses to read, and he continued to meet with his men, but the routine felt empty. He began to spend more and more time on the plot of land the Iraqis had given him to grow vegetables that he brought home for Reem to cook.

For the Palestinians in Iraq, Abu al-Abbas remained the Godfather, the man who could get things done. He still had power to intercede with the Iraqi government. He received visits from supplicants like a Palestinian woman who came to the house for protection from Uday Hussein, Saddam's despotic oldest son, who told her he would release her husband from jail if she sent her daughter to one of his orgiastic "parties," where raping women was part of the entertainment. Through his connection with Saddam, Abbas was able to smuggle her and her children out of Iraq within forty-eight hours. Most of the favors, however, while important to the people making the requests, were mundane, involving jobs and domestic disputes.

That spring, however, Abu al-Abbas received an invitation from Yasser Arafat that, his wife Reem said, "brought him back to life." Abbas was to be one of five hundred delegates to the first meeting of the Palestine National Council to be held in Gaza, not in exile. He would now enter the land that his parents fled with permission of the State of Israel, under amnesty agreements that followed Oslo. The anticipation turned him into a nervous wreck, smoking even more than usual.

The purpose of the council was to keep Oslo alive by carrying out a critical component of the Accords, to amend the 1964 Palestinian covenant by deleting warmongering articles like No. 15, which declared it a duty "to repulse the Zionist, imperialist invasion from the great Arab homeland and to purge the Zionist presence from Palestine." Israeli Prime Minister Shimon Peres insisted that the PLO remove all references to the destruction of the Jewish state from its charter before peace negotiations could begin.

The PLO meeting in Gaza took place despite escalating violence in the region. Several Palestinian officials, including PFLP leader George Habash, boycotted the meeting, which coincided with an Israeli bombing of southern Lebanon that killed scores of civilians. The Israelis were retaliating against rockets launched into northern Israel by Hezbollah, a violation of a 1993 cease-fire brokered by Washington in conjunction with the Oslo talks. Gaza itself had been under tight restrictions following a series of Palestinian suicide bombings in Israel. Jewish as well as Arab hard-liners objected to the Gaza meeting, for opposing reasons. The Palestinians saw the gathering as undermining their ambition of taking back the land; the Israelis viewed it as legitimizing terrorists by recognizing them as politicians. Jerusalem Mayor Ehud Olmert, of the opposition Likud party, said having the PLO leaders in Israel was like giving a kosher certificate to murderers.

"At first glance, the gray-haired men swarming seaside Gaza in blazers and windbreakers and exchanging brotherly kisses look like Arab businessmen arriving at a trade show," wrote Marjorie Miller in the *Los Angeles Times*, of the gathering that began April 23, 1996. "They suck in their paunches, sit down to cigarettes and strong coffee and say how very good it is to meet again."

Miller continued, "These are no average conventioneers. They are old time guerillas, the authors of the 1972 Munich Olympics massacre, the 1985 *Achille Lauro* hijacking and numerous other terrorist attacks during more than two decades of war against Israel."

She interviewed Abu al-Abbas, who said he would support the motion that effectively recognized the legitimacy of the State of Israel. "Arafat is my close friend," Abbas told reporters. "If he needs my help in getting the votes he needs for serving the Palestinian people, I will help him." He openly wept as he spoke of Haifa, whence his family fled in 1948. "It is my right to return to my homeland and live here," he said.

Abbas apologized for the *Achille Lauro* and said he was a different man now. "The *Achille Lauro* was a mistake," he declared. "My mentality has changed from military to political." Yet even at this moment of reconciliation, Abbas kept his options open. "The struggle of the Palestinian people should continue in the present and carry on into the future," he said.

Rome, 1996

FOR THE men who hijacked the *Achille Lauro*, there had been only one struggle for the past decade, the struggle for survival. The grinding dullness of prison offered limitless opportunity to think about their failed mission and what its purpose had been. As their youth slipped away, each of them was alone with his thoughts; except for a brief overlap, they were kept in separate prisons in different cities. Each had time to ponder whether he would be assassinated by the Mossad. Each could wonder what had happened to Abu al-Abbas's promise, right before they were taken off the plane at Sigonella: "Do not fear, I will not abandon you," he told them.

One by one, they realized they were on their own. Two months before the Palestinian summit in Gaza, and ten years into his thirty-year prison sentence, on February 26, 1996, Majid al-Molqi, Leon Klinghoffer's killer, escaped to the Costa del Sol in Spain. He didn't have to break out of prison: he was already on a twelve-day furlough for good behavior from Rebibbia, a high-security prison in Rome. Molqi was a beneficiary of a law passed in 1986, the year he was convicted, aimed at humanizing the Italian prison system, that gave inmates who qualified the chance to work outside jail and have brief holidays with their families. It was his fifth furlough; under the law he was free between 8 a.m. and 8 p.m., but this time he was allowed to stay overnight with other workers at a Catholic shelter where he had previously volunteered. Molqi had been a model prisoner. He now spoke Italian like a Roman. He learned to sew. Though Muslim, he became friends with a priest, who encouraged him to work at this shelter in Rome. He corresponded with women who wrote to him, intrigued by his story; eventually he would marry one of them, Carla Biano, a member of Guerriglia Metropolitana per il Comunismo, an Italian terrorist group.

The escape set off an uproar. The U.S. government offered a $2 million reward for Molqi's capture. Jewish groups protested, and the ADL issued a press release in the name of the Klinghoffer sisters. By happenstance, Ilsa was on vacation in Rome with her husband, Paul Dworin; through the ADL, she was put in contact with an American embassy official in Rome. He arranged a series of meetings between her and Paul and various Italian government officials, as well as one with the U.S. ambassador. In a thank-you note to Ambassador

Reginald Bartholomew, dated July 8, 1996, Ilsa praised the Italians. "The officials with whom we met appear to be genuinely interested in extraditing Al-Molqi and in helping to find, and ultimately extradite, Abu al-Abbas."

Molqi's freedom was short-lived. Within a month, he was arrested in Estepona, a town just twelve miles from the Spanish resort city of Marbella, where Monzer al-Kassar kept a lavish home, which may or may not have been a coincidence. Molqi was extradited to Italy and returned to prison, but in Palermo, Sicily, not Rome. He remained there until April 30, 2009, when he was released for good behavior, having served almost twenty-four years of his thirty-year sentence. Carla Biano, his wife, learned that he was in Syria, living with his family. They stayed in touch for a while and then she didn't hear from him anymore.

Three years before Molqi's escape, Bassam al-Ashker, the youngest of the hijackers, had also slipped out of custody, on December 14, 1992. His escape came as a shock to Minors Court Judge Francesco Mazza Galanti, who had met Ashker a year earlier, when the prisoner asked to be transferred into an alternative program where he could work outside prison during the day. "I was struck by his seriousness, unusual for a boy of then twenty-three, the tranquility with which at least apparently he handled the isolation of prison," recalled Galanti, who had recommended Ashker for supervised release. Ashker began working for the Red Cross in Genoa.

While he was there, a journalist named Edoardo Pusillo met Ashker and asked whether he could interview him for a book. Ashker was more than willing; he had spent five years working on a book himself. He had given the manuscript to his lawyer and then it vanished. He and Pusillo met several times over a period of months. The last time they got together, Ashker was contemplative.

"I have many friends," he told Pusillo. "I try to be as serene as possible, to forget the darkness of the cell and to think about tomorrow, though it is impossible to erase certain experiences from my soul as a Palestinian fighter." He said what he wanted most was to hug his parents again, to sit next to them and see their faces. He expressed his hope for peace in the Middle East but reaffirmed his willingness to battle on. "If necessary I will return to fight and I will be ready anew to die so that my people and Palestine can live," he said.

"Often I am asked if I ever feel like running away," he told Pusillo. "Yes, I have thought about it, but I will not do it." When Pusillo arrived at the Red Cross building for their next session, Ashker was gone. Pusillo put the interviews in a drawer for several years and then decided to publish what he had.

Ashker made his way to Algeria, where his parents came to see him. His mother had been able to visit him once in Italy; he hadn't seen his father in more than seven years. Abu al-Abbas brought Ashker to Iraq and rewarded him for his loyalty by making him a top lieutenant.

Over the years, Ashker would replay the *Achille Lauro* disaster in his mind. Decades later, when the slender boy had become a solid, middle-aged man, he was asked what the hijacking meant to him. "It was meant to show the world that Palestinians are there and are rebelling against the enemy," he said. "[The ship] was just a vehicle that was taking us home."

He didn't regret taking part in the mission; it was "just part of what they had to do to liberate their occupied land." But he did regret the outcome. "It did not succeed," he said.

Ashker felt sorrow for Leon Klinghoffer, whose murder he insisted was never part of the plan. "What happened was very painful, the killing of Klinghoffer," he said. "It was not intended. This was not a boat, it was like a village with hundreds of people on board. You cannot say, I want to kill this one and leave this one. Klinghoffer, they did not kill him intentionally. The intention was not to kill anybody."

After the hijacking, he saw the other *fedayeen* from the *Achille Lauro* only when he was taken to Genoa to testify at their trial—except for one month, when he was reunited with Omar al-Assadi, who kept trying to get him to change his story. By then, Ashker had been interrogated repeatedly, by Italians and by Americans. He never wavered. "The operation was clear," he said. "We went on board this boat to use it as a vehicle to reach Palestine and to fight the Israeli military soldiers."

Assadi, the hijacker who turned state's evidence, remained in jail for fifteen years, though he benefited from his cooperation. Between 1989 and 1994, he estimated he went on about eighty furloughs. During his first outing from prison, he returned to Genoa, where he and the other three hijackers had boarded the *Achille Lauro*. "I wanted to relive those sensations," he said. "I wanted to better understand what I had believed in, and what I had felt getting on the ship."

Assadi continued to insist that Abu al-Abbas had tricked the hijackers into believing Ashdod was the goal rather than the real objective, which was to hijack the ship to obtain the release of Samir Kuntar and the other Palestinians held in custody by Israel for the murders at Nahariyya. "He sent us on the *Achille Lauro* like animals for slaughter," Assadi told Cristina Rogledi, a journalist for the Italian magazine *Oggi*, in 1998. Rogledi remembered him as a slight man, who seemed younger than he was, "a gentle kid who was caught up in something much larger than himself."

Assadi explained his motives. "We were *fedayeen* committed to fighting for our land and we had gotten on the ship to complete a very specific military operation: to arrive in Israel and kill our enemy," he said. "It had nothing to do with the shameful kidnapping of innocents organized to force the release of the relative of Abu al-Abbas. I was supposed to die to return freedom to another man?"

During his years in prison, Assadi had time to elaborate on his story, though none of his fellow hijackers ever corroborated his version of what happened—quite the opposite. But Assadi continued to try to make sense out of an event whose rationale and disposition seemed less and less logical as the years passed. Under either scenario, the hijacking was a poorly devised scheme, doomed to futility. For Assadi, Abbas was not just a failed leader, he was self-serving. Recalling the hours on the plane at Sigonella, waiting for a resolution of his fate, Assadi was bitter. "Within the hour we [he and the other hijackers] were at the police station of Syracuse," he said. "Abu al-Abbas stayed in the plane and from that day I never saw him again. I know only that he was able to return to Tunis placid and free."

Abdellatif Fataier, the hijacker the passengers called Rambo, received the harshest sentence after Molqi—twenty-four years—not because he had done anything worse than the other two who hadn't killed anyone, but because he was neither a minor like Ashker nor a witness for the prosecution like Assadi.

Both Fataier and Molqi continued to be represented by Gianfranco Pagano, the defense lawyer, who persevered in making appeals for them over the years. The lawyer felt special sympathy for Fataier, who genuinely seemed to regret his involvement. He was about to be granted a furlough when Molqi escaped to Spain. Once again, Fataier was harshly judged for Molqi's actions. His furlough was withdrawn, and he was transferred to a maximum-security prison, where he was placed in solitary confinement. In one year he lost forty pounds, before his lawyer was able to have him moved to another prison. He never had visitors, except once, when he saw his mother. He had been forgotten by Arafat and the PLO and by Abu al-Abbas.

In 2000, under Pagano's guidance, Fataier sent an impassioned letter to the president of Italy, requesting a pardon. Noting that he had been in jail more than fourteen years, almost half his life, he took responsibility for his role in the hijacking, acknowledging that it was an act of terrorism, while explaining what he thought it was supposed to be. "In our eyes at the time it represented...a heroic act to free our people from oppression," he wrote. "None of us was gifted then with the cultural tools to understand that this was not the right way to try to change things, and that no protestation, not even the most noble, can take on such importance as to cost human life. For this reason, today it is of great relief to me that I never stained my hands with blood and that I had nothing to do with the killing of the American Leon Klinghoffer, even though, I cannot deny, that homicide resulted from an operation to which I had contributed."

He accepted his punishment but asked if it hadn't been sufficient. "What weighs on me most of all today is the sense of futility of my continued protracted incarceration," he wrote. "I am a new man. That boy of twenty no longer exists. After all, even the international political climate has much changed. Today I am a profound and sincere supporter of Arafat's efforts in the direction of peace. Thanks to this new period of dialogue, I feel able to say that the war between Palestinians and Israelis is a thing of the past. A sign of this is the fact that Abu al-Abbas, then leader of the PLF, the extremist wing of the PLO of which I was a part, and the designer of the terrorist action of which I was part, who was condemned to life in prison in the same court as mine, today sits respectably in the Palestinian parliament."

The request was denied. Pagano kept trying, unsuccessfully, to persuade other politicians to help release Fataier from prison. Fataier remained in prison for twenty years and eventually ended up in Algeria. The harshness of Fataier's fate frustrated the lawyer more than watching his clients be abandoned by their leaders. The murder of Klinghoffer made that inevitable. "I am sorry, but you killed this guy," he once said to Molqi. "You understand that Palestine does not want to present itself as a place where they kill paralytic people. It is indefensible."

Pagano was never paid for his service, though he once spoke to Abu al-Abbas by telephone and was assured that compensation would be forthcoming. The money never came, but the lawyer felt he was rewarded in other ways. "It was a personal and professional experience that helped me grow as a lawyer," he said. "To speak with people who are different from the others—political prisoners instead of common prisoners." There were practical returns as well. "It gave me notoriety and work," he acknowledged. Becoming known as "the *Achille Lauro* lawyer" was good for business.

15

The Optimist

Throughout the eighteen years Reem lived in Baghdad with Abu al-Abbas, the strictures of Saddam Hussein's ruthless and unpredictable dictatorship kept her on edge. But her sons remembered those years warmly. Most of their happy recollections centered around Abbas. Whenever he wasn't traveling, they all ate dinner together. They remembered meals full of lively conversation, a forum that expanded during school vacations, when Omar and Khaled came to Iraq from Canada. "We discussed how we were doing in school, what we want to do in the future, like any father talking to a kid, not what he was doing with his political life," Reef Ghadban recalled. "We never discussed what he was doing."

Living with Abbas made Loaye, the oldest of the blended family's five sons, feel safe in a way he never had. His stepfather had a strength unlike anyone he had ever known. "It was the way he walks, the way he enters a room, the way he smiles, the tone of voice," Loaye said. "He had lots of power but when you saw him walking around talking to the guards, or to the maids, he treated everyone the same. He had this kind of humility. Saddam Hussein was a powerful person, but you didn't feel the humility. He would spread fear in you. You wouldn't dare challenge him, you would be scared of that guy. With Abu al-Abbas, you wanted to tell him your problems, you felt he would want to help you."

In the private schools they attended in Tunis, Beirut, Montreal, and Baghdad, the young men were groomed to be citizens of the world, fluent in multiple languages. At Baghdad International School, Reef mingled with the children of Czech and Romanian diplomats, and businesspeople from countries around the globe. None of his close friends was Palestinian. He and his brothers knew the men who worked for Abu al-Abbas and the families who asked his stepfather for favors, but the children of these people lived in poor neighborhoods and attended government schools, not expensive private institutions like Baghdad International. Sometimes there was a community celebration and the boys visited the PLF training camps, a special thrill, watching Abu al-Abbas in his element. In most ways, however, the lives of Reef and his brothers were as remote from those of other Palestinians who lived in Iraq as from those of the Palestinians in Gaza and the West Bank of Israel, or in refugee camps in Jordan, Syria, and Lebanon, or the 380,000 Palestinians expelled from Kuwait after Saddam's invasion in 1990, punishment for the PLO's alliance with the Iraqi dictator.

Yet the sons of Abu al-Abbas were steeped in Palestinian identity, which formed the household's spiritual core, rather than any religious belief. From an early age they learned about the land of their forefathers and saw how much it meant to Abbas, who was respected not just by them but by an entire community. The house was filled with the photographs of Palestine that Abu al-Abbas paid people to send him—exorbitant amounts, his wife felt—including images of the town near Haifa that his parents were from. He spent hours placing them next to one another to create a panoramic view. He planted saplings someone brought from Palestine in their garden. The boys were constantly reminded of the significance of this mythic place.

In the summer of 1999, Abu al-Abbas took his younger Canadian son, Omar, on a three-week visit to Gaza and the West Bank. It was an eye-opening experience for the nineteen-year old, who had lived most of his life in Montreal. They flew from Jordan to Gaza on a propeller plane, a piece of junk that shook the entire time, everybody praying to God that it wouldn't crash. Omar remembered his emotional reaction to being surrounded by Palestinians for the first time. "It was the first time I saw Palestinian people everywhere, speaking that familiar accent," he said. "It was quite amazing."

The familiarity was accompanied by a sense of alienation. "It was the first time I was physically in the place of my roots," he said. "Yet even in Gaza and the West Bank afterward, I felt somehow distanced from other Palestinians by my Western upbringing and disconnected to some extent by my imperfect Arabic. This saddened me as it was something that kept me from feeling fully immersed in my homeland."

Omar was horrified at the conditions he saw there—what he heard from people about their treatment by the Israeli government and observing Israeli soldiers holding Uzis standing guard everywhere they traveled. "It felt like all of our people were being forced into subjugation at the barrel of a gun," he said. "I saw neighborhoods with massive concrete blocks positioned outside of them ready to close them off at a moment's notice should trouble arise. It was a dystopian reality, right in front of my eyes."

He saw metal shutters on shops that could be easily shut down when the army rolled in. He felt the tension in Gaza and saw support for Hamas building. "You could feel they were getting more support because there wasn't an answer and the PLO wasn't doing enough," he said. "For me, I could never relate to Hamas but for people there, they were the alternative."

It was a difficult trip, filled with poignancy and disillusionment. Abu al-Abbas took Omar to Tirat Carmel, the Israeli city populated with Jewish settlers following the 1948 War after the destruction of al-Tira, the Palestinian town that Omar's grandparents came from. Omar and his brothers had heard about this town for so many years, regarding it as a holy site for their family, part of the stirring history they'd learned from Abu al-Abbas. Yet what the young man saw was depressingly prosaic. "The old village where his parents came from was a bunch of suburban duplexes," he said. "[We knew] this was where the village was, but it had just been erased off the face of the earth and replaced with Anywheresville, U.S.A. kind of thing, duplexes with no character."

However, when they visited Birzeit, where his other grandmother—Samia's mother—was from, Omar was able to understand better the previous generation's attachment. The town remained Palestinian and held vestiges of the past. "It felt like a memory I never had, having heard all about it from my mom," he said. "There was a warmth to it, and a deep sadness, too."

Despite the bittersweet experience of witnessing a landscape overtaken by Israeli development and seeing the desperate struggle for survival of his people, Omar observed a peacefulness in his father during their travels. "It was like he was finally at home," he said, "even if it was a home that was broken and occupied."

A year later, Abu al-Abbas returned to Palestine with Reem and Ali, their fourteen-year-old son. They took a road trip to Jerusalem, Haifa, Ramallah, and Nablus, before returning to Gaza. There were no roadblocks then; they drove through checkpoints without stopping, though Reem was conscious of the young Israeli Army soldiers standing by, about the same age as her own sons, holding automatic rifles. Reem enjoyed visiting the historic sites but found Gaza dispiriting. She was embarrassed by the way their entourage of visiting PLO dignitaries entered the city, as though they were liberators, honking their horns and waving from the windows. "In reality, however, we never really 'liberated' Gaza," she wrote. "Palestinian officials who flocked from Tunisia, Jordan, Iraq, Lebanon and Syria arrived with plenty of money and purchased comfortable villas for their families—which stood empty much of the time. PLO officials would visit Gaza to attend periodic meetings of the Palestinian Council or to spend summers on the beach. Few PLO members became permanent residents. Gaza City was overcrowded. The infrastructure was crumbling. Public health was poor."

They returned to Baghdad just before the start of the second *intifada*, the Palestinian uprising that marked the utter collapse of the peace process. It was instigated by Ariel Sharon's provocative decision on

September 29, 2000, to visit Haram al Sharif, the holy Muslim site in East Jerusalem referred to by the Israelis as the Temple Mount. Sharon led the right-wing opposition to Prime Minister Ehud Barak, who supported Rabin and the Oslo Accords. In the second *intifada*, the unarmed youth of the first uprising had been supplanted by Islamists carrying guns, far more inspired by Hamas than the PLO, whose leadership had failed them. Hamas's founding charter in 1988 calls unequivocally for Islamic control of Palestine, stating, "In face of the Jews' usurpation of Palestine, it is compulsory that the banner of Jihad be raised." The charter also rejects the secularism of the Palestine Liberation Organization: "without belittling its role in the Arab-Israeli conflict, we are unable to exchange the present or future Islamic Palestine with the secular idea. The Islamic nature of Palestine is part of our religion and whoever takes his religion lightly is a loser." The second *intifada*, a violent uprising that lasted more than four years, was marked by suicide bombings that took the lives of one thousand Israelis, including the lynching of two reservists, and reprisals that killed almost four thousand Palestinians.

After that trip, Arafat warned Abbas to stay clear of the occupied territories. In December 2000, the peace process collapsed with Arafat's outright rejection of the plan proposed at Camp David by President Bill Clinton and supported by Prime Minister Ehud Barak. "This was the shattering moment for many Israelis who believed in the possibility of resolving the conflict," wrote Yossi Klein Halevi, a writer who would later become codirector of the Hartman Institute's Muslim Leader Initiative in Jerusalem. Ariel Sharon, the militant general and longtime champion of the expansionist Israeli settlement movement, became prime minister of Israel in 2001. Yasser Arafat was struggling for political survival; he didn't need another reason to clash with Sharon. Abu al-Abbas was effectively grounded. He stayed in Baghdad, growing gray and portly. "His good looks suffered from too much food, too little exercise, too many Marlboros, too much drinking—and a life of stress," Reem recalled. He suffered the ailments of middle age—high blood pressure and angina; in 1996 and 1999 stents were inserted to open the blocked arteries leading to his heart.

Through political circumstance rather than desire, he appeared to be preparing for retirement, watching his sons graduate from high school and college, spending more and more of his time surfing the web. Though internet use was tightly restricted in Saddam's Iraq, as a privileged official, Abbas was given an upgrade. He became obsessed with his computer, reading the U.S. and Israeli press—*Maariv*, *Ha'aretz*, and the *New York Times*. He acquired a new companion, a dog named Rocky, who remained by his side, standing guard beside Abbas's desk while he worked, accompanying him to his farm, walking with him by the river. His stepson Reef had brought the golden retriever as a puppy from Beirut over his mother's objections when he returned to Iraq after graduating from college. When Reem was growing up, dogs were not customarily welcomed as pets in the Middle East. She told her son the dog could stay only if he was confined to Reef's room when he was inside the house. But Rocky was a cunning and affable creature; he wore down Reem's resistance with unrelenting affection. She fell in love with him, especially when she saw how much he meant to her husband. As a joke, Reef told her he had named the dog after Rocky Balboa, the fictional prize fighter Sylvester Stallone made famous the world over as the triumphant underdog. She believed him, not realizing that half the dogs in the Middle East were named Rocky (the other half were called Max). In Reem's imagination, the name became symbolic, representing the characteristics shared by Abu al-Abbas and the dog and Rocky Balboa. "He was forgotten and counted out," she wrote, "but then surprised everyone by returning to triumph in one sequel after another."

Israeli intelligence, not surprisingly, offered a different analysis of Abu al-Abbas's next act. "A tool of the Iraqi regime for carrying out terrorist attacks against Israel," concluded the Military Intelligence unit of the Israel Defense Forces (IDF) in a report dated September 20, 2002.

The accusation stemmed from interrogations of PLF squads arrested in Israel in 2001–2002, after the second *intifada* ended whatever hope remained for the Oslo Accords. The Middle East was on fire again, in the wake of the 9/11 attacks on the United States. The PLF prisoners told their captors that they trained in military camps in Iraq, under the guidance of Abu al-Abbas and his lieutenant Bassam al-Ashker.

The Israelis cited documents revealing that Yasser Arafat personally approved financing PLF activities, but also noted that Palestinian counterintelligence didn't trust the PLF and "is watchful of PLF activity due to internal PLF conflicts and a suspicion that the Israeli Security service and Jordanian Intelligence penetrated the organization."

The IDF report connected the PLF to Iraqi-trained terrorist cells in the West Bank, including one that was behind the kidnapping and murder of Yuri Sushchin, a nineteen-year-old student from Jerusalem, as well as a plot to carry out mass killings at Ben Gurion International Airport and crowded places in Jerusalem, and an additional attack in Tel Aviv—at the Dophinarium discotheque, where a lethal attack had been carried out previously, killing 21 Israelis, mostly high school students, and wounding 132.

The report quoted Iraqi Deputy Prime Minister Tariq Aziz responding to a speech by U.S. President George W. Bush. "The Iraqi leadership believes that the Palestinians—and it does not matter who they are and how we [in Iraq] view one figure or another—are not terrorists," Aziz said on September 14, 2002. "The Palestinians fight and struggle with legitimate means...it is legitimate activity which we support explicitly and not in secret."

A year after 9/11 and the subsequent U.S. invasion of Afghanistan, Abu al-Abbas told Reem al-Nimer that an American war with Iraq would be coming soon. The Bush administration had turned its sights on Saddam Hussein, accusing him of supporting Al Qaeda and developing an illegal nuclear weapons program. In a speech on October 7, 2002, as President Bush made his case for using force against Iraq, he invoked the *Achille Lauro*: "Over the years, Iraq has provided safe haven to terrorists such as Abu Nidal, whose terror organization carried out more than 90 terrorist attacks in 20 countries that killed or injured nearly 900 people including 12 Americans. Iraq has also provided safe haven to Abu Abbas [sic], who was responsible for seizing the *Achille Lauro* and killing an American passenger."

Abu al-Abbas took the American president's threat seriously. In early 2003, he urged Reem and Reef, who was doing business in Baghdad, to leave Iraq, to join Ali and Loaye in Beirut.

Reem was alarmed in a way she had never been before. She and Abbas had lived through many wars, but his tone was different this time. Even more unsettling was the bundle of papers he told her to take with her, containing birth certificates, real estate papers, bank statements, diplomas, and passports.

Crying, Reem asked him why he was giving her the documents. "Is this our last time together?" she asked.

"We'll be together soon," he reassured her. "It's safer to take them with you to Lebanon."

Two months later, on April 9, 2003, twenty-four days after the American invasion of Iraq, Baghdad was controlled by the U.S. Army. Abu al-Abbas was captured a week later, after trying to flee to Syria with his bodyguard. "One of our key objectives is to search for, capture, and drive out terrorists who have found safe haven in Iraq," said the U.S. Army Central Command in a statement. "The capture of Abu al-Abbas in Iraq removes a portion of the terror network supported by Iraq and represents yet another victory in the global war on terrorism."

The PLO issued its own statement, noting that under the Oslo agreement, no member of the PLO should be arrested for actions occurring prior to September 13, 1993. Newspaper reports observed that the American indictment against Abbas for the *Achille Lauro* had expired, though a warrant for his arrest remained outstanding in Italy. Lisa and Ilsa Klinghoffer issued a statement as well: "We are delighted that the murderous terrorist Abu Al-Abbas is in U.S. custody," it read.

"While we personally seek justice for our father's murder, the larger issue is terrorism. Bringing Abbas to justice will send a strong signal to terrorists anywhere in the world that there is no place to run, no place to hide."

Abbas was imprisoned in Camp Cropper, a detention center near Baghdad International Airport, referred to by the U.S. Army bureaucracy as a "high value detainee confinement center." Prisoners included many high-ranking Iraqi government officials; Saddam Hussein was held there before his execution.

Abbas's family thought he would be released soon. "He was part of the deal done for the Oslo agreement," said Reef, his stepson. "We thought the history is gone, finished. It's a new phase. I wasn't surprised they caught him, but I was surprised they kept him. What was the legal reason? We never knew."

Letters began to come to the family from Abbas via the Red Cross, actually fragments of letters; they had been cut up and mangled by prison censors. Abu al-Abbas let them know he was delighted to hear that his dog Rocky had survived the invasion and occupation of Baghdad and was reunited with the family in Beirut. He asked Reem to send books. He provided continually upbeat assessments of his circumstances. In a January 16, 2004, letter to his youngest son, Ali, he wrote: "I don't know how long my absence will be, but I do know that life never pursues one single path. It is often marked by severe ups and downs. What is important is to always be optimistic, and to place before our eyes very high and noble goals; not letting life pass without achievements." He urged his youngest son to study hard and to respect his family. He retained a sense of humor in a PS. "My weight is now 95 kg [210 pounds]—no extras and my letter has to be like that as well."

Two months after writing that letter, at 12:30 a.m. on March 8, 2004, Abu al-Abbas was pronounced dead by a U.S. Army physician. According to a sixty-page investigative report filed by the army, Abbas failed to respond to CPR and other treatment following an apparent heart attack.

The report quotes from an interview with a civilian Arabic translator who worked at Camp Cropper. He is referred to as 67C-4, 664; all names were redacted. 67C-4, 664 told investigators he had been called to the clinic shortly before midnight to translate for a detainee who was complaining of chest pains. Within a half hour, despite receiving mouth-to-mouth resuscitation and defibrillator shocks, the detainee did not survive. The report contained a Q&A between 67C-4, 664 and the investigator.

Q: What was the detainee's name?
A: I don't know his name, all I know is that he is #39.

Q: How long has this detainee been at Camp Cropper?
A: A good 10 months, if not longer.

Q: Has he made any complaints about his health?
A: Yes, he went to the clinic two or three times before. The first time was around August, 2003, September, 2003, and I am not sure of the other time. He said he was "under the weather."

Q: What does "under the weather" mean?
A: He had a cold or flu-like symptoms. I don't recall what kind of prescription he was given.

Q: Has he ever complained about exhibiting any chest pains or ever having any problems breathing?
A: No.

Q: Did you see the detainee at all yesterday, 7 March 2004?
A: Yes. I seen [sic] him sometimes between 3 and 4 p.m.

Q: Describe his demeanor.
A: I was just a short distance away. He looked pretty normal and pretty happy. He did not look sick at all.

Q: Did the detainee have any prior heart problems or have a heart condition?

A: Yes. When he came in to get treated for the flu-like symptoms, I looked at his record and seen he had previous heart attacks. I cannot remember the exact dates this occurred.

Q: Did the medical staff take any kinds of precautions for this detainee knowing he had previous heart problems?

A: Yes, because when he came in for treatment of his flu-like symptoms, he was asked how his heart was doing. He would always say he was feeling good. He was always smiling and easy going.

Q: Did he have any problems with any detainees that you are aware of?

A: No.

Q: Do you have anything else that you would like to add to this statement?

A: No.

Ali Abbas would be turning eighteen and had been accepted for admission to Concordia University in Montreal. The Canadian embassy in Beirut wasn't issuing embarkment visas, so he needed to go to Damascus. Although the Syrian capital was only an eighty-five-mile drive from Beirut, it was a dangerous trip.

Despite Reem's reservations about Monzer al-Kassar, she knew he was a useful connection and he was living in Damascus. She reached out to him and left for Damascus on March 7, 2004, leaving Ali behind with her parents. The next evening, Reem met Kassar for dinner, in the old part of Damascus. Halfway through the meal, Kassar's driver came in and whispered something in his boss's ear. He became unearthly pale but when Reem asked him what was wrong, he refused to say anything. Reem's cell phone rang. She learned that Abu al-Abbas was dead.

In the blur that followed she experienced what she always suspected about Kassar. "Part of him is good and part of him is very evil," she said. Like a real friend, he accompanied her to Beirut and offered to assist with the funeral arrangements. But she soon learned firsthand that Kassar's help came with a price.

The dissolution of their relationship began with a disagreement about where Abu al-Abbas should be buried. Reem wanted her husband laid to rest in Ramallah, so that finally he would find a place in the land he had fought for his entire life. But she quickly realized that there would be no peaceful repose for Abu al-Abbas. Before transporting the body, the Red Cross needed approval from the Israeli government. Days passed and there was still no answer. Kassar began pressuring Reem to bury her husband in Syria, arguing that he still had siblings there, in the Yarmouk refugee camp where he had grown up. He reminded her that Islamic ritual required quick burial. Reem felt Kassar had additional motives, that he would gain political advantage if he brought the Palestinian hero to Syria. "He was just trying to sell something," she said. "He wanted to improve his relations with the Syrians. They thought if they buried Abu al-Abbas in Syria in front of the Palestinians, they would look like patriots, like they cared about the Palestinian cause."

She told him she would not have Abu al-Abbas sent to Syria until the Israelis gave her an answer. "Let them say no," she told Kassar. "I want them to say no, so nobody will blame me, why I didn't try to bury him in Ramallah."

He started shouting at her and then left for Damascus. When he returned to Beirut that evening, he told Reem he had asked the family of Abu al-Abbas living in Syria to alert the Palestinian press that the funeral would be in Damascus and the funeral would be the next day.

Reem gave up. She had resisted Kassar's badgering for an entire week, the time it took for the Israelis to finally say no. Then everything happened very fast. Kassar was with Reem in Beirut on March 23, when the Red Cross called and said the coffin would be arriving in Damascus in one hour. Even speeding, it would take more than an hour to make the trip. They quickly arranged a convoy of cars to transport various PLF men as well as Kassar, Reem, and her family—including her father and brother and all the boys except Khaled, who was in Canada with his mother. As the cars raced toward the Syrian border, forty-two miles away, Kassar called local members of the PLF, telling them the funeral would be at 4 p.m. in the Yarmouk camp.

The sons of Abu al-Abbas were turned back at the border. Reef, Loaye, and Ali didn't have passports; they traveled on refugee identity cards, issued by the United Nations. Omar's Canadian passport required a visa. There wasn't time to make arrangements for any of them. Reem had a Jordanian passport, as did her brother and father. As she had so many times in her life, she was forced to make a split-second decision. It didn't feel right, but Reem sent their sons back to Beirut, while she and the rest continued to Damascus.

When they reached the airport, a Red Cross official offered condolences and handed her the official sixty-page death report from the U.S. Army. The Red Cross man said she had to identify the body. Reem refused. Her husband had been in a refrigerator for two weeks by then. She knew from his letters that he had lost a great deal of weight since she had seen him a year before. Whatever he looked like now was not what she wanted to remember. "I did not want this picture to stay in my mind," she said. She asked her brother-in-law to verify his brother's identity.

Back in the cars for the final leg of the trip, they were speeding against the clock from the airport to Yarmouk, just outside Damascus. Reem knew in advance this wasn't going to be just a funeral, but a political demonstration. That's why she had told her mother and sister not to come. In a daze, she felt she was swimming in the sea of people who accompanied her husband's casket through the streets of the refugee enclave. Reem tried to control her sobs, knowing everyone was looking at her, the martyr's widow, her streaked blond hair noticeably uncovered amid women wearing head scarves and burkas, throwing rice, according to Syrian custom. The casket was wrapped in the Palestinian flag, embossed with a photo of Abu al-Abbas. Reem was swept along in a current of three thousand people marching through the streets. Shops were closed as a sign of mourning; American and Israeli flags were set on fire as the crowd chanted slogans:

Our souls and blood, we will shed for Abu al-Abbas.
Hey Bush, listen there, Palestine will not kneel.
Palestinians are not afraid of death.
God is great [Allah Akbar], say it loud.

After the procession stopped, Reem stepped up to a microphone and faced the crowd of mourners and protesters. "He's a loss to us as a family and to every Palestinian, but he chose the path of martyrdom," she said, "just like every Palestinian boy who wishes to defend their land with their life."

Even as Reem fulfilled her responsibility as a political widow, Kassar was freezing her out. Throughout the afternoon, he spoke to her brother, he spoke to her father, but he looked past her, as if she didn't exist. Exhausted and overwhelmed as she was, the insult sparked her fury, which was evident years later, when she remembered that time. "If someone really loved Abu al-Abbas, he wouldn't have done this to his wife for a very stupid reason, shall we wait another two days or forget about Israel," she said. "This is not a good reason for someone to stop talking to you, someone who is supposed to be a very good friend, someone who feels for you because you lost your husband, someone who cares about the kids. No, it was a big lie."

They didn't speak for two years. Reem began to suspect another motive for Kassar's behavior as PLF members dependent on her husband started importuning her for money. Reem said that Kassar "wanted to have a distance between me and him so that every time a member of the PLF would go to him to ask for money he said, 'Why don't you go to the wife of Abu al-Abbas, she has the money.'"

Kassar remained in touch with her sons, but not with Reem. The lack of respect intensified her anger. "I am the head of this family," she said. Then one day she received a call from one of Kassar's bodyguards, with a message from his boss. An Iraqi man, a businessman who had been in the same cell as Abu al-Abbas at Camp Cropper, wanted to meet Reem. Would she join them for lunch?

She couldn't refuse. This was her chance to hear what one of the last people to see Abbas alive had to say. Kassar was polite but formal when he greeted her at his home in Damascus and introduced her to Aseel Tabra. Part of a wealthy Iraqi family, Tabra was a powerful businessman who, until 2003, was deputy chairman of the Iraqi National Olympic Committee, working for Uday Hussein, who had a reputation for physically abusing athletes who displeased him. Tabra became the official the Iraqi government sent to meet foreign delegations, or for discussions about accommodating the handicapped, or to welcome planes carrying humanitarian aid. Many athletes believed the Iraqi Olympic Committee was a front for Uday's criminal operation and suspected that Tabra must be involved by association. Just before the U.S. invasion, Uday threw Tabra in jail. Then Uday was killed by the Americans, and Tabra ended up in a cell with Abu al-Abbas.

Reem saw a broken man. Tabra's wife and two of his children had been killed in a rocket attack; his youngest child, a baby when the United States attacked, had been taken in by a relative. When Tabra was arrested by the Americans for his association with Uday, he had already reached bottom. He had lost his family, his money, everything. "Abu al-Abbas was my healer," he told Reem. "He was my doctor, my father, my brother. He made me go back to being a human."

He told her he witnessed the massive heart attack that killed her husband, reiterating what Reem had read in the U.S. Army report. While the confirmation that Abu al-Abbas had died of natural causes came as a relief, Reem couldn't shake the suspicion that this wasn't the full story. "Was it a coincidence that Abu al-Abas and three other Palestinian leaders who had lived within reach of Israeli arms for decades suddenly died in 2004, including Yasser Arafat?" she asked.

Before lunch was over, she exchanged contact information with Tabra. They called each other for a while and then lost touch, after he moved to Egypt, then Dubai, and then Jordan. As for Monzer, she never saw him again. When she heard in 2007 that he had been arrested again in Spain and extradited to the United States, facing charges that could put him in prison for the rest of his life, she wasn't surprised. "People like that always end up being killed or going to jail," she said. "Very few of them would ask God to forgive them and then stay at home and live the rest of their lives in peace. Usually such characters would keep going in very dangerous roads. They never give up. They always want more money and more deals and more power."

16

Operation Legacy

New York City, 2008

The trial of Monzer al-Kassar began in U.S. federal court in lower Manhattan at 9 a.m. on November 5, 2008. For two weeks jurors heard testimony implicating Kassar in arms sales to the Revolutionary Armed Forces of Colombia, a rebel group designated by the U.S. government as a foreign terrorist organization and known by its Spanish acronym, FARC. The weapons, worth millions of dollars, included fifteen surface-to-air missiles, four thousand grenades, nearly nine thousand assault rifles, and thousands of pounds of C-4 explosives. The missiles, the jurors were told, would be used to shoot down American helicopters in Colombia, leading to charges against Monzer of conspiracy to kill American citizens and employees.

The chief witness for the prosecution was John Archer, an agent for the Drug Enforcement Agency (DEA). Agent Archer, a man in his thirties, helped plan and execute the sting operation that finally snared Kassar, who had been pursued by the DEA for more than fifteen years, ever since he had been acquitted in Spain of charges related to the *Achille Lauro*. Throughout the three-week trial in New York, Archer was acutely aware of two stylishly dressed middle-aged women watching from the gallery for the general public. They were Lisa and Ilsa Klinghoffer. Archer had been introduced to them in the U.S. attorney's office shortly before Kassar's arrest. "We met with them to let them know something was coming soon, just to let them know that no one [had] forgotten about them," Archer said.

The sisters were in federal court because of the allegation against Kassar that was not on the docket or even mentioned by prosecutors: supplying weapons for the *Achille Lauro* hijacking. Unwilling to risk the same fate as the Spanish prosecutors, the federal attorneys accused him "only" of being part of a powerful, international illicit arms and drug trade that profited from violent disruption and war. Above the surface, he ran an import-export business, but prosecutors said Kassar made his vast fortune in a clandestine netherworld, as a trafficker serving a diverse clientele. The U.S. attorney for the Southern District of New York charged Kassar with providing military equipment to armed factions "engaged in violent conflicts around the world," in countries including Nicaragua, Brazil, Cyprus, Bosnia, Croatia, Somalia, Iran, and Iraq. He was accused of providing weapons for "known terrorist organizations, such as the Palestinian Liberation Front, the goals of which included attacking United States interests and United States nationals." Besides omitting the *Achille Lauro*, the indictment also didn't mention Kassar's client Oliver North, and the weapons the arms dealer supplied to the American government during the Iran-Contra affair.

In the courtroom, the defendant played the part of a sophisticated, successful businessman—a confident-looking man of sixty-three with a shock of gray hair and deep, intelligent eyes, wearing a well-tailored suit. Kassar was a billionaire, known as the Proud Peacock for his ostentation. He had settled with his wife and four children in one of his many residences, a white marble mansion, sitting on a luxurious estate with a twelve-car garage and swimming pool shaped like a four-leaf clover, overlooking the resort town of Marbella, on the southern coast of Spain. A CIA weapons specialist who negotiated the Iran-Contra munitions deal, paid for via a Swiss bank account controlled by Oliver North, told a reporter that Kassar was a gracious host, who invited him into his home and, though there was a chef on staff, made breakfast for him.

It was reasonable to envision the defendant as a wealthy bon vivant, but there was a hardness, too, that made the charges seem plausible. "Kassar was a menacing figure," said a juror. "Refined but scary." Not surprising for a man in Kassar's line of work, he had done his share of jail time, including more than a year before the mid-1990s trial in Spain, prior to his release upon posting $15.5 million bail.

Lisa Klinghoffer was at the federal courthouse in lower Manhattan every day. Though a silent witness to the proceedings, she became a noticeable presence, even to jurors who didn't know who she was. Ilsa came as often as she could, going back and forth to work. For the Klinghoffer sisters, the trial was their final chance to bring Abu al-Abbas to justice, even if by proxy, four years after his death in an American Army prison.

For James Soiles, a senior DEA agent, the trial also offered vindication. Soiles likewise looked his part—tall and lean with a graying ponytail. He had been hunting Kassar for so long he called the investigation Operation Legacy. Kassar had appeared on Soiles's radar in the early 1980s, when he was a young agent working the streets in New York, and later, when he was transferred to Paris, following the heroin trade. Drug smugglers he arrested kept bringing up a Syrian named Kassar. "Everybody we snatched would mention his name," Soiles recalled. Thus began the investigation that led Soiles to make the connection between Monzer al-Kassar and Abu al-Abbas and the *Achille Lauro*. At the Spanish trial, Soiles was a primary witness against Kassar, one of the few who hadn't been sidelined for mysterious reasons. As evidence, Soiles had presented photos of Abbas and Kassar together on board a private jet; another showed Abu al-Abbas at Monzer al-Kassar's wedding. He presented a copy of an Iraqi passport, with a photo of Abbas but a different name; the same alias appeared on a joint bank account set up by Kassar just before the *Achille Lauro* hijacking, and on a Bank of America credit card.

It hadn't been enough. Kassar had gone free. Soiles wasn't going to risk losing him again. He flew to Spain following Kassar's latest indictment and extradition, to personally escort the arms dealer to the United States on a government jet.

Both John Archer and James Soiles distinguished between Kassar and Abu al-Abbas. "Most people who knew Abu al-Abbas personally liked him," said Soiles. "With Abu al-Abbas everybody says he was a nice guy and sometimes you forget he was a terrorist, the way people talk about him." Monzer was different, said Soiles. "When you meet Monzer, he's a very charismatic guy but a real despicable person."

Archer felt Kassar admired Abu al-Abbas and supported the cause, up to a point. "Monzer would never walk away from everything he had," Archer said. "He would assist but not give his life to it. 'And by the way, if I can make money on both ends of the deal, I'm going to do it.' He had the ideology only to a degree."

Kassar always denied any role in Iran-Contra, or any illegal activities, including the one that brought the Klinghoffer sisters to his trial, supplying weapons for the *Achille Lauro* hijacking. He never stopped condemning Soiles and Archer. In a blog post response to a TV news report about his capture, Kassar wrote, "It's a shame how a few bad apples from the D.E.A., like Agent John Archer, and Chief Agent James Soiles, deceived CNN and the American taxpayers, hiding in sheep's clothing, when they are the real criminals."

Kassar couldn't understand why he was a criminal when the U.S. government was the single largest purveyor of arms in the world (followed by the Russians). He told his lawyer that he was being persecuted because of the *Achille Lauro*—not directly, but because of DEA Agent Soiles's obsession. This was payback for the failure of the earlier trial in Spain.

The erudite arms dealer invoked the medieval Sunni Muslim theologian and scholar Ibn Taymiyyah, and the words he uttered when he was held prisoner at the Damascus Castle prison in the fourteenth century: "What my enemies could do to me! If they kill me, it's martyrdom for the sake of God. And if they imprison me for life, it's solitude with my God."

For years Ilsa and Lisa had felt like lonely crusaders against terrorism. That changed, along with everything else, with the attacks on the

World Trade Center in New York, less than two miles from where they lived. The murder of three thousand civilians at one blow put the entire country on alert. The Bush administration's War on Terror became the justification for the invasion of Iraq and an escalation in the U.S. military presence abroad. Leon Klinghoffer was no longer a solitary symbol, the emblematic innocent caught in the crossfire of endless war.

A month after 9/11, Lisa and Ilsa met Joel Levy, who had just been hired as a regional director for the Anti-Defamation League (ADL). Levy introduced himself and Yoni Fiegel, a visiting Israeli terrorism expert who had asked Levy if he could arrange an expedition into the pit where the World Trade Center had stood. The Klinghoffer sisters asked if they could go along. They squeezed into a jeep with Levy, the Israeli, and an officer from the New York Police Department. Ilsa sat on Levy's lap; he was a small man, but she was even smaller. They rode in silence into the smoldering devastation, smoke rising from fires—a vision from Dante's *Inferno*, was how Levy described it.

Levy had joined the U.S. Foreign Service in 1974, after college and the Peace Corps. He knew of the State Department's reputation for being anti-Semitic, but he never experienced it. Terrorism and the Palestinian-Israeli conflict, however, were never far from his consciousness. Between 1982 and 1987 he was stationed in Malta—a Mediterranean island south of Sicily and only sixty miles from Libya, a listening post on Qaddafi. The embassy periodically received threats against Levy, who established a tiny synagogue on the island for Malta's small Jewish community; his daughter celebrated her bat mitzvah there. The Israeli chargé d'affaires in Malta was shot in an assassination attempt, on her way to someone's house for Sabbath dinner. Then came the *Achille Lauro* hijacking and Klinghoffer's murder, followed six weeks later, on November 23, 1985, by the Abu Nidal terrorist group's attack that forced an EgyptAir passenger plane en route to Libya to land on Malta. Levy, by then deputy chief of the U.S. mission, stood by in horror as an Egyptian commando unit botched a rescue attempt, igniting a fireball that destroyed the airplane and killed sixty people.

One day, in the aftermath of the back-to-back hijackings, a Maltese artist came to the embassy. He told Levy he had made a painting of the *Achille Lauro* and wanted to send it to the family. Levy passed the painting along to someone in the State Department in Washington. He didn't know what happened after that (the Klinghoffers never received the painting).

That was the closest connection he had to the family until 9/11. Levy found it fitting and humbling to confront the fiery remains of the World Trade Center with Lisa and Ilsa, all those years later. "They were very concerned and curious, like any New Yorker, about what had happened right here in New York," he said. "But for them it had a depth that was much much greater, and a context that was much much greater. As horrible as it was for everyone else, for them it had personal meaning beyond anyone else. I'll just never ever forget that experience."

The U.S. government and the ADL found a new role for Lisa and Ilsa in the wake of 9/11. In 2003, after the capture of Abu al-Abbas, the sisters came on the radar of Kathryn Turman, the assistant director of the FBI's office of victims' assistance. Turman had been dealing with victims of terrorism since the late 1980s, when she worked for Republican Senator John Heinz of Pennsylvania. Turman's portfolio included meeting family members of people killed in the explosion of Pan Am 103 in 1988. Then, in a cruel coincidence, the senator died in an airplane crash and Turman began running a victim assistance program for the Department of Justice. She met Ilsa and Lisa at a meeting with the ADL and Justice Department, right after she moved to the FBI.

Turman saw the Klinghoffer sisters as embodiments of the psychological journey she often talked about with her colleagues dealing with victims. "We used to talk about from pain to power," she said. "They always take that tragedy with them, they always feel that loss, but they can move forward in ways that make them better people, make their lives more meaningful and purposeful. Sometimes people become very focused on a memorial project, an initiative, or advocacy."

Long before she met the Klinghoffer sisters, Turman was aware of them. She had been particularly interested in their lawsuit against the

PLO, which set the stage for victims' rights laws that began developing in the 1990s. "They were the first terrorism victims that I was aware of who really became activists," said Turman. "Who tried to make something good come out of what had happened in their family and to educate others and to make the world safer for other people. The loss was personal, but they went beyond that."

In 2003, the ADL began sponsoring an antiterrorism training program in Washington, D.C.; it was open to members of the FBI, the new federal Department of Homeland Security, and local police. In 2006 the ADL invited Lisa and Ilsa to participate in the trainings, three-day seminars which took place twice a year, featuring Israeli and other antiterror experts. "Their voice is one of the most powerful pieces of that training," Turman said. "Everyone I know, and there have been hundreds of FBI folks who have been to it over the years, talk about the quality of the training and the fact they bring out that human side in such a powerful but quiet way."

It was gratifying for the sisters. They heard from FBI agents and police officers, who thanked them for sharing their story, and told them it motivated them to know how much their other work means for families. In subsequent years, the semiannual trip to Washington became for them a sacred pilgrimage.

When Kathryn Turman told Lisa and Ilsa in 2004 that Abu al-Abbas had died in captivity, Lisa felt empty inside. "Justice wasn't about killing him," she said. "Justice was him being convicted of the crime." Few people understood. When Abbas had been captured, people kept asking her and Ilsa, "Aren't you thrilled?" The question itself spoke to a lack of understanding of what they had been trying to achieve all these years, collaborating with the ADL, giving speeches about terrorism, finding justice for their father's death—thinking about what justice might look like. Monzer al-Kassar wasn't an adequate substitute for Abu al-Abbas, but his trial gave Lisa satisfaction, the feeling that her and Ilsa's efforts hadn't been in vain.

She was deeply moved when, on the last day of testimony, she and Ilsa received an affirming email from DEA Agent Archer: "Four years ago when I got this case, my goals were driven by a family who had suffered for twenty years," he wrote. "I'm happy knowing that my presence gave you comfort as yours did for me. I've heard agents say that testifying is like being on an island. For me, it's like being in the middle of the ocean alone in the water with a large shark, and everyone else is on the boat praying for you to swim faster. Seeing you in the courtroom during the course of the trial really helped me keep things in perspective and gave me great motivation to stay focused knowing good would win in the end."

For Ilsa, justice was something one could define. It was process, the system doing its work, as she'd been taught to believe. Kassar's trial represented that definition of justice, a proceeding that brought out facts and asked strangers to evaluate them according to a set of rules that could be articulated. She wasn't interested in "closure," and became impatient when sympathetic people uttered the word. As if she and Lisa could ever put what happened to their family behind them! All Ilsa asked for was accountability. When she heard Abu al-Abbas had died, she was upset, but not because she felt sorry for him. "There was another bad actor gone," she said. "We would rather have seen him at trial, go through the process, be held accountable in public so the public could understand the horrible things he had orchestrated."

The sisters had always wanted a by-the-books legal proceeding for Abu al-Abbas. From the time he was arrested in Iraq, they had pushed to have him extradited to the United States for trial. With the help of the ADL, they went to Washington for meetings with the senators from New York, Charles Schumer and Hillary Clinton. Clinton was warm and friendly, but when they listened to the meaning behind her carefully chosen words, they understood she couldn't help. "She was saying why he couldn't be extradited here because it was political, and it wasn't going to happen," Lisa said.

They had to settle for Monzer al-Kassar. Yet even though he had been brought to trial, as they had hoped, they had an emotional, contrary response to the brute reality of a legal proceeding, grounded in the elegant ideals of the U.S. Constitution. Every day when they saw

Kassar's lawyer, Ira Sorkin, in the court cafeteria, they wondered how he could defend someone like Kassar.

One day they walked over to him, carrying their lunch trays. "I have to ask you a question," Lisa said. "How could you represent this man? How could you do this?"

Sorkin's response was something like "Everyone deserves representation, don't you think?"

Theoretically, yes, the sisters believed that. But, said Ilsa on reflection, "Sorkin didn't have to take the case. He had a choice."

Sorkin was tough, an old-school lawyer who got his start when elite New York firms didn't deign to touch criminal cases. Those same firms didn't accept Jews, which for a long time explained the disproportionate number of Jewish lawyers in the defense bar. He was sixty-five years old and had been practicing law for forty years, having worked both sides of the courtroom, beginning as a prosecutor and enforcer for the Securities and Exchange Commission before switching to the defense. He knew that often when people said they wanted "justice," what they really longed for was vengeance. He had received his first death threat in 1975, when he was a prosecutor. He understood the unasked part of Lisa Klinghoffer's question: How could you *as a Jew* represent this man? His own law firm wasn't all that happy when he agreed to represent Kassar.

Before agreeing to take the case, Sorkin and his associate had flown to Madrid to meet Kassar in jail, where he was awaiting extradition to the United States. After pleasantries, Sorkin said to his prospective client: "You need to understand that one, I'm Jewish, and two, I'm very involved in the Hebrew University of Jerusalem and a supporter of the university." Not a problem, Kassar assured the lawyer.

Sorkin felt he didn't have to apologize to anyone for representing Kassar. His job wasn't to make judgments on the moral fallibility of his clients, but to make the government prove its case "beyond a reasonable doubt." Real outrage erupted against Sorkin with another client he took on while defending Kassar, Bernard Madoff, who was also Jewish, the man accused of concocting the largest financial fraud in history, costing investors $65 billion. Sorkin received numerous death threats, including one that said, "As one Jew to another, I deeply regret that the Sorkin family did not perish in the Nazi death camps."

Kassar saw the Klinghoffers during the trial and resented them. "My opinion of the two daughters is based on reading and seeing their actions," he said later. "They are full of envy, [and] have been trying to make a name, garner fame for themselves, with financial benefits—out of the death of their father, even on the cause of innocent people who have nothing to do with the death of their father."

He understood they had suffered a loss but implied that it was nothing compared with the loss suffered by Palestinians. "No doubt losing their father left a large wound in the same way [that] hundreds of thousands of innocent Palestinians had the same large wound for losing their loved ones and their homes."

He denounced their association with the ADL, which he described as a Zionist organization, and then he offered his definition of Zionism: "Subtle, elusive, cunning, crafty, sagacious, discerning."

He dismissed the ADL's history of promoting civil rights in the United States. "They mask their features in America so that African Americans and others will not turn against them," he said. "When so-called Israeli [sic] discriminates against their own people...the Whites are first, followed second by Africans generally, and third, the Arabs."

Elaborating on the Klinghoffer sisters' relationship to the ADL, Kassar said: "The best I can say of them, they have been used."

Kassar's own daughter, twenty-four-year-old Haiffa, was called to the stand by Sorkin as a character witness, as well as to address the accusation that her father wished to harm Americans. "All my teachers were American," she said. "All my friends are Americans." She testified that she had no idea what the Colombian insurgent group FARC was or even what business her father was in.

A *New Yorker* article captured her affection for her father. "Haiffa described her father as warm and playful," wrote Patrick Radden Keefe. "She was allowed to visit him on only a few occasions when she was in New York for the trial, but at seven o'clock some evenings she would stand outside the lower-Manhattan jail where he was being held. Kassar's cell was on the ninth floor and had a high window. He would switch the light on and off, so that Haiffa knew which window to watch. Then he would jump up high enough to catch a glimpse of his daughter blowing him a kiss from the sidewalk below."

On February 24, 2009, Lisa and Ilsa watched as Monzer al-Kassar was sentenced to thirty years in prison. In delivering the sentence, U.S. District Judge Jed S. Rakoff expressed a kind of admiration for the defendant, calling him "a very sophisticated person, a very complicated person." It was a tragedy, said the judge, "that a person of his intelligence has spent so much of his life in activities that certainly were not calculated to advance the human race."

Lisa and Ilsa Klinghoffer felt satisfied if not happy that day. After all they had been through and the losses they had suffered, they had learned to take solace where they could find it. They knew the conviction of Monzer al-Kassar wouldn't de-escalate the international arms trade or dissolve the hatred that led to terrorism or bring their parents back to life. They had watched with alarm the growth of what Ilsa called the terrorism industry, the security measures that were now everywhere, in office buildings, train stations, apartment houses, and hospitals. Sometimes it felt like the human need for conflict was ingrained as deep as the sea that swallowed Leon. They knew that no miracles were in sight that could part the waters and set the world free. But they had done everything in their power to honor the memory of their mother and father.

Coda

2018

Children listen to their parents' parables and then reach their own conclusions as they observe the world around them.

At his bar mitzvah speech, Max Klinghoffer Dworin (son of Ilsa and Paul) declared, "I don't believe in God." The thirteen-year-old boy explained his reasoning to the family and friends gathered in the Village Temple in Greenwich Village on February 9, 2002, five months after 9/11. "Part of my difficulty in a belief in a divine power springs from the fact that so much evil and hatred in this world is perpetrated in the name of God; Jewish, Christian, Muslim and other faiths," he said. "How can I believe in God when God's creation is so flawed and still has not mastered the simple acts of living peacefully together?"

Then he enumerated examples of God's absence.

—Six million Jews died in the Holocaust
—There are wars.
—There is famine.
—There are bombings.
—There is suffering and poverty.
—When friends and family die before their time and
—When my grandfather Leon, that I never met, was killed on the *Achille Lauro*.

Fifteen years later, Max recalled that speech while talking to me about how he would tell his family's story, conscious that the legacy would one day fall to him and his cousin Michael. "I've felt excited about that but also nervous because it's not really my fight, my mission, my cause," he said. "I never knew my grandfather."

What do you see as the mission and the cause, I asked him. He replied, "I think it's drawing attention to hatred and the harm that hatred can lead to. I think it's trying to prevent these things before they happen, though we're in a day and age when I don't think that's possible, supporting other families who are going through this experience of having someone snatched away unexpectedly."

What about justice and revenge? Speaking about his mother and his aunt, Lisa, he said, "I would say they don't want revenge, but they are also never going to get justice. They'll never get emotional compensation. To me it isn't about—but I don't think it's about justice either. It's about making it meaningful."

He reconsidered. "Actually, making it not meaningless is better," he said. "This is the hand we're dealt so let's just play the card."

As I was writing this coda, a news alert appeared on my cell phone screen. "At Least 28 Palestinians Die in Protests as U.S. Prepares to Open Jerusalem Embassy."

It was May 14, 2018, the seventieth anniversary of Israel's declaration of statehood. I noticed on Facebook that it was also Lisa Klinghoffer's birthday.

As the day progressed, the casualty estimates grew to several dozens dead, and at least 2,700 wounded. For seven weeks Palestinians had been protesting Israel's economic blockade of Gaza, culminating in a mass attempt orchestrated by Hamas to cross the border wall, followed by Israeli retaliation.

The provocative relocation of the U.S. embassy had been engineered by President Donald Trump, Israeli Prime Minister Benjamin Netanyahu's acquaintance from his days in New York in the 1980s. For the opening, Trump's team chose Robert Jeffress, an evangelical pastor from Texas, to deliver a prayer. Jeffress, a prominent figure in conservative politics, had once said in a television interview that Islam "is a heresy from the pit of hell." As for Judaism, the minister said in the same interview, "You can't be saved being a Jew." He added, "Not only do religions like Mormonism, Islam, Judaism, Hinduism—not only do they lead people away from the true God, they lead people to an eternity of separation from God in hell."

The concurrence of these two events, separated by forty miles, represented a stark divide that was also commonplace in Israel. The country bustles with prosperity, marked by an unemployment rate of 3.6 percent. The occupied territories—the land Israel took over after its victory in the 1967 Six-Day War—tell a different story, one of humiliation and checkpoints and diminished opportunity. Unemployment as of October 2017 was 29 percent—44 percent among Gaza's 1.8 million residents, more than double the overall rate in the West Bank, which had a population of 2.6 million. Unemployment was worse for the young: more than 60 percent of those aged fifteen to twenty-nine in Gaza were out of work.

Israel technically no longer occupied Gaza. In 2005, Israeli troops and settlements were removed from the Gaza Strip, the narrow enclave bordering the Mediterranean on the west and Egypt on the south. Soon thereafter, the militant Hamas won a popular election and wrested control from Fatah after a bloody civil war. Subsequently, rather than build the economy or govern, Hamas focused on destruction, attacking Israel underground and overhead, via tunnels and rockets, causing few casualties but creating enormous tension and instigating multiple wars between the two entities. In 2007 Israel retaliated with a blockade supported by Egypt, which led to a humanitarian crisis in Gaza. There were more rocket attacks from Gaza engineered by Hamas, fierce reprisals, cease-fires, and wars.

The violent outbreak of May 2018 occurred two months after I was in Jerusalem, interviewing Carmi Gillon, the former head of Shin Bet, or Shabak, Israel's internal security force, an organization that routinely used torture and other illegal tactics against Palestinians and extremist Jews. Gillon was in charge when Yitzhak Rabin was assassinated; later he became a diplomat and outspoken critic of Netanyahu, who has been prime minister since 2009. Gillon and I had been introduced by Ira Sorkin, Monzer al-Kassar's lawyer; Sorkin and Gillon had served as trustees for Hebrew University together.

Gillon liked to say he was the Israeli equivalent of an American descendant of the *Mayflower*. His maternal great-grandfather arrived in Jerusalem in 1859 and established the first Hebrew-language newspaper in what would become Israel.

"I think occupation is terrible for the sake of Israel," said Gillon. "I don't care about the Palestinians. I care only about Israel, I am very selfish, you can quote me. I think the occupation will destroy us, because of the price we pay for occupying other people. It begins to influence civil rights, the law system inside Israel."

He continued, "That was the only motivation Yitzhak Rabin had [to pursue] Oslo. He didn't believe a word of Arafat. Rabin had no romantic ideas; he was a fighter. But he realized in 1993 there is no future in the country. He wanted to invest money in education and infrastructure, not in security, fighting fifteen-year-old terrorists. This is not a future for a country. This was against his vision and the vision of Peres. Our current prime minister has no vision. He cares only what happens an hour from now, not even a day from now."

I asked him how Abu al-Abbas, known in Israel as Mohammed Zaidan, was regarded in Israel. "Just another terrorist," said Gillon. "Not important."

What about the *Achille Lauro*? "It was a big story for a few days," he said. "Another episode. For Americans it was different. Without the *Achille Lauro* Americans didn't even know about terror attacks in Europe. But when an American citizen was involved and was killed, it became a big story in America."

Four months before I met Gillon, my son and I traveled to Beirut.

"You have picked the worst time to come here" was Reem al-Nimer's greeting to us when we arrived, though arguably it was business as usual in the Middle East. That day Saad Hariri, prime minister of Lebanon, showed up in Saudi Arabia, announcing unexpectedly from Riyadh that he was quitting, while accusing Iran of meddling in other Arab countries and increasing tensions in Lebanon through its proxy Hezbollah.

Throughout the week my son and I kept checking on Hariri's status. "He has not been back since, and no one is sure when, or if, he is returning," wrote the *New York Times* Beirut correspondent, three days after we arrived.

"Maybe there will be war, maybe not," Reem told us with a shrug. Meanwhile, my son and I took a few uneventful day trips to marvelous historic sites around the country. We were warned not to head south, toward Israel. I checked my Google maps; it was eighty miles to Haifa from our hotel.

Reem was a gracious guide through Beirut, a city she loved and hated, showing us the places where Abu al-Abbas had courted his wives and escaped assassination attempts. In the years since her husband's death, she had resumed the life into which she was born, living in an elegant apartment near the Four Seasons Hotel when she wasn't traveling to India on yoga retreats, or to Prague to see her grandchildren, or somewhere else to visit friends. We visited Dar el-Nimer, her family's foundation, which promotes the work of Palestinian artists, historians, filmmakers, and musicians.

Most of Lebanon's population of six million exists outside the bubble of prosperity. An estimated 986,000 Syrian refugees from Syria's civil war, ongoing since 2011, have taken up residence in the country. More than half of the 450,000 Palestinians in Lebanon remain in refugee camps where they have lived for generations by now; poverty, overcrowding, and unemployment are pervasive.

Even the most elegant neighborhoods in Beirut carried markers of violence. Reem's apartment was a couple of blocks from where Prime Minister Hariri's father had been assassinated in 2005. She told us that her son Reef, now a Czech citizen, was reluctant to visit with his family, because the last time they'd been in Beirut in 2013, a bomb had gone off and shattered the windows in Reem's apartment. Her sons had left the Middle East behind and for that she was happy.

In the prologue to her book, Reem made a plea for coexistence between Arabs and Jews. "I hate war," she wrote. "I cannot imagine losing more friends and family in yet another battle. And, late at night, I imagine that our opponents in these conflicts share my grief. I have to admit that they, too, have lost children, women, and young men in the prime of life."

The publisher of the Arabic edition removed this call for reconciliation as well as a photo showing Abu al-Abbas sitting under a photo of Saddam Hussein—it would kill sales in Kuwait, she was told.

While I was in Beirut, I kept trying to visit Samia Costandi, who was quite ill. She had bone cancer, diagnosed as a secondary recurrence from an earlier bout with breast cancer. She had moved back to Beirut to be with her father after her mother died; her son Khaled lived with them. Despite her illness, she had spent hours talking to me via Skype in the spring and summer of 2017, eager to share her story. In July we made plans to meet when I came to Lebanon. But each time I called, Khaled said she was too weak for visitors. Less than a month after I returned to New York, Reem called to tell me Samia had died.

As I wrote Omar Abbas a condolence note, I remembered something he told me about his heritage. From his mother, he said, he learned empathy, kindness, love. "It's very important for me to look at someone else and recognize that they are not so different," he said.

"My father taught me that we have unlimited potential," he continued. "My father taught me how one person can actually change the world. My father also taught me how different people can regard you. He said anyone who actually makes a difference is bound to have enemies. It was almost his way of explaining why his image is so contradictory, controversial."

For Omar, his father's death marked the end of the *Achille Lauro*. "That was the ending of the story, the series of events that was set in motion on the day my father decided to go ahead with this operation," he said. "That operation ended with him dying in an American jail for all the wrong reasons. The entire sequence that led me to losing my father was already in place and was already playing out and we didn't know it. That sequence that started with the *Achille Lauro*. It affected everything in our lives."

When we began to speak in 2017, Omar was thirty-seven and had been living in Dubai for ten years, working as a commercial film director, making advertising for soft drinks, automobiles, health care. As we got to know each other, he gave me a virtual tour of his office via Skype, carrying his computer through his high-tech workplace, introducing me to colleagues along the way. The charming little boy had grown into a charming man.

But as he told his family's story, the pain he had experienced was palpable. After his father died he went through an angry phase. For a while he posted photos coming out of the ongoing war between Gaza and Israel, but he found the constant arguments exhausting and turned his attention to his career and his immediate family. He envied his half brother, Ali, who found an outlet for his feelings in writing and performing rap, including a piece called "AK 48," a riff on the assault rifle the *Achille Lauro* hijackers used and the year his father (and the State of Israel) were born.

One day, visiting Beirut, Omar went to a kitschy counterculture bar with a filmmaker friend, a hole-in-the-wall where a few aging activists of his parents' generation still hung out. He and his friend struck up a conversation with an older man sitting on a bar stool. The man started reminiscing about days past and great warriors and then said, "I was with Abu al-Abbas."

Omar told me the words sent a chill down his back.

"That was a great man and there will be no one like him," the man said.

Omar's friend said, "You're sitting next to his son."

The man turned to Omar and started to cry.

That chance encounter clarified Omar's struggle to understand his father's legacy. "This was a man who was vilified, turned into a monster," said Omar. "But he was a leader. If you go on Facebook, all these people I knew when I was a little kid are on Facebook, people who loved my father, worked with him, they have his picture as their profile picture. Or his picture with them. I don't have anyone in my life that inspires that kind of devotion. That's the wrong word. Love. Love is a better word."

What about Leon Klinghoffer? I asked. "The family of Leon Klinghoffer suffered the loss of their father, which is something we Palestinians know all too well," said Omar. "They were dragged into the spotlight and their lives were turned upside down. I can't begin to count the number of times I was told the story of somebody in our family who was affected by Israelis in a similar way but their story was never broadcast to the Western world. I always had a sense of injustice at the fact that our stories were kind of relegated. It felt unfair, especially as a kid. But that doesn't make Leon Klinghoffer's story any less real or important."

When Marilyn Klinghoffer was first diagnosed with cancer, long before she planned the cruise on the *Achille Lauro*, an uncomfortable thought nagged at Ilsa and Lisa. "How are we going to deal with this if our mother doesn't make it?" "This" was their invalid father. They kept that question at bay, but periodically it would creep in.

As difficult as that alternative reality seemed, it would have been comprehensible. But they could never come to grips with Leon's death at the hands of a terrorist. No matter how often they thought about it, or how much they read, they couldn't understand why their father had been chosen.

The Israelis almost immediately had promoted the idea that Klinghoffer was killed because he was Jewish. Eventually this became accepted as the reason. However, this motive is not substantiated by the firsthand accounts of Captain De Rosa and Seymour Meskin, Klinghoffer's friend, or by testimony from the hijackers. Neither the Italian prosecutor nor defense attorney I interviewed believed that the victim's religion explained why he was killed. Leon Klinghoffer's passport was part of a pile of U.S. passports, which do not indicate the religion of the passport holder. His captors did not speak English, except for Bassam al-Ashker, the youngest hijacker.

"Klinghoffer was not killed on purpose," Ashker told me when I interviewed him for this book via Skype. "He was unlucky."

Ashker's story was consistent with his testimony in court, as well as with numerous interrogations and his own memoir. He seemed credible when he said that, as far as he knew, killing a passenger was not part of the plan—even though it was probably inevitable if he had thought it through. The hijackers isolated the passports of the American and British people and threatened to start killing them if the Israelis didn't agree to release Palestinian prisoners and the Syrians didn't allow the hijackers to disembark at Tartus. But Ashker believed what he had been told by Molqi, that the threats were a trick, meant to get the international community involved in what was happening on board the *Achille Lauro* and provide safe haven to the hijackers.

Still, the initial purpose of the mission was to take and threaten Israeli lives—Jewish lives—at Ashdod. The plan's vagaries would have made it impossible to distinguish between military personnel and civilians.

Ashker said he wasn't aware that anyone had been killed until later. It was a large ship—"like a town," he said—and he stayed by Captain De Rosa's side throughout the hijacking. "Until we left the boat, nobody heard of Klinghoffer," he said and then corrected himself. "One of the others must have done it but refused to say he has done it."

When I spoke to him, Ashker was living in Lebanon, in a Palestinian camp, where his ability to work was restricted by Lebanese law. He was living with his second wife and had four children from his two marriages. He drew a small salary from the PLO and found work when he could.

When I asked him his hopes for the future, he answered, "I would like to go back to Palestine or at least be buried under a tree or in the mountains of my own homeland," he said. "For my grandchildren, I hope they will live a life with peace."

The one person who knew why Leon Klinghoffer had been killed was Majid al-Molqi and he had vanished, along with the others. His lawyer, Gianfranco Pagano, told me they had stayed in touch on and off after Molqi was released from prison and expelled from Italy. He ended up in Syria, where he spent some time in the military. The last time Pagano heard from Molqi had been five or six years earlier, when Molqi called because he needed help to start a business. He was broke.

Pagano said he truly believed there was no strategy behind the decision to kill Klinghoffer. "Molqi lost his mind," he said. "From what he told me, Klinghoffer had a cane and he even tried to hit them with it, lashing out," Pagano said. But the lawyer acknowledged that even this explanation was just a theory. Molqi's story kept changing. "We were not dealing with a terrorist who knows what he is doing," said Pagano.

In *The Death of Klinghoffer*, Alice Goodman created a combative Leon Klinghoffer, who confronts his captors with articulate anger. "I've never been a violent man," this Leon sings, "Ask anyone. I'm a person who'd just as soon avoid trouble, but somebody's got to tell you the truth. I came here with my wife. We both have tried to live good lives. We give gladly, receive gratefully, love, and take pleasure in small things. Suffer and comfort each other. We're human. We are the kind of people you like to kill."

In real life, by the time he was wheeled on board the *Achille Lauro*, Leon Klinghoffer had difficulty saying the simplest things. Only those closest to him could understand what he was uttering.

But the opera was never meant to be a documentary, though it would become—for many—what was remembered. Often as not, when I mentioned that I was working on a book about Leon Klinghoffer and the *Achille Lauro*, people responded, "Oh, right, they made an opera about it." And the opera itself has become as well-known for the controversy it has elicited as for its content.

Indeed, it was *The Death of Klinghoffer* that brought the *Achille Lauro* back into my consciousness in 2014, when it was about to be performed in

New York for the first time in twenty-three years, at the Metropolitan Opera House. Reflecting the partisan times, the revival drew vehement protests, much uglier than the objections offered in Brooklyn in 1991, when the contretemps played out largely in the press. This time, the opposition showed up on opening night at Lincoln Center to picket the opera—which many confessed they hadn't seen.

Hundreds of demonstrators gathered, carrying signs that said "The Met Opera Glorifies Terrorism" and "Gelb, Are You Taking Terror $$$?," referring to Peter Gelb, general manager of the Met. Among them was former New York mayor Rudy Giuliani, who years later became President Donald Trump's lawyer. About one hundred of the protesters arrived in wheelchairs, many holding signs saying "I Am Leon Klinghoffer." Ticket holders had to walk through a line of police barricades as demonstrators shouted, "Shame on you."

Inside the theater, once the performance began, there were a few sporadic shouts, gamely ignored by the conductor. Most of the audience listened and watched receptively, and when composer John Adams walked onstage during the final curtain call, he received a warm ovation. "In the end, the vituperation led to the opposite of the desired outcome: listeners who had been berated on the plaza were more inclined to support the work," concluded Alex Ross, the *New Yorker* music critic, in his review.

Opening night had been preceded by long negotiations between Peter Gelb of the Met and Abraham Foxman of the ADL. They made a deal. The Met program would include a statement from the Klinghoffer sisters and the Met agreed to cancel the live simulcast of the opera scheduled in two thousand venues in cities around the world.

An editorial in the *New York Times* criticized the Met for caving in and opponents of the opera lambasted Foxman. "I was called Kapo, quisling, collaborator," Foxman told me. "Look, I think it's a bad opera, but I'm not a music maven. The opera is not anti-Jewish. Peter Gelb is not an anti-Semite. People went berserk. People didn't recognize that in a democracy you compromise, that no one is a winner or a loser. It was one of the ugliest things in my career."

This wasn't the only possible outcome. When the opera was performed in St. Louis in 2011, the Opera Theater of St. Louis also included a statement from Lisa and Ilsa Klinghoffer in the program. But rather than stop with a conciliatory gesture, the company cosponsored (with a local Jewish group) a series of interfaith discussions, led by a Jew, a Muslim, and a Christian. "In other cities, outrage at *The Death of Klinghoffer*" has caused picketing, controversy and, sometimes, canceled performances," wrote a reporter for the *St. Louis Post-Dispatch*. "In St. Louis, where the opera is receiving its first staged North American production in 20 years, it has caused an outbreak of interfaith understanding and civility."

At least for a moment.

There remains the unsolved murder of Alex Odeh.

When I met Norma Odeh, it was evident that she was proud of the life she had built on her own. Despite everything, the three girls she and Alex had brought into the world were grown and were doing well. She had found strength within her that she didn't know existed.

But in some ways time had stopped for her in 1985, the day that Alex was killed. "Everybody said, 'You'll move on,'" she said. "But it hurts every day. It hurts when I look at my girls, when I look at my grandkids."

By the time we had this conversation, in the fall of 2017, more than thirty years had passed since her husband's death. She told me she was convinced that she would feel differently if someone had been legally convicted for Alex's murder. Just as Lisa and Ilsa Klinghoffer were not satisfied by learning that Abu al-Abbas had died in a U.S. Army jail, Norma gained no solace from knowing that Robert Manning, the chief suspect in Alex's murder, was spending his remaining days in federal prison for another crime. It didn't make her feel better to know that the FBI still considered Alex's murder an open case. She couldn't shake the feeling that the world cared more about Leon Klinghoffer than about Alex, because he was Palestinian.

Her fierceness didn't align with her appearance—a small, middle-aged woman with worried dark eyes, who spoke in a soft voice. She met

me together with her oldest daughter, Helena, who was thirty-nine, almost the same age as her father—whom she resembles—when he was
killed. They appeared to be a loving mother and daughter, teasing each
other and supplementing one another's answers with easy familiarity.
Helena and her husband, who was born in Palestine, lived with Norma
in Santa Ana.

Helena had already become the guardian of her father's legacy. Her
two younger sisters, both of whom had children, had lingering fears
about possible backlash, though they always attended the annual Alex
Odeh Memorial Banquet sponsored by the Orange County chapter
of the American-Arab Anti-Discrimination Committee (ADC), where
Helena was a member of the board.

A nine-foot-high bronze statue of Alex Odeh stands outside Santa
Ana's main public library. The statue's pedestal is inscribed with an excerpt from one of his poems: "Lies are like still ashes. When the wind
of truth blows, they are dispersed like dust and disappear."

More than five hundred people had gathered for the statue's unveil-
ing on April 11, 1994, which drew speakers from a cross section of the
Orange County community—including Jews, Arabs, blacks, and Lati-
nos. During the speeches, Irv Rubin, national chairman of the JDL,
stood across the street yelling "Alex Odeh deserved to die" while FBI
agents guarded the Odeh family. Two years later, vandals poured red
paint on the statue, repeating the violation a second time months later,
after the statue had been cleaned. The second vandalism was designated a hate crime by the FBI but no arrests followed.

In 2015, for the thirtieth anniversary of Odeh's death, the local
ADC raised money to refurbish the statue, which had been worn by
time and the weather. "They keep his memory alive in Santa Ana,"
said Helena Odeh. "People walk by every day. It's made us a little bit
stronger as a family. His memory is alive no matter what."

As for Irv Rubin, he died violently in 2003—after authorities said
he slashed his own throat and fell eighteen feet over a railing—while
detained in a Los Angeles jail, awaiting trial for plotting to blow up a
mosque in Culver City.

In the week following the murders of Leon Klinghoffer and Alex Odeh, a cartoon appeared on the editorial page of the *Los Angeles Times*. Drawn by three-time Pulitzer Prize winner Paul Conrad, it shows Odeh in heaven, pushing Klinghoffer's wheelchair companionably through the clouds. They both look peaceful.

The caption is a masterstroke of heartbreaking understatement.

"Small world, wasn't it?"

Acknowledgments

The original title for this book was *Klinghoffer's Daughters*, when the only story I knew was the American one, which itself was suspenseful, heart wrenching, and intellectually engaging. But as my research widened to encompass other perspectives — especially those of the Palestinians and Italians, but also Lebanese, Iraqi, Israeli, Egyptian, Syrian, and Tunisian — the obvious asserted itself: terrorism can't be understood without taking a panoptic view. Nor could the political be disentangled from the personal, because grave decisions of life-and-death consequence are made by individuals governed by their own histories and passions, no matter where they sit in the chain of power.

From the day I suggested writing a book about the *Achille Lauro*, Lisa and Ilsa Klinghoffer could not have been more forthcoming or more helpful — even after I told them the scope of the book had widened to include the family of Abu al-Abbas. That same generosity of time and spirit was reflected in numerous interviews with them as well as their husbands, Jerry Arbittier and Paul Dworin.

Max Klinghoffer Dworin told me he was most interested in the "ticktock" — what exactly happened to his grandfather, when and why. Throughout the writing of this book, I kept that thought in mind, coming to realize that in this story, as in life, the ticktock gets faster as time progresses. So more than half the book takes place in a two-week period; the rest stretches over two decades.

Early in my research I learned about Alex Odeh from *The Achille Lauro Hijacking*, a book written by Michael Bohn, who had been the director of the White House Situation Room at the time of the hijacking. I reached out to Norma Odeh, Alex's widow, who was reluctant to speak at first but eventually both she and their eldest daughter, Helena, were willing to share their stories.

Around the same time, while compulsively Googling the name Abu al-Abbas, I came across a memoir written by Reem al-Nimer, titled *Curse of the Achille Lauro.*

After reading her book, I found Nimer on Facebook and sent her a message, not really expecting a reply. But she answered quickly and thus began a conversation that continued for several months via Skype and eventually face-to-face in Beirut. Through Reem I met her sons, Ali Abbas, Reef Ghadban, and Loaye al-Ghadban, as well as her stepsons, Khaled Abbas and Omar Abbas. Omar introduced me to his mother, Samia Costandi, with whom I had two lengthy interviews by Skype and several email exchanges. When she died, I felt the loss of her gracious humanity and fiercely probing intellect.

Like the Klinghoffers, these were resilient people with a fierce resolve to protect and preserve their families. They told me their stories in hours of conversations, as I collected pieces of remembered history directly from people who were part of it, including U.S. military officers, intelligence agents, and diplomats; Italian jurists and politicians; Monzer al-Kassar, the arms dealer who had been a close friend of Abbas; and Bassam al-Ashker, one of the *Achille Lauro* hijackers. These interviews took place in person as well as by Skype, email, and telephone in New York City; Los Angeles; Montreal; Prague; Genoa; Rome; Washington, D.C.; LaFollette, Tennessee; the United States Penitentiary in Marion, Illinois; Boston; McLean, Virginia; Jerusalem; Dubai; and Beirut.

In addition to all the people who took the time for interviews, I was helped enormously by many dedicated archivists and librarians, especially Jennifer Newby and Ray Wilson at the Ronald Reagan Presidential Library, Leanora Lange and Ilya Slavutskiy at the Center for Jewish History, and Marianne Benjamin at the Anti-Defamation League.

Reverend Thomas Faulkner, who served as a chaplain at Ground

Zero following the September 11, 2001, attacks, provided insights into the trauma suffered by families of victims of terrorism.

For the Italian portions of the research, Jane Tylus and Sally Fischer came to my aid and introduced me to Brian DeGrazia and Sybil Fix. Brian's translation of Gerardo De Rosa's book *Terrorism Forza 10* was impeccable. Sybil became an important partner, interpreting the Italian interviews as I conducted them, and then transcribing and translating the recordings of those interviews. She provided critical research assistance, reading piles of documents and translating them, as well as Italian newspapers and books—most notably, Edoardo Pusillo's interviews with Bassam al-Ashker, *Cucciolo di leone*; Bettino Craxi's *La Notte di Sigonella*; and Matteo Gerlini's *Il Dirottamento dell'Achille Lauro e i suoi inattesi e sorprendenti risvolti*. Deep appreciation goes to Gianfranco Pagano, the defense attorney who provided access to necessary documentation as well as his recollections, and to Alessandra Gagliardi for pointing me in his direction. To Antonio Badini I owe much gratitude for his memories and insights.

A trusted circle of advisers took on the perilous task of being early readers: Debbie Abrams, Bobby Cohen, Madeline deLone, Noelle Hannon, Rabbi Deborah Hirsch, and Sara Krulwich. Jack Schwartz gave me the precious benefit of the rigorous questioning that I had already come to value so deeply when he was my editor at the *New York Times*.

I never underestimate the value of those friends who endured many hours of *Achille Lauro* conversation: Megan Barnett, Charles Durfee, Trish Hall, Stephanie Kanarek, Jennifer Oddliefson, Susan Merlucci Reno, Janet Taxin, Ann Temkin, Jill Weber, and Pat Winter. Zahra al-Zubaidi, part of this group, also translated documents and videos from Arabic. Thanks, too, to Marsha Berkowitz and Wayne Kabak for support when I needed it.

Kathy Robbins has guided me from the beginning of my book-writing career three decades ago. It has been a joyful and productive partnership that goes well beyond a business venture. She and David Halpern, along with Janet Oshiro and the terrific staff at the Robbins Office, are true advocates, friends, and allies.

This is my first book with Little, Brown editor Vanessa Mobley, and it has been a wonderful experience every step of the way. Her passion and intelligence, combined with unwavering diligence, have provided a constant and deeply appreciated touchstone. At Little, Brown, thanks are also due to Peggy Freudenthal and Trent Duffy, for astute editorial guidance; Joseph Lee and Sareena Kamath, for help with production questions; Craig Young, Ira Boudah, Elizabeth Garriga, and the marketing team; and Lucy Kim, for the exquisite jacket design.

My family read first drafts of the book and much more. My mother, Lilly Salcman, and sister, Suzanne Salamon, listened patiently to my stories and ruminations, no doubt more than once. Roxie and Eli Salamon-Abrams were travel companions, sounding boards, interpreters, and—possibly most important—sweet distractions when needed. Bill Abrams, my husband, was my first editor as always and remains my steadfast and beloved adviser about writing and everything else.

Finally, a note about Maggie, our dear dog who was by my side for the writing of four books, including this one. She died the day I turned in the final draft, reminding me that loss is the price we pay for love.

Notes and Sources

The *Achille Lauro* hijacking in 1985 attracted voluminous worldwide media coverage and dominated U.S. news headlines for weeks. My research began with a deep dive into this vast reportage, much of it remarkable for its thoroughness, especially given the limitations imposed by deadlines and the prevailing technology. That initial reading helped me understand what information was available in real time and formed the background to this story. I have not listed every news article; the list would be longer than this book.

Numerous books and research papers emerged from the hijacking and Leon Klinghoffer's murder. I have included those that provided significant insight into the history and geopolitics in the Bibliography. The notes that follow cite specific books, articles, and websites that were of special importance in sections of this narrative. I was able to interview each of the authors who wrote firsthand accounts of the events described herein, except Captain Gerardo De Rosa, who died in 2014. The two Case Program reports *The Achille Lauro Hijacking [A]* and *[B]* by Vlad Jenkins were also hugely helpful, as was Robert Fink's "*Klinghoffer* in Brooklyn Heights," an examination of *The Death of Klinghoffer* and its reception.

Documents from the hijacking trial in Italy, as well as pretrial interrogatories, depositions, and sentencing were provided by Gianfranco Pagano, defense attorney for Majid al-Molqi and Abdellatif Fataier, and translated by Sybil Fix.

Three archives were invaluable. First, the Klinghoffer Family Papers at the American Jewish Historical Society, part of the Center for

Jewish History in New York City, contains background material on the Klinghoffer family; news reports of the hijacking; Marilyn Klinghoffer speeches, testimony, and notes; television and newspaper accounts of the hijacking; and eulogies, condolence letters, and documents relating to the Klinghoffer Foundation.

Second, the Anti-Defamation League Resource Library has a sizable collection of news clippings about the hijacking and the opera, as well as copies of legal proceedings, including the Klinghoffer lawsuit against the PLO and various civil lawsuits related to the hijacking.

Finally, the archive at the Ronald Reagan Presidential Library in Simi Valley, California, administered by the National Archives and Records Administration, contains thousands of documents, including many that were previously classified, pertaining to the *Achille Lauro*. This collection guided my understanding of the Reagan administration's thought process and handling of the diplomatic, military, political, and personal issues presented by this crisis.

Other useful material came from the Library of Congress digital collection Frontline Diplomacy: The Foreign Affairs Oral History Collection of the Association for Diplomatic Studies and Training; the Fondazione Bettino Craxi; and the Vanderbilt University Television News Archive. In addition, Lisa and Ilsa Klinghoffer, Omar Abbas, Carol Hodes, Kenneth Meskin, and Lynda Gould opened personal collections of news clippings, lawsuits, and letters connected with the hijacking.

The two made-for-television movies about the hijacking were useful, especially *Voyage of Terror: The Achille Lauro Affair* (1990), which was filmed on the actual ship. Penny Woolcock's 2003 film rendition of *The Death of Klinghoffer* was helpful as well.

Individual interviews provided the lifeblood of the research. A few of the eighty people I interviewed asked not to be named; the rest are listed below.

For the Leon Klinghoffer story: Jerry Arbittier, Casey Donohue, Paul Dworin, Max Klinghoffer Dworin, Dennis Gralla, Larry Gralla, Ilsa Klinghoffer, Lisa Klinghoffer, Joel Levy, Larry List, Lana Mayer,

Jeff Okun, Rayna Ragonetti, Sara Rimer, Roz Schacknow, Letty Simon, Neva Small. I had the opportunity to interview June Cantor, the one surviving member of the Beach People, as well as several children of the group, now roughly the age their parents were when they took the Mediterranean cruise in 1985: Robert Cantor, Frank Gould, Lynda Gould, Carol Hodes, Steven Hodes, Kenneth Meskin, Maura Spiegel.

At the Anti-Defamation League: Steven Freeman, Abraham Foxman, Kenneth Jacobson, Susan Heller Pinto, Bluma Zuckerbrot-Finkelstein.

For the Abu al-Abbas story: Sami Abouyed, John Archer, Khaled Abbas, Omar Abbas, Bassam al-Ashker, Samia Costandi, Carmi Gillon, Loaye al-Ghadban, Reef Ghadban, Tony Horwitz, Monzer al-Kassar, Reem al-Nimer, Edward Schumacher-Matos, James Soiles, Ira Lee Sorkin.

For the Alex Odeh story: Senator James Abourezk, Khalil Bendib, Michael Bohn, Richard Habib, Rusty Kennedy, Helena Odeh, Norma Odeh.

Crucial parts of the narrative took place in Italy. These interviews were conducted by Skype and email with interpretation and translation by Sybil Fix: Antonio Badini, Carla Biano, Luigi Carli, Gianfranco Pagano, Edoardo Pusillo.

For help understanding U.S. government actions: Michael Bohn, Laurence Neal, Carl Stiner, Nicholas Veliotes.

On the subject of terrorism: Heather Cartwright, Christopher J. Fuller, Claire Finkelstein, Jennifer Levy, Kathryn Turman, David Wills.

Regarding *The Death of Klinghoffer:* John Adams, Robert Fink, Peter Sellars.

EPIGRAPH

xvii **My friends, I must insist:** J. T. Rogers, *Oslo* (New York: Theatre Communications Group, 2017).

PROLOGUE

3 **This was the moment that:** Omar Abbas's memory of becoming conscious of the *Achille Lauro* came from interviews with Omar Abbas, Feb. 20, 2017, and Samia Costandi, Apr. 25, 2017.

3 **The divorce had been modern:** Beirut University College became Lebanese American University in 1994. The school operates under a charter from the Board of Regents of the University of the State of New York.

I: A WEEK EARLIER…

6 **The *Achille Lauro* had a tendency to tilt:** Historic and nautical background from www.ssmaritime.com/achillelauro.htm.

6 **The Italians replaced the name:** "Achille Lauro, the Neapolitan Political Boss and Industrialist Who…," UPI archives, Nov. 15, 1982.

6 **During the next twenty years:** Information about mishaps that befell the ship from Ralph Blumental, "Hijacking at Sea, *The Achille Lauro:* Over Half a Century, a Series of Crises and Mishaps," *New York Times,* Oct. 9, 1985.

7 **"Whilst at sea you will savour":** 1980s brochure for the *Achille Lauro.*

7 **Captain Gerardo De Rosa was at the helm:** Details in this chapter about Gerardo De Rosa and the ship *Achille Lauro*, including his thoughts and direct quotes, come from his memoir, *Terrorismo Forza 10* (Milan: Arnoldo Mondadori, 1987). Other facts from Indictment Order issued Apr. 15, 1986, by Consigliere Istruttore F. Paolo Castellano; and Sentenza di Primo Grado (1st document), courtesy of Gianfranco Pagano.

7 **On a luxury liner, however, seafaring expertise was merely the baseline competency:** Additional information about the *Achille Lauro*—passenger lists, crew, etc.—from *Klinghoffer v. SNC Achille Lauro*, United States District Court, Southern District of New York, 85 Civ. 9708.

9 **The captain always tried to shake hands:** There were many conflicting accounts of the number of passengers and crew. I've used the shipping company documents cited

in various court proceedings, including the Sentenza di Primo Grado issued by the Italian justice system in the hijacking trial.

13 **The man holding the assault rifle was Bassam al-Ashker:** Biographical material about Bassam al-Ashker comes from my interview with him, Mar. 23, 2018; Bassam al-Ashker, statement to investigators, Nov. 4, 1985; *Cucciolo di leone: Biografia di un giovane fedayin* (Lion's Cub: Biography of a young *fedayin*), based on a series of interviews with Italian journalist Edoardo Pusillo, edited by Pusillo and Francesco Mazza Galanti (Milan: Franco Angeli, 2000); and court documents.

16 **"television terrorism":** Judith Miller, "Yasir Arafat, Palestinian Leader, Dies at 75," *New York Times,* Nov. 10, 2004.

18 **When he traveled through Palestinian military camps:** Interview with Ali Abbas, Feb. 4, 2017.

18 **In Israel, Abbas was denounced as a ruthless terrorist:** Interviews with Samia Costandi, Feb. 25 and Apr. 25, 2017; and Smadar Haran Kaiser, "The World Should Know What He Did to My Family," *Washington Post,* May 18, 2003.

2: THE ONES WAITING BACK HOME

28 **As the *Achille Lauro* sailed toward Tartus:** Information about the Klinghoffer family from extensive interviews with family members and numerous friends, and material from the Klinghoffer archive at the American Jewish Historical Society, New York City.

30 **"What's a Roto-Broil, you might ask?":** Mark Bittman, "Diners Journal: Bringing Back the Roto-Broil," *New York Times,* May 1, 2008.

36 **Reem al-Nimer was having her morning coffee:** Information about Reem al-Nimer and her family from interviews, and from Nimer's memoir, *Curse of the Achille Lauro: A Tribute to Lost Souls* (Seattle: Cune Press, 2014).

39 **This guarantee set the stage:** General background on the establishment of the State of Israel from wide reading, but a most useful source was Daniel Gordis, *Israel: A Concise History of a Nation Reborn* (New York: HarperCollins, 2016). For demographic information about Palestine before 1948, I turned to Justin McCarthy, *The Population of Palestine: Population History and Statistics of the Late Ottoman Period and the Mandate. Institute for Palestine Studies Series.* (New York: Columbia University Press, 1990), 26.

43 **Samia Costandi had much in common:** Information about Samia Costandi and her family from interviews; Costandi, "Exile in Lebanon," in *Women and the Politics of Military Confrontation: Palestinian and Israeli Gendered Narratives of Dislocation,* ed. Nahla Abdo and Ronit Lentin (New York: Berghahn Books, 2002); and Costandi, *A*

Palestinian Canadian Educator's Narrative Inquiry (Saarbrücken, Ger.: Lambert Academic Publishing, 2006).

44 **Still, with Palestinians as with Israelis, it is rare:** Ronen Bergman, *Rise and Kill First: The Secret History of Israel's Targeted Assassinations*, trans. Ronnie Hope (New York: Random House, 2018), 168–70; and Costandi interview.

44 **Even as a girl, living a comfortable life:** Costandi, "Exile in Lebanon," 40.

46 **When her parents realized:** Letters from Abu al-Abbas to Samia Costandi (and to her parents) throughout the book provided by Omar Abbas.

3: BIG GUNS

51 **Two weeks before the 1980 election:** Douglas E. Kneeland, "Reagan Calls Peace His First Objective in Address to Nation," *New York Times*, Oct. 20, 1980; and Ronald Reagan, "Televised Address by Governor Ronald Reagan: 'A Strategy for Peace in the '80s,'" Oct. 19, 1980, at John Woolley and Gerhard Peters, The American Presidency Project, www.presidency.ucsb.edu/ws/?pid=85200.

52 **"Traveling with Ronald Reagan, as I have just done":** Anthony Lewis, "Reagan on War and Peace," *New York Times*, Oct. 20, 1980.

53 **However, the Reagan team would soon discover:** David C. Wills, *The First War on Terrorism: Counter-Terrorism Policy During the Reagan Administration* (Lanham, Md.: Rowman and Littlefield, 2003), 6–7.

54 **"They have this ability to move around":** Interview with Caspar Weinberger on "Target America," *PBS Frontline*, Oct. 4, 2001, www.pbs.org/wgbh/pages/frontline/shows/target/interviews/weinberger.html.

54 **It didn't help that Secretary of State:** Jane Mayer and Doyle McManus, *Landslide: The Unmaking of the President 1984–1988* (Boston: Houghton Mifflin, 1988), 53, 54.

54 **Their disagreements were not just ideological:** Armitage's account is taken from his interview with Wills, *The First War on Terrorism*, 222.

55 **Robert McFarlane, assistant to the president for national security affairs:** Ibid., 38.

55 **This was fine with CIA Director Casey:** Y. Smith, "Former CIA Director William J. Casey Dies," *Washington Post*, May 7, 1987.

55 **Terrorism was a distraction:** "Remarks at the Annual Convention of the National Association of Evangelicals in Orlando, Florida," Mar. 8, 1983, Ronald Reagan Presidential Library, Simi Valley, Calif., www.reaganlibrary.gov/research/speeches/30883b.

55 **The Middle East combatants:** "Flashback: April 18, 1983: U.S. Embassy Attacked in Beirut," Central Intelligence Agency Featured Story Archive, https://www.cia.gov/news-information/featured-story-archive/2014-featured-story-archive/flashback-april-18-1983-u-s-embassy-bombed-in-beirut.html

56 **"What was our mission?":** Thomas L. Friedman, "America's Failure in Lebanon," *New York Times,* Apr. 8, 1984.

57 **Seven months later:** "Terror in the Sky—Hezbollah Seizes TWA Flight 847," Foreign Affairs Oral History Collection, Association for Diplomatic Studies and Training, Arlington, Va., https://adst.org/2015/06/terror-in-the-sky-hezbollah-terrorists-seize-twa-flight-847/.

58 **This ritualized cycle of violence became part of the expanding portfolio:** Jonathan Fuerbinger, "McFarlane Backs Aide on Contra Role," *New York Times,* Sept. 6, 1985; "The Iran-Contra Report: Chronology," www.nytimes.com/books/97/06/29/reviews/iran-chronology.html; and "Final Report of the Independent Counsel for Iran-Contra Matters," https://fas.org/irp/offdocs/walsh/.

59 **Officially called the deputy director of military affairs:** Oliver L. North with William Novak, *Under Fire* (New York: Harper Paperbacks, 1991), 232.

60 **A CIA publication described the qualifications:** Michael Donley, Cornelius O'Leary, and John Montgomery, "Inside the White House Situation Room: A National Nerve Center," Apr. 14, 2007, Central Intelligence Center Library, www.cia.gov/library/center-for-the-study-of-intelligence/csi-publications/csi-studies/studies/97unclass/whithous.html.

60 **When Michael Bohn, the director of the Situation Room:** Interview with Michael Bohn, Mar. 10, 2017.

61 **"Give this a chance":** Memo, Oliver North to Robert McFarlane, Oct. 8, 1985, Collection: Crisis Management Center, NSC: Records, File Folder: Achille Lauro [19 of 23], box 91131, Reagan Library.

61 **Within a few hours:** Vlad Jenkins, *Achille Lauro Hijacking Incident [A]*, Case Program C16-88-863.0 (Cambridge, Mass.: Kennedy School of Government/Harvard College, 1988).

4: THE NIGHTMARE

66 **"See," he said, "the sun still rises":** Gerardo De Rosa, *Terrorismo Forza 10* (Milan: Arnoldo Mondadori, 1987), 108.

66 **Seymour Meskin woke up that Tuesday morning:** From handwritten account by Seymour Meskin, courtesy of Kenneth Meskin.

67 **They had been enjoying themselves:** Interview with Carol Hodes (Mildred's daughter), Sept. 17, 2016.

68 **The authenticity quickly became apparent:** Joseph Berger, "Italy Said to Free Two P.L.O. Aides: U.S. Issues Warrant for One; Hostages Tell of 'Death List'; Account of Ordeal," *New York Times,* October 13, 1985.

68 **People followed their instincts:** Sylvia Sherman drawings, October 1985; Klinghoffer Family Papers, P-1002, box 3, folder 12, American Jewish Historical Society, New York.

68 **Meanwhile, an Austrian woman:** E. J. Dionne, "Hostage's Death: 'A Shot to the Forehead,'" *New York Times*, October 11, 1985.

69 **Accordingly, when the passengers:** Hodes interview; and interview with Kenneth Meskin, Sept. 23, 2016.

71 **Her memory later distilled the moment:** Marilyn Klinghoffer Recollections, Klinghoffer Family Papers, P-1002, box 3, folder 1, American Jewish Historical Society.

78 **Rimer was in a mild panic:** Interview with Sara Rimer, Oct. 6, 2016.

5: LIES, THEN HEARTBREAK

81 **For Abbas, the *Achille Lauro* operation was part of the long game:** Reem al-Nimer, *Curse of the Achille Lauro: A Tribute to Lost Souls* (Seattle: Cune Press, 2014), 20.

82 **Yasser Arafat now had different goals:** Interview with Reem al-Nimer and Sami Moubayed, Nov. 6, 2017.

82 **On Tuesday evening, around three hours after:** Valuable sources for the details of the hijacking are Vlad Jenkins, *The Achille Lauro Hijacking [A]*, Case Program, C16-88-863-0 (Cambridge, Mass: Kennedy School of Government/Harvard College, 1988); and Vlad Jenkins, *The Achille Lauro Hijacking [B]*, Case Program, C16-88-864-0 (Cambridge, Mass.: Kennedy School of Government/Harvard College, 1988). Documents from the Ronald Reagan Presidential Library's Achille Lauro and Oliver North files supplemented and corroborated the account.

83 **Someone in the State Department found:** Samir Murtada, "Palestinian Liberation Front's Abbas Interview," *Al-Watan Al-Arabi*, Sept. 20–26, 1985, 33–34.

84 **Similarly, the Italian government balanced:** "L'Espresso Reveals Hidden Diaries of Arafat," *L'Espresso*, Feb. 2, 2018; and Bettino Craxi, *La Notte di Sigonella* (Milan: Arnoldo Mondadori, 2015).

86 **Transcripts reveal a jittery Molqi:** Jenkins, *The Achille Lauro Hijacking [A]*, exhibit 2.

87 **"[It was] crazy in the way that the whole ordeal":** Gerardo De Rosa, *Terrorismo Forza 10* (Milan: Arnoldo Mondadori, 1987), 161.

87 **Marilyn Klinghoffer hadn't been able to sleep:** Marilyn Klinghoffer Recollections, Klinghoffer Family Papers, P-1002, box 3, folder 1, American Jewish Historical Society, New York.

91 **That Wednesday morning, when Sara Rimer:** Interview with Sara Rimer, Oct. 6, 2016.

93 **Rimer could not know she had witnessed:** Murder and rape statistics for New York City and the United States were taken from Uniform Crime Reporting Statis-

tics of the Department of Justice and the FBI, www.bjs.gov/ucrdata/Search/Crime /Local/RunCrimeJurisbyJuris.cfm and www.bjs.gov/ucrdata/Search/Crime/State /RunCrimeStatebyState.cfm.

93 **The day before, as part of its coverage:** "Middle East and Violence: Summary of One Year's Toll," *New York Times,* Oct. 8, 1985.

6: COWBOYS AND TERRORISTS

96 **The U.S. ambassador to Egypt, Nicholas A Veliotes:** Recollections and quotes attributed to Nicholas Veliotes come from interview on Apr. 25, 2017, or from an interview on January 29, 1990, conducted with Veliotes by Charles Stuart Kennedy for the Association for Diplomatic Studies and Training, available at www.adst.org/OH%20TOCs/Veliotes,%20Nicholas%20A,toc.pdf.

96 **The blunt message strayed:** Martin Snapp and Media News, "Snapp Shots: Remembering Johnny Otis and His Roots," *The Mercury News,* Jan. 26, 2012.

98 **The Israeli government continued to play:** Thomas L. Friedman, "End of a Hijacking: Israel Bitter at 'Murder of a Jew'; Israel Urges Egyptians to Prosecute Hijackers," *New York Times,* Oct. 10, 1985.

101 **Mubarak said the hijackers:** Loren Jenkins, "U.S. Jets Intercept Hijackers' Plane," *Washington Post,* Oct. 11, 1985.

101 **Then, openly pandering:** Ibid.

102 **The White House soon realized:** Michael K. Bohn, *The Achille Lauro Hijacking: Lessons in the Politics and Prejudice of Terrorism* (Dulles, Va.: Brassey's, 2004).

102 **Throughout the day:** David C. Wills, *The First War on Terrorism: Counter-Terrorism Policy During the Reagan Administration* (Lanham, Md.: Rowman and Littlefield, 2003), 150–51.

103 **Stark tried out the idea:** Ibid., 151, 152; Bohn, *The Achille Lauro Hijacking,* 23, 24.

103 **The Yamamoto variation gained momentum:** Wills, *The First War on Terrorism,* 152, 153.

104 **President Reagan's next destination was a Sara Lee plant:** "Remarks to Employees at the Kitchens of Sara Lee in Deerfield, Illinois," Oct. 10, 1985, Ronald Reagan Presidential Library, Simi Valley, Calif., www.reaganlibrary.gov/research/speeches /101085b.

105 **Reagan cut him off:** Wills, *The First War on Terrorism,* 155.

106 **For the people in Washington:** Recollections of Laurence Neal in this chapter from interview on Apr. 14, 2017, and follow-up emails; and Neal's remarks at "A Special Evening Commemorating the 30th Anniversary of the Murder of Leon Klinghoffer Aboard the *Achille Lauro,*" presented by the American Jewish Historical Society and the Center for Jewish History at the Center for Jewish History, New York City, Oct. 8, 2015. Details about the USS *Saratoga* from *Dictionary of Ameri-*

can Fighting Ships and United States Naval Aviation, 1910–1995, Naval Historical Center, www.navy.mil/navydata/nav_legacy.asp?id=65.

108 **After three hours of circling:** Neal interview; and Bohn, *The Achille Lauro Hijacking,* 27–32.

109 **It wasn't just the lights:** "Hostages and Hijackers; an Egyptian Pilot Reports a U.S. Threat to Shoot," Reuters, Oct. 17, 1985.

110 **When Larry Neal looked at photographs:** General Stiner material taken from Tom Clancy, with General Carl Stiner and Tony Koltz, *Shadow Warriors: Inside the Special Forces* (New York: Putnam, 2002); interview with Carl Stiner, May 25, 2017; and Edwin Chen, "Panama: The Road to Recovery: Stiner—'Right Guy' to Lead Complex Invasion of Panama," *Los Angeles Times,* Dec. 26, 1989.

114 **None of them—neither the military men on the ground nor the diplomats:** Vlad Jenkins, *The Achille Lauro Hijacking [B],* Case Program, CI6-88-864-0 (Cambridge, Mass: Kennedy School of Government/Harvard College, 1988).

114 **George Shultz and Caspar Weinberger called their counterparts:** Vlad Jenkins, *The Achille Lauro Hijacking [A],* Case Program, CI6-88-863-0 (Cambridge, Mass: Kennedy School of Government/Harvard College, 1988).

115 **The mysterious "diplomatic guests":** Material about Badratkan's relationship with Abu al-Abbas and Abbas's feelings about death from interviews with Samia Costandi, Apr. 25, 2017, and Reem al-Nimer, May 5, 2017.

115 **Abu al-Abbas often told his wives:** Reem al-Nimer, *Curse of the Achille Lauro: A Tribute to Lost Souls* (Seattle: Cune Press, 2014), 16.

116 **As daylight filtered in through the airplane's windows:** Edoardo Pusillo and Francesco Mazza Galanti, eds., *Cucciolo di leone: Biografia di un giovane fedayin* (Lion's Cub: Biography of a Young Fedayin) (Milan: Franco Angeli, 2000), ch. 10.

7: FULMINATIONS

117 **While former Senator James Abourezk was sympathetic:** Unless otherwise indicated, material regarding James Abourezk from interview with Senator Abourezk, Oct. 24, 2016.

118 **He didn't feel much discrimination in South Dakota:** Elisabeth Bumiller, "Abourezk's Arab Defense," *Washington Post,* July 3, 1982.

118 **Abourezk came home with an altered perspective:** Ibid.

118 **His message cost him:** Ibid.

120 *Exodus* **became the political and emotional template:** Bradley Burston, "The 'Exodus' Effect: The Monumentally Fictional Israel That Remade American Jewry," *Ha'aretz,* Nov. 9, 2012.

120 **the nadir may have been Abscam:** Bumiller, "Abourezk's Arab Defense."

121 **Born Iskander Michael Odeh:** Alex Odeh material from Michael K. Bohn, *The Achille Lauro Hijacking: Lessons in the Politics and Prejudice of Terrorism* (Dulles, Va.: Brassey's, 2004); interviews with Norma Odeh (June 27 and Sept. 12, 2017), Helena Odeh (July 3 and Sept. 12, 2017), Rusty Kennedy (May 12, 2017), and Richard Habib (Oct. 20, 2016); Hisham Ahmed, "An Interview with Ellen Nassab," *The Link* 22, no. 3 (July–August 1989); as well as news reports, notably, Jay Mathews, "Alex Odeh: Arab-American Victim of Hate," *Washington Post*, Oct. 13, 1985; and Dave Palermo and Gary Jarson, "'Santa Ana Bombing Kills Arab Committee Director," *Los Angeles Times*, Oct. 12, 1985.

122 **He became a U.S. citizen:** Norma Odeh interviews.

125 **And then the president delivered:** "Remarks and a Question and Answer Session with Reporters," Oct. 11, 1985, Ronald Reagan Presidential Library, Simi Valley, Calif., www.reaganlibrary.gov/sspeeches/101185a.

125 **drug-related arrests up:** Ronald Reagan: "Radio Address to the Nation on Federal Drug Policy," Oct. 2, 1982, at John Woolley and Gerhard Peters, The American Presidency Project, www.presidency.ucsb.edu/ws/?pid=43085.

126 **SUBJECT: Phone Call to Family:** Memo to Robert McFarlane from Oliver L. North, Collection: North, Oliver L., box 22, Reagan Library.

130 **They arrived at the Cairo Hilton:** From handwritten account by Seymour Meskin, courtesy of Kenneth Meskin.

131 **General Stiner greeted Marilyn Klinghoffer:** Interview with Carl Stiner, May 25, 2017; and Tom Clancy, with General Carl Stiner and Tony Koltz, *Shadow Warriors: Inside the Special Forces* (New York: Putnam, 2002), 293.

8: MACHINATIONS

133 **Craxi was a wily operator:** John Tagliabue, "Bettino Craxi, Italian Prime Minister Who Was Tainted by Corruption, Dies at 65," *New York Times*, Jan. 20, 2000.

134 **The U.S. government had become determined:** Vlad Jenkins, *The Achille Lauro Hijacking [B]*, Case Program, C16-88-864-0 (Cambridge, Mass.: Kennedy School of Government/Harvard College, 1988).

134 **Arafat sent Craxi a letter:** Bettino Craxi, *La Notte di Sigonella* (Milan: Arnoldo Mondadori, 2015), 109–11.

134 **That Friday morning, Hussein al-Aflak:** Ibid., 114–18; and Tagliabue, "Bettino Craxi, Italian Prime Minister."

134 **Enter Antonio Badini, Craxi's top foreign policy aide:** Multiple interviews with Antonio Badini, 2017; Craxi, *La Notte di Sigonella*; and Badini pretrial deposition, courtesy of Gianfranco Pagano.

136 **They arrived at the NATO base:** Tom Clancy, with General Carl Stiner and Tony Koltz, *Shadow Warriors: Inside the Special Forces* (New York: Putnam, 2002), 290–91; interview with Carl Stiner, May 25, 2017; and Badini interviews.

140 **"Sons of bitches":** Jenkins, *The Achille Lauro Hijacking [B]*; and interview with Nicholas A. Veliotes, January 29, 1990, conducted by Charles Stuart Kennedy for the Association for Diplomatic Studies and Training, available at www.adst.org/OH%20TOCs/Veliotes,%20Nicholas%20A.toc.pdf.

140 **Stiner took this defeat philosophically:** Clancy, Stiner, and Koltz, *Shadow Warriors*, 294–96.

141 **Craxi was squeezed on all sides:** "Chronology of Incidents Related to the Israeli Attack on PLO Headquarters in Tunis and the Achille Lauro Hijacking" [internal White House report by anonymous State Department analyst, Oct. 1985], Crisis Management Center, NSC: Records, File Folder: Achille Lauro [1 of 23], box 91131, Ronald Reagan Presidential Library, Simi Valley, Calif.

142 **For Badini, the deception was painful but necessary:** Antonio Badini, email to author, May 3, 2018.

144 **In Egypt, student protesters marched in the streets:** Memo from American Embassy Cairo to Secretary of State; Collection: Crisis Management Center, NSC: Records, File Folder: Achille Lauro [19 of 23], box 91131, Reagan Library.

144 **Veliotes requested that all administration participants:** Ibid.

145 **"Al-Abbas is not a marginal figure in the PLO":** Mark Lavie, "Israel Plays Taped 'Proof' of PLO Role," *Chicago Tribune*, Oct. 18, 1985.

145 **When he spoke by telephone:** Edward Schumacher, "Hostages and Hijackers: An Affront to Egypt's Pride…," *New York Times*, Oct. 14, 1985. Schumacher-Matos's byline appeared as Edward Schumacher because the *Times* policy didn't allow any of its reporters to use hyphenated names.

146 **Schumacher-Matos was based in Madrid:** Interview with Edward Schumacher-Matos, May 24, 2017.

9: CORPORA DELICTI

148 **She was told not to look:** Interview with Norma Odeh, June 27, 2017. Unless otherwise indicated, direct quotes from Norma Odeh in this section came from this interview, another one on Sept. 12, 2017, or follow-up emails.

148 **She kept thinking:** Kristina Lindgren, "'I Never Thought This Could Happen in America': Widow of Slain Leader Prays Killer Is Captured," *Los Angeles Times*, Nov. 11, 1985.

148 **Yet political violence and racism were embedded:** Mark Pinsky, "The 'Quiet'

Death of Alex Odeh: Terrorism Comes to Orange County," *Present Tense: The Magazine of World Jewish Affairs* 13, no. 2 (Winter 1986): 11.

149 **"I have no tears for Mr. Odeh":** Jay Mathews, "Alex Odeh: Arab-American Victim of Hate," *Washington Post*, Oct. 13, 1985.

149 **President Reagan called the bombing "heinous":** "Statement by Principal Deputy Press Secretary Speakes on the Murder of Iskander Odeh," October 12, 1985, Ronald Reagan Presidential Library, Simi Valley, Calif., www.reaganlibrary.gov/research/speeches/101285b.

150 **One of the friends who had dinner with Alex:** Pinsky, "The 'Quiet' Death of Alex Odeh."

150 **American and Palestinian flags:** Ibid., 11–12.

151 **Ellen Nassab, Alex's sister:** Hisham Ahmed, "An Interview with Ellen Nassab," *The Link* 22, no. 3 (July–August 1989).

153 **Leon's miraculous reappearance:** Bernard Gwertzman, "Hostage's Body Clearly Identified with Signs of Two Gunshot Wounds," *New York Times*, Oct. 17, 1985; and Thomas Friedman, "A Double Blow to Arafat," *New York Times*, Oct. 16, 1985.

153 **Like many religions, Orthodox Judaism:** "Autopsy Shows Gunshots Killed Klinghoffer," Associated Press, Oct. 18, 1985.

154 **Leon's remains arrived:** Marilyn Haig, "Body of American Slain in Hijacking Arrives in New York," Associated Press, Oct. 21, 1985.

156 **Tattelbaum was an impassioned orator:** Eulogy courtesy of Ilsa and Lisa Klinghoffer.

10: ILSA'S WEDDING

161 **When Ilsa and Lisa had met Marilyn:** Unless otherwise indicated, recollections in this chapter are from interviews with Ilsa and Lisa Klinghoffer between late 2015 and the spring of 2018.

161 **They were reassured that she:** John J. Goldman and Tony Robinson, " 'God Bless You,' Reagan Tells Her: Klinghoffer's Widow Spit in Killers' Faces," *Los Angeles Times*, Oct. 13, 1985.

162 **unexpected visitor was Benjamin Netanyahu:** Interview with Maura Spiegel, Oct. 19, 2016.

163 **Soon Marilyn was invited to testify:** Robin Toner, "Widow Urges World Fight on Terror," *New York Times*, Oct. 31, 1985.

164 **How do you feel now?:** Klinghoffer Family Papers, P-1002, box 3, folder 1, American Jewish Historical Society, New York.

165 **North prepared a memo:** Memo, Collection: North, Oliver L., box 100, folder:

Terrorism: Achille Lauro Hijacking 10/7/1985 II: White House Memos, Ronald Reagan Presidential Library, Simi Valley, Calif.

167 **The president's words had been chosen carefully:** "Remarks Following Discussions with Prime Minister Shimon Peres of Israel," Oct. 17, 1985, Reagan Library, www.reaganlibrary.gov/research/speeches/101785c.

167 **A memo signed by Robert McFarlane before the meeting:** Memo (rough draft), Robert McFarlane to Ronald Reagan in advance of Oct. 17, 1985, meeting with Shimon Peres, file SRB 0350, Achille Lauro File (8), box 93211, Reagan Library.

168 **Sunday, October 20, Deputy Secretary of State John C. Whitehead:** Handwritten note by Ronald Reagan (signed RR), Achille Lauro File (8), box 93211, Reagan Library.

168 **Reagan dealt personally with Italy:** "Craxi Is Positive on U.S. Relations," *New York Times*, Oct. 25, 1985.

169 **Yet a White House report:** Memo to Deputy Secretary of Defense from Leonard M. Perroots, Lieutenant General, USAF, Oct. 23, 1985, Collection: Crisis Management Center, NSC: Records box 1, Folder: Achille Lauro [1], Reagan Library.

169 **Marilyn's embrace of the political:** Sara Rimer, "Klinghoffer Family Finds Pressures Hard to Escape," *New York Times*, Oct. 31, 1985; and "Commemorating the 30th Anniversary of the Murder of Leon Klinghoffer Aboard the *Achille Lauro*," American Jewish Historical Society, Oct. 8, 2015, http://ajhs.org/commemorating30th-anniversary murder-leon-klinghoffer-aboard-achillelauro-evening-conversationand.

172 **"I believe that my husband's death":** Toner, "Widow Urges World Fight on Terror."

11: TRIALS

176 **"In the beginning, our operations":** Terrorism/Abbas Interview, reported by Henry Champ, aired May 5, 1986, NBC Evening News, Vanderbilt University Television News Archive, Nashville, Tenn., https://tvnews.vanderbilt.edu/siteindex/1986-5.

178 **After receiving a polite kiss-off:** Jerry Arbittier, letter to the editor, *New York Times*, May 18, 1986.

178 **Grossman responded with his own letter:** Lawrence Grossman, letter to the editor, *New York Times*, May 25, 1986.

180 **Even before Gianfranco Pagano entered the Palazzo di Giustizia:** Unless otherwise indicated, Gianfranco Pagano perspective and quotes come from interviews with Gianfranco Pagano on Jan. 2 and Oct. 4, 2017, or from follow-up emails. Unless otherwise indicated, additional material about the trial in this chapter from Vincenzo Curia, "Genova Will Relive the Terrible Days of the Lauro Hijacking," *Il Lavoro*, June 4, 1986; Maria Latella, "An Eye on the Press, an Eye on Security,"

Il Secolo, June 13, 1986; and Roberto Suro, "Achille Lauro Trial of 15 Opens in Italy," *New York Times,* June 19, 1986.

182 **For Carli, this case was merely a job:** Luigi Carli, email to author, Sept. 17, 2017.

183 **Pagano knew that in Molqi's case:** Defendant and witness statements given to U.S. and Italian investigators in the fall of 1985, submitted as evidence in the trial, courtesy of Gianfranco Pagano.

185 **In this instance, Pagano agreed with Carli:** Carli to author, Sept. 17, 2017.

185 **It had already been made clear:** Loren Jenkins, "Italians Accuse Abbas in Hijacking Trial," *Washington Post,* June 10, 1986.

186 **Although the power of the Red Brigades:** "Mapping Militant Organizations: Red Brigades" (Stanford University project funded by the National Science Foundation and the Department of Defense, 2009–2012), https://web.stanford.edu/group/mappingmilitants/cgi-bin/groups/view/77?highlight=Red+Brigades.

186 **This violent backdrop as well as more ancient histories:** Historic detail about Palazzo di Giustizia from http://it.wikipedia.org/wiki/Portoria#Ospedale_di_Pammatone. Details of opening day of trial from Associated Press, "Achille Lauro Hijacking Trial Opens in Italy; Five Defendants in Court, Nine Still at Large," *Los Angeles Times,* June 19, 1986; and Suro, "Achille Lauro Trial of 15 Opens."

187 **Dozens of reporters packed the press section:** Francesco Paterno, "Achille Lauro: It Is an Immediate Brawl; Four Germans Interrupt the First Hearing; Beaten and Arrested; The Requests of the Defense Are Rejected," *Il Manifesto,* June 19, 1986.

188 **The following day, June 19:** Roberto Suro, "Hijacker of the Achille Lauro Recants Confession of Killing," *New York Times,* June 20, 1986.

188 **The prosecutor called Ahmad "Omar" Maruf al-Assadi:** Roberto Suro, "Achille Lauro Hijacker Testifies Against Comrades," *New York Times,* June 21, 1986.

188 **The accusation acted as a trip wire for Molqi and Fataier:** Maria Latella, "'Rambo' Issues Threats; He Yells but the Interpreter Refuses to Translate," *Il Secolo,* June 21, 1986.

189 **Carli played it cool:** Maria Latella, "New Trial for Contempt Against the Prosecutor; the Lauro Case Comes to Milan; Threats by the Defendants Against Judge Carli; the Magistrate Is the Victim," *Il Secolo,* Dec. 9, 1986.

190 **Though Fataier and Molqi were partners in fury:** Defendant and witness statements submitted as evidence in the trial; and Fataier interrogation of Oct. 11, 1985, courtesy of Gianfranco Pagano.

190 **Antonio Badini, Prime Minister Craxi's diplomatic adviser:** Interview with Antonio Badini, Oct. 5, 2017, and follow-up emails; and Badini's pretrial deposition, courtesy of Gianfranco Pagano.

192 **The captain was impressive, a solid witness:** United Press International, "Captain Denies Cover-Up in Klinghoffer's Murder," *Los Angeles Times*, June 24, 1986.

192 **The story became more coherent every day:** Defendant and witness statements submitted as evidence in the trial; and Vincenzo Curia, "Ashker Repents Having Repented; Andreotti Will Not Attend the Trial," *Il Lavoro*, June 26, 1986.

194 **The trial wound down on July 5:** Interview with Gianfranco Pagano, Jan. 2, 2017.

195 **Carlo Pisacane, Duke of San Giovanni:** Jeff Matthews, "The Gleaner, Carlo Pisacane and the Failed Revolution," Naples: Life, Death and Miracles, Oct. 2011, www.naplesldm.com/pisacane.php.

195 **Invoking the Pisacane legend:** United Press International, "Hijack Jury Asked to Ignore Cause," *Chicago Tribune*, July 6, 1986.

197 **On July 10, 1986, the judge read the verdict:** Roberto Suro, "Italian Jury Gives Cruise Ship Killer 30-Year Sentence," *New York Times*, July 11, 1986; background material for sentencing from Sentenza di Primo Grado (1st document), courtesy of Gianfranco Pagano.

198 **For Pagano, the verdict was a victory:** Pagano interview.

198 **At a press conference Ilsa and Lisa summoned Marilyn's ferocity:** Robert Carroll, "Someone Will Pay," *New York Daily News*, July 11, 1986.

199 **The previous December, after the end of the fall school semester:** Recollections in this section from multiple interviews with Reem al-Nimer and from Reem al-Nimer, *Curse of the Achille Lauro: A Tribute to Lost Souls* (Seattle: Cune Press, 2014).

200 **Saddam had welcomed them in Baghdad:** "Palestinian Displacement," Forced Migration Review (University of Oxford), Aug. 2006, www.fmreview.org/palestine. For U.S. secret aid to Iraq, see Seymour M. Hersh, "U.S. Secretly Gave Aid to Iraq Early in Its War Against Iran," *New York Times*, Jan. 26, 1992; and Julian Borger, "Rumsfeld 'Offered Help to Saddam,'" *The Guardian*, Dec. 31, 2002.

201 **After the Iranian arms deal emerged publicly:** Malcolm Byrne, ed., "Becoming Enemies," National Security Archive Electronic Briefing Book, No. 394, Document 6 #8635961, Oct. 12, 2012, https://nsarchive2.gwu.edu/news/20121012/

202 **After the interview first aired on American television:** Interview with Nimer, May 5, 2017.

202 **Abu al-Abbas left Iraq shortly after Tariq's warning:** Nimer, *Curse of the Achille Lauro*, 125.

202 **"a quiet, gentle man":** C. Robert Zelnick, "How the Rug Was Pulled from Under Zafer al-Masri," *Christian Science Monitor*, Mar. 11, 1986.

203 **Extremists on all sides of the conflict exulted:** Henry Kamm, "West Bank Mayor, Named by Israel, Killed by Gunman," *New York Times*, Mar. 3, 1986.

203 **Reem felt that her uncle's murder:** Nimer, *Curse of the Achille Lauro*, 128.

204 **In the days after the hijacking:** Interviews with Samia Costandi; and Jonathan C. Randal, "Israelis Down Guerrillas' Balloon," *Washington Post*, Apr. 17, 1981.

206 **As they talked, she believed him:** Costandi interviews; Randal, "Israelis Down Guerrillas' Balloon."

12: PRESENTING… *THE DEATH OF KLINGHOFFER*

207 **In the six years that had passed:** Interview with Kenneth Jacobson, June 27, 2016; interview with Susan Heller Pinto, associate director of international affairs division, ADL, June 8, 2016; and interview with Abraham Foxman, June 16, 2016.

209 **Crucial players of the Reagan team:** "Iran-Contra Affair," www.britannica.com/event/Iran-Contra-Affair.

210 **Later that year, in November:** Daniel Cariaga, "S.F. Opera Commissions 'The Death of Klinghoffer,'" *Los Angeles Times*, Nov. 12, 1989.

210 **"Jewish menaces and ghosts and phantoms and memories":** "Israel and Operation Shylock" (Philip Roth interview), Web of Stories, www.webofstories.com/play/philip.roth/23.

210 **The sisters were thrilled when they heard about the opera:** Material about Lisa and Ilsa Klinghoffer's experience with the opera derives from my interviews with them.

211 **Sellars was the most exciting component:** Ira Krasnow, "Entertainment Wunderkind-Director Revamps Kennedy Center," UPI, Feb. 2, 1985.

214 **"I was reminded throughout the Gulf War":** Peter Catalano, "Opera," *Washington Post*, Mar. 21, 1991.

215 **The opera itself elicited a respectful, if muted, response:** Manuela Hoelterhoff, "Opera: Adams/Sellars 'Klinghoffer,'" *Wall Street Journal*, Mar. 29, 1991.

215 **John Rockwell in the *New York Times*:** John Rockwell, "Review/Opera; From an Episode of Terrorism, Adams's 'Death of Klinghoffer,'" *New York Times*, Mar. 21, 1991.

217 **Not all the children of the Beach People:** Interview with Kenneth Meskin, Sept. 23, 2016; and interview with Steven Hodes, Dec. 7, 2016.

217 **The Rumor scene, the "odd little prologue":** Raymond Sokolov, "Adamsweek: Klinghoffer Dies Again," *Wall Street Journal*, Sept. 18, 1991; and Edward Rothstein, "Seeking Symmetry Between Palestinians and Jews," *New York Times*, Sept. 7, 1991.

218 **Even Edward Said, a prominent Palestinian American scholar:** Edward Said, "Music: Die Tote Stadt, Fidelio, The Death of Klinghoffer," *The Nation*, Nov. 11, 1991, 597–600.

218 **For Peter Sellars, outrage and debate:** Unless otherwise specified, Peter Sellars material in this chapter from our interview of Sept. 11, 2017.

219 **He'd been an unusual child:** John O'Mahony, "The Mighty Munchkin," *The Guardian*, May 19, 2000.

220 **Adams, also Harvard-educated, was the oldest of the three:** Unless otherwise indicated, John Adams material comes from his memoir, *Hallelujah Junction: Composing an American Life* (New York: Farrar, Straus and Giroux, 2008), or from John Adams, email to author, Nov. 1, 2017.

221 **Goodman, already resentful:** "An Interview with Alice Goodman with Michael Dervan," Chamber Choir Ireland, Apr. 13, 2017, www.chamberchoirireland.com/alice-goodman-interview/.

222 **It quickly became evident that the inherent tension:** Adams to author, Nov. 1, 2017.

223 **As she was writing, she was filled with fervor:** Stuart Jeffries, "Alice Goodman: The Furore That Finished Me," *The Guardian*, Jan. 29, 2012.

223 **With the help of Alice Goodman's spiritual upheaval:** Robert Fink, "*Klinghoffer* in Brooklyn Heights," *Cambridge Opera Journal* 17, no. 2 (2005): 173–213; and interview with Robert Fink, Sept. 12, 2017.

224 **For Lisa and Ilsa, in September 1991:** Allan Kozinn, "Klinghoffer Daughters Protest Opera," *New York Times*, Sept. 11, 1991, C13.

13: FINDING THEIR PLACE IN THE STORY

226 **The hijacking of the Achille Lauro became, for Robert I. Friedman:** Larry Cohler-Esses, "A Tough Reporter," *New York Jewish Week*, July 12, 2002; and "Robert I. Friedman," *The Nation*, July 18, 2002.

226 **For Friedman, Kahane's terrorist underground:** Robert I. Friedman, *The False Prophet: Rabbi Meir Kahane* (London: Faber and Faber, 1990); and George Ramos, "L.A. Born JDL Man a Suspect in '85 Slaying of Alex Odeh," *Los Angeles Times*, June 25, 1988.

229 **according to an American Jewish Committee 1986 survey:** "Most Jews Concerned About Israel, Accept Criticism of the State," Jewish Telegraphic Agency, Apr. 27, 1987, https://www.jta.org/1987/04/27/archive/most-u-s-jews-concerned about-israelaccept-criticism-of-state. The American Jewish Committee report this article cites, "Ties and Tensions: The 1986 Survey of Jewish Attitudes Toward Israel and Israelis," was conducted by a team led by Steven M. Cohen, professor of sociology, Queens College, City University of New York; more than 1,100 Jewish Americans were interviewed in October and November 1986.

229 **A few months after Friedman's book was published:** Kenneth Reich, "Bombing Suspect Returned to U.S.: Extradition: Robert Manning leaves Israel to face trial in the killing of a Manhattan Beach secretary. Officials also believe that

he is responsible for the death of an Arab activist," *Los Angeles Times,* July 19, 1993, http://articles.latimes.com/1993-07-19/news/mn-14708_I_manhattan-beach; Michael Parks, "Jailed California Woman Dies in Israel: Mideast: Settler Rochelle Manning, 54, was awaiting extradition for trial in a letter-bomb murder. She was a friend of Baruch Goldstein, who massacred about 30 Arabs." *Los Angeles Times* March 19, 1994, http://articles.latimes.com/1994-03-19/news/mn-35856_I_baruch-goldstein; "Gabriel San Roman, "Convicted Bomber Robert Manning Denies any Role in Alex Odeh's Murder in Lawsuit," *OC Weekly,* July 19, 2017, https://ocweekly.com/convicted-bomber-robert-manning-denies-any-role-in-alex-odehs-murder-in-lawsuit-8266765.

230 **But there was no resolution in the Alex Odeh Case:** Robert I. Friedman, "The California Murder Case That Israel Is Sweeping Under the Rug," *Los Angeles Times,* May 13, 1990; and interviews with Norma Odeh, June 27 and Sept. 12, 2017.

232 **On that same visit to Jifna:** "Police Are Criticized in Israel for Handling of Temple Mount Riots," *Jewish Telegraphic Agency,* Oct. 10, 1990, www.jta.org/1990/10/10/archive/police-are-criticized-in-israel-for-handling-of-temple-mount-riots; and Kenneth Roth, ed., *Human Rights Watch World Report 1990,* www.hrw.org/reports/1990/WR90/MIDEAST.BOU-04.htm.

233 **In March 1991, as** *Klinghoffer's* **creators:** Samia Costandi recollections from interviews with her and from Costandi, *A Palestinian Canadian Educator's Narrative Inquiry* (Saarbrücken, Ger.: Lambert Academic Publishing, 2006), 212–24.

233 **Omar's strongest memories:** Omar al-Abbas recollections from interviews with him.

14: SIDELINED BY HISTORY

239 **Just as the Klinghoffer sisters saw Abu al-Abbas's freedom:** Walter Ruby, "Abul Abbas's Other Remarks," *New York Times,* Dec. 7, 1988.

239 **the PLF leader was dropped:** Michael Ross, "PLO Drops Terrorist Abbas from Panel," *Los Angeles Times,* Apr. 23, 1987.

240 **In November 1988, just one year later:** Reem al-Nimer, *Curse of the Achille Lauro: A Tribute to Lost Souls* (Seattle: Cune Press, 2014), 131.

240 **Arafat was cagey as always when discussing Abbas's status:** Michael K. Bohn, *The Achille Lauro Hijacking: Lessons in the Politics and Prejudice of Terrorism* (Dulles, Va.: Brassey's, 2004), 106–7.

240 **Abbas, tall and imposing in a businessman's suit:** Youssef M. Ibrahim, "PLO Proclaims Palestine to Be an Independent State; Hints at Recognizing Israel," *New York Times,* Nov. 15, 1988.

241 **Abbas's words had repercussions for Arafat:** Robert Pear, "U.S. Denies Arafat Entry

for Speech to Session of U.N.," *New York Times*, Nov. 27, 1988; and Don Oberdorfer, "U.S. Denies Entry Visa to Arafat," *Washington Post*, Nov. 27, 1988.

241 **Even as Arafat was making overtures toward peace:** Nimer, *Curse of the Achille Lauro*, 134.

241 **Crazy perhaps, but strategic:** Neil MacFarquhar, "An Erratic Leader, Brutal and Defiant to the End," *New York Times*, Oct. 20, 2011.

242 **Abu al-Abbas traveled to Tripoli, Libya:** Nimer, *Curse of the Achille Lauro*, 134.

242 **Abbas convinced himself:** Seymour Hersh, "The Iran Pipeline: A Hidden Chapter/ A Special Report; U.S. Said to Have Allowed Israel to Sell Arms to Iran," *New York Times*, Dec. 8, 1991.

243 **The meeting with Qaddafi:** Nimer, *Curse of the Achille Lauro*, 138–40.

243 **Abbas was determined to get it right this time:** Ibid., 135–40.

244 **For Abbas, the episode became a nightmarish repeat:** Daniel Williams, "Guerrilla Says Raid Aimed to Kill Civilians," *Los Angeles Times*, June 6, 1990.

245 **"He was always positive":** Interview with Reef Ghadban, Jan. 16, 2018.

245 **Horwitz was strip-searched and driven to the meeting:** Claire Zulkey, "The Tony Horwitz Interview: Somewhere Under Twenty Questions," Zulkey, May 9, 2008, http://zulkey.com/2008/05/-where-do-you-keep.shtml#.WlfeE6inGUk.

245 **Once inside, however, Horwitz:** Tony Horwitz, "A Terrorist Talks About Life, Warns of More Deaths," *Wall Street Journal*, Sept. 10, 1990.

246 **It would strike Horwitz:** Tony Horwitz, email to author, Jan. 15, 2018.

246 **But a cold side emerged:** Horwitz, "A Terrorist Talks About Life."

246 **As if to prove Abbas's point:** Unless otherwise indicated, Monzer al-Kassar material taken from interviews with him over a period of months in 2017.

248 **Reem did not return the compliment:** Interview with Reem al-Nimer, May 5, 2017.

248 **Kassar spent more than a year:** Patrick Radden Keefe, "The Trafficker," *The New Yorker*, Feb. 8, 2010.

248 **While Monzer al-Kassar was awaiting trial in Spain:** Nimer, *Curse of the Achille Lauro*, 153.

249 **The handshake between Arafat and Rabin:** Thomas L. Friedman, "Rabin and Arafat Seal Their Accord as Clinton Applauds 'Brave Gamble,'" *New York Times*, Sept. 14, 1993.

249 **Optimism was the officially sanctioned mood:** Nimer, *Curse of the Achille Lauro*, 152–53.

250 **Hamas and other extremist Islamic groups:** Statistics from B'Tselem: The Israeli Information Center for Human Rights in the Occupied Territories, www.btselem.org/statistics/first_intifada_tables. General background on Goldstein from Daniel Gordis, *Israel: A Concise History of a Nation Reborn* (New York: HarperCollins, 2016), 366–67.

251 **The *Achille Lauro* remained a metaphor:** Associated Press, "Achille Lauro Sinks off the Coast of Somalia," *New York Times*, Dec. 3, 1994.

251 **Captain De Rosa had retired:** Giorgio Dell'arti, "Gerardo De Rosa," Cinquantamila.it, updated Oct. 4, 2013.

251 **Less than a year later:** Joel Greenberg, "Arafat Visits Israel to Give Condolences to Leah Rabin," *New York Times*, Nov. 10, 1995; and Mary Curtius, "Israel's Likud Rejects Blame in Rabin's Death," *Los Angeles Times*, Nov. 14, 1995.

251 **For the Palestinians in Iraq:** Nimer, *Curse of the Achille Lauro*, 149–50; interview with Reef Ghadban, Jan. 18, 2018.

252 **That spring, however, Abu al-Abbas received an invitation:** Nimer, *Curse of the Achille Lauro*, 154–55.

252 **The purpose of the council:** Serge Schmemann, "Palestinians Meet to Rethink Calls for Israel's Destruction," *New York Times*, Apr. 23, 1996.

252 **The PLO meeting in Gaza:** Ibid.

253 **"Arab businessmen arriving at a trade show":** Marjorie Miller, "PLO Old Guard Returns to Gaza for Charter Vote," *Los Angeles Times*, Apr. 23, 1996.

254 **One by one, they realized they were on their own:** Philip Willan, "Mario Gozzini: He Reformed Italy's Prisons," *The Guardian*, May 16, 1999; and John Tabliabue, "Italy Opens Inquiry into Jail Escape by Achille Lauro Gunman," *New York Times*, Mar. 5, 1996.

255 **Molqi's freedom was short-lived:** Peter Shadbolt, "Achille Lauro Hijacker Arrested in Spain," UPI Archives, Mar. 22, 1996; and Carla Biano, email to author, Oct. 22, 2017.

255 **Bassam al-Ashker, the youngest of the hijackers:** Edoardo Pusillo and Francesco Mazza Galanti, eds., *Cucciolo di leone: Biografia di un giovane fedayin* (Lion's Cub: Biography of a Young Fedayin) (Milan: Franco Angeli, 2000), 147–50.

255 **While he was there, a journalist named Edoardo Pusillo met Ashker:** Interview with Bassam al-Ashker, Feb. 23, 2018; and Edoardo Pusillo, email to author, June 12, 2017.

256 **Ashker made his way to Algeria:** Interview with Ashker.

257 **Assadi, the hijacker who turned state's evidence:** Cristina Rogledi, "So I Understood That Abbas Had Fooled Us," *Oggi*, Mar. 13, 1998.

258 **In 2000, under Pagano's guidance:** Documents provided by Gianfranco Pagano.

15: THE OPTIMIST

260 **"We discussed how we were doing":** Interview with Reef Ghadban, Jan. 16, 2018.

260 **"It was the way he walks":** Interview with Loaye al-Ghadban, Jan. 28, 2018.

261 **remote from those of other Palestinians:** Information on Palestinian expulsion from Megan O'Toole, "Palestine-Kuwait Relations: 'Ice Has Started to Melt,'" *Al Jazeera*, Aug. 6, 2015.

261 **In the summer of 1999:** Interview with Omar Abbas, Feb. 20, 2017; and Omar Abbas, email to author, Feb. 12, 2018.

263 **A year later, Abu al-Abbas returned to Palestine:** Interviews with Reem al-Nimer; and Reem al-Nimer, *Curse of the Achille Lauro: A Tribute to Lost Souls* (Seattle: Cune Press, 2014), 158.

264 **Hamas's founding charter:** "Hamas Covenant 1988: The Covenant of the Islamic Resistance Movement," Avalon Project: Documents in Law, History and Diplomacy, Yale Law School, http://avalon.law.yale.edu/20th_century/hamas.asp. Casualty estimates resulting from the second *intifada* vary and, like everything else in the conflict, become politicized. I am using statistics provided by B'Tselem: The Israeli Information Center for Human Rights in the Occupied Territories; its tally of 2000–2006 casualties relies on numbers provided by both Israelis and Palestinians: see "Six Years of Intifida," Sept. 28, 2006, www.btselem.org/press_releases/20060928.

264 **After that trip, Arafat warned Abbas:** Nimer, *Curse of the Achille Lauro*, 153, 154, 163, 164; Nimer interviews; and Yossi Klein Halevi, *Letters to My Palestinian Neighbor* (New York: HarperCollins, 2018).

265 **Israeli intelligence, not surprisingly, offered:** Israel Defense Forces Military Intelligence, "The Palestinian Liberation Front: Headed by Abu al-Abbas as a Tool of the Iraqi Regime for Carrying Out Terrorist Attacks Against Israel," Israel Ministry of Foreign Affairs, Sept. 30, 2002, http://mfa.gov.il/MFA/MFA-Archive/2002/Pages/The%20Palestinian%20Liberation%20Front-%20Headed%20by%20Abu%20al.aspx.

267 **"Over the years":** "Transcript: Confronting Iraqi Threat 'Is Crucial to Winning War on Terror,'" *New York Times*, Oct. 8, 2002.

267 **Two months later, on April 9, 2003:** David Ensor, "U.S. Captures Mastermind of Achille Lauro Hijacking," CNN, Apr. 16, 2003.

268 **Abbas's family thought he would be released soon:** Reef al-Ghadban interview; and Nimer, *Curse of the Achille Lauro*, 184–86.

268 **Two months after writing that letter:** United States Army, Criminal Investigation Command, 75th Military Police Detachment, "CID Report of Investigation—Final (C)—0050-04-CID259-80155-5H9A," The Torture Archive: A Project of the National Security Archive, Oct. 10, 2012, http://gwdspace.wrlc.org:8180/xmlui/handle/2041/64839.

270 **Ali Abbas would be turning eighteen:** Interview with Reem al-Nimer, Feb. 10, 2018; and Nimer, *Curse of the Achille Lauro*, 177.

272 **Back in the cars for the final leg of the trip:** "Funeral for Achille Lauro Hijacker Abul Abbas," AP Archive, July 21, 2015, www.youtube.com/watch?v=f7yy0HgIXhw.

273 **They didn't speak for two years:** Tom Farrey, "Iraq's Olympic Chief Turned on Top Aide," ESPN, Mar. 8, 2003, http://a.espncdn.com/oly/news/2003/ 0308/1520173.html; Nimer interview, Feb. 10, 2018; and Nimer, *Curse of the Achille Lauro*, 178.

16: OPERATION LEGACY

276 **The trial of Monzer al-Kassar:** Steve Cohen, "Inside a Terror Trial," *City Journal*, Summer 2009; and Benjamin Weiser, "An Arms Dealer Is Sentenced to 30 Years in a Scheme to Sell Weapons to Terrorists," *New York Times*, Feb. 24, 2009.

276 **The chief witness for the prosecution:** Interview with John Archer, Apr. 27, 2017.

277 **The sisters were in federal court:** Press release, Office of the United States Attorney, Southern District of New York, June 8, 2007.

277 **In the courtroom, the defendant played the part:** Steve Cohen, email to author, Feb. 6, 2017; and Patrick Radden Keefe, "The Trafficker," *The New Yorker*, Feb. 8, 2010.

278 **"Kassar was a menacing figure":** Cohen interview.

278 **For James Soiles, a senior DEA agent:** Keefe, "The Trafficker"; and interview with James Soiles, May 12, 2017.

279 **Archer felt Kassar admired Abu al-Abbas:** Archer interview.

279 **Kassar always denied any role in Iran-Contra:** Monzer al-Kassar, blog post on convictpals.com/blog, Aug. 19, 2017 (copy provided by Kassar, email to author, Aug. 1, 2017).

280 **A month after 9/11, Lisa and Ilsa met Joel Levy:** Interview with Joel Levy, May 25, 2016.

281 **The U.S. government and the ADL found a new role:** Interview with Kathryn Turman, July 14, 2016.

282 **When Kathryn Turman told Lisa and Ilsa:** The Klinghoffer sisters discussed their reactions to Abu al-Abbas's death and Monzer al-Kassar's trial in interviews on June 27, 2017, and Feb. 12, 2018.

282 **"Four years ago when I got this case":** John Archer, email to Lisa and Ilsa Klinghoffer, courtesy of Lisa and Ilsa Klinghoffer and John Archer.

284 **Sorkin was tough, an old-school lawyer:** Interview with Ira Lee Sorkin, Feb. 22, 2018; and Diana B. Henriques, "Madoff Lawyer Absorbs Part of the Rage," *New York Times*, Mar. 10, 2009.

285 **Kassar saw the Klinghoffers:** Monzer al-Kassar's feelings about the Klinghoffer sisters and the ADL from his email to author, Mar. 12, 2017.

285 **Kassar's own daughter:** Keefe, "The Trafficker."

286 **On February 24, 2009, Lisa and Ilsa:** Weiser, "An Arms Dealer Is Sentenced."

CODA

287 **"I don't believe in God":** Bar mitzvah speech courtesy of Max Klinghoffer Dworin and Ilsa Klinghoffer; and interview with Max Klinghoffer Dworin, Jan. 5, 2017.

288 **The provocative relocation of the U.S. Embassy:** Matthew Haag, "Despite Past Remarks on Jews, Two Pastors Bless New American Embassy in Jerusalem," *New York Times,* May 15, 2018.

289 **The concurrence of these two events:** The World Bank, "Palestine's Economic Outlook—Oct. 2017," Oct. 11, 2017, www.worldbank.org/en/country/west bankandgaza/publication/palestine-s-economic-outlook—october-2017.

290 **Gillon was in charge:** Interview with Carmi Gillon, Mar. 11, 2018.

291 **"He had not been back since":** Anne Barnard, "Where's Said Hariri? Lebanon Wants to Know," *New York Times,* Nov. 7, 2017.

291 **Most of Lebanon's population of six million:** U.N. Refugee Agency, "Syria Regional Refugee Response," Apr. 20, 2018, http://data2.unhcr.org/en/situations /syria/location/71; "Where We Work," July 1, 2014 www.unrwa.org/where-we -work/lebanon

292 **"I cannot imagine losing more friends":** Reem al-Nimer, *Curse of the Achille Lauro: A Tribute to Lost Souls* (Seattle: Cune Press, 2014), 1.

292 **he learned empathy, kindness, love:** Interview with Omar Abbas, Feb. 20, 2017.

295 **"Klinghoffer was not killed on purpose":** Interview with Bassam al-Ashker, Mar. 23, 2018.

297 **Inside the theater, once the performance began:** Alex Ross, "Long Wake: 'The Death of Klinghoffer' at the Met," *The New Yorker,* Nov. 3, 2014.

297 **"I was called Kapo":** Interview with Abraham Foxman, June 16, 2016.

297 **This wasn't the only possible outcome:** Rabbi Howard Kaplansky, "Commentary: Opera Serves as Springboard for Interfaith Discussion," *St. Louis Jewish Light,* June 15, 2011.

299 **More than five hundred people had gathered:** Gabriel San Roman, "Activists and Family Members Keep the Memory of Alex Odeh Alive, 30 Years After His Unsolved Assassination," *OC Weekly,* Oct. 7, 2015.

299 **he died violently in 2003:** Francie Grace, "JDL Leader Dies After Suicide Attempt," Associated Press, Feb. 5, 2003.

300 **In the week following the murders:** Paul Conrad, "Small World, Wasn't It?" (cartoon), *Los Angeles Times,* Oct. 16, 1985, II:5.

Bibliography

Abdo, Nahla, and Ronit Lentin, eds. *Women and the Politics of Military Confrontation: Palestinian and Israeli Gendered Narratives of Dislocation.* New York: Berghahn Books, 2002.

Adams, John. *Hallelujah Junction: Composing an American Life.* New York: Farrar, Straus and Giroux, 2008.

Adams, John, and Alice Goodman. *The Death of Klinghoffer: An Opera in Two Acts with Prologue.* Milwaukee: Boosey and Hawkes, 2009.

Al-Ali, Naji. *A Child in Palestine.* London: Verso, 2009.

Anderson, Scott. *Lawrence in Arabia: War, Deceit, Imperial Folly and the Making of the Modern Middle East.* New York: Doubleday, 2013.

Anderson, Sean K., and Peter N. Spagnolo. "Case Study: The Achille Lauro Hijacking." www.isu.edu/~andesean/AchilleLauroCaseStudy.htm#_edn2.

Bacevich, Andrew. *America's War for the Greater Middle East.* New York: Random House, 2016.

Barnes, Julian. *A History of the World in 10½ Chapters.* New York: Knopf, 1989.

Bergman, Ronen. *Rise and Kill First: The Secret History of Israel's Targeted Assassinations.* Translated by Ronnie Hope. New York: Random House, 2018.

Bohn, Michael K. *The Achille Lauro Hijacking: Lessons in the Politics and Prejudice of Terrorism.* Dulles, Va.: Brassey's, 2004.

Chomsky, Noam. *Who Rules the World?* New York: Metropolitan Books/Henry Holt, 2016.

Ciezadlo, Anna. *Day of Honey: A Memoir of Food, Love, and War.* New York: Free Press/Simon and Schuster, 2011.

Clancy, Tom, with General Carl Stiner and Tony Koltz. *Shadow Warriors: Inside the Special Forces.* New York: Putnam, 1988.

Costandi, Samia. *A Palestinian Canadian Educator's Narrative Inquiry.* Saarbrücken, Ger.: Lambert Academic Publishing, 2006.

Craxi, Bettino. *La Notte di Sigonella.* Milan: Arnoldo Mondadori, 2015.

De Rosa, Gerardo. *Terrorismo Forza 10*. Milan: Arnoldo Mondadori, 1987.

Fink, Robert. "*Klinghoffer* in Brooklyn Heights." *Cambridge Opera Journal* 17, no. 2 (2005): 173–213. doi:10.1017/S0954586705001989.

Fisk, Robert C. *The Great War for Civilisation: The Conquest of the Middle East*. New York: Vintage, 2007.

Friedman, Robert I. *The False Prophet: Rabbi Meir Kahane*. London: Faber and Faber, 1990.

Friedman, Thomas. *From Beirut to Jerusalem*. New York: Anchor Books, 1990.

Fuller, Christopher J. *See It, Shoot It: The Secret History of the CIA's Lethal Drone Program*. New Haven: Yale University Press, 2017.

Gerlini, Matteo. *Il Dirottamento dell'Achille Lauro e i suoi inattesi e sorprendenti risvolti*. Milan: Mondadori Universitá, 2016.

Gooding, Gregory V. "Fighting Terrorism in the 1980s: The Interception of the Achille Lauro Hijackers." *Yale Journal of International Law* 12 (1987). http://digitalcommons.law.yale.edu/yjil/vol12/iss1/7.

Goodman, Alice. *History Is Our Mother: Three Libretti*. New York: NYRB Classics, 2017.

Goossens, Ruben. ssMaritime.com. www.ssmaritime.com/achillelauro.htm.

Gordis, Daniel. *Israel: A Concise History of a Nation Reborn*. New York: HarperCollins, 2016.

Gratch, Alon. *The Israeli Mind: How the Israeli National Character Shapes Our World*. New York: St. Martin's, 2015.

Grossman, David. *Death as a Way of Life: Israel Ten Years After Oslo*. New York: Farrar, Straus and Giroux, 2003.

—. *Horse Walks into a Bar*. London: Vintage/Penguin, 2017.

—. *Sleeping on a Wire: Conversations with Palestinians in Israel*. New York: Picador, 2003. First published 1993 by Farrar, Straus and Giroux.

Habib, Richard. "The Murder of Alex Odeh." *The Link* 49, no. 3 (June–July 2016).

Halberstam, Malvina. "Convention on Maritime Safety." *The American Journal of International Law* 82, no. 2 (Apr. 1988): 269–310.

Halevi, Yossi Klein, *Letters to My Palestinian Neighbor*. New York: HarperCollins, 2018.

Harris-Gershon, David. *What Do You Buy the Children of the Terrorist Who Tried to Kill Your Wife?* London: Oneworld, 2013.

Helmer, Daniel Isaac. *Flipside of the Coin: Israel's Lebanese Incursion Between 1982–2000*. Fort Leavenworth, Kans.: Combat Studies Institute Press/U.S. Army Combined Arms Center, 2007.

Heymann, Philip B. *Terrorism and America: A Commonsense Strategy for a Democratic Society*. Cambridge, Mass.: MIT Press, 1998.

Hoffman, Bruce. *Inside Terrorism*. New York: Columbia University Press, 2017.

Holz, Josephine, Eric Cardinal, and Dennis Kerr. "The Achille Lauro: A Study in Terror." *Public Opinion Quarterly* 51, no. 3 (Jan. 1, 1987): 448–54.

Jenkins, Brian Michael, "The Aftermath of the Achille Lauro." Santa Monica, Calif.: RAND Corporation, 1985. www.rand.org/pubs/papers/P7163.html.

Jenkins, Vlad. *The Achille Lauro Hijacking [A].* Case Program, C16-88-863-0. Cambridge, Mass.: Kennedy School of Government/Harvard College, 1988.

———. *The Achille Lauro Hijacking [B].* Case Program, C16-88-864-0. Cambridge, Mass.: Kennedy School of Government/Harvard College, 1988.

Kamalipour, Yahya R. *The U.S. Media and the Middle East: Image and Perception.* Westport, Conn.: Greenwood Press, 1995.

Kennedy, Charles Stuart. Interview with Nicholas A. Veliotes, Jan. 29, 1990. Association for Diplomatic Studies and Training. www.adst.org/OH%20TOCs/Veliotes,%20Nicholas%20A.toc.pdf.

Liput, Andrew L. "An Analysis of the Achille Lauro Affair: Towards an Effective and Legal Method of Bringing International Terrorists to Justice." *Fordham International Law Journal* 9, no. 2, article 5 (1985).

Martin, David C., and John Walcott. *Best Laid Plans: The Inside Story of America's War Against Terrorism.* New York: Harper and Row, 1988.

Mayer, Jane, and Doyle McManus. *Landslide: The Unmaking of the President 1984–1988.* Boston: Houghton Mifflin, 1988.

McCullough, Lt. Commander Larry A., JAGG, USN. "International and Domestic Criminal Law Issues in the Achille Lauro Incident: A Functional Analysis." *Naval Law Review* 36. 53 (1986).

McFarlane, Robert C., and Zofia Smardz. *Special Trust.* New York: Cadell and Davies, 1994.

Meyer, Herbert E., ed. *Scouting the Future: The Public Speeches of William J. Casey.* Washington, D.C.: Regnery Gateway, 1989.

al-Nimer, Reem. *Curse of the Achille Lauro: A Tribute to Lost Souls.* Seattle: Cune Press, 2014.

North, Oliver L., with William Novak. *Under Fire: An American Story.* New York: Harper Paperbacks, 1991.

Oz, Amos. *A Tale of Love and Darkness.* Translated by Nicholas de Lange. New York: Harvest, 2004.

Pillar, Paul R. *Terrorism and U.S. Foreign Policy.* Washington, D.C.: Brookings Institution, 2001.

Prashad, Vijay, ed. *Letters to Palestine: Writers Respond to War and Occupation.* London: Verso, 2015.

Pusillo, Edoardo, and Francesco Mazza Galanti, eds. *Cucciolo di leone: Biografia di un giovane fedayin.* Milan: Franco Angeli, 2000.

Roth, Philip. *Operation Shylock: A Confession.* New York: Simon and Schuster, 1993.

Russell, Bertrand. *The Will to Doubt.* New York: Philosophical Library, 1958.

Said, Edward W. *Orientalism.* New York: Vintage, 1979.

Sattouf, Riad. *The Arab of the Future: A Childhood in the Middle East, 1978–1984.* Translated by Sam Taylor. New York: Metropolitan Books/Henry Holt, 2015.

—. *The Arab of the Future 2: A Childhood in the Middle East, 1984-1985.* Translated by Sam Taylor. New York: Metropolitan Books/Henry Holt, 2015.

Shavrit, Ari. *My Promised Land: The Triumph and Tragedy of Israel.* New York: Spiegel and Grau, 2013.

Sheehan, Jack. *The TV Arab.* Bowling Green, Ohio: Bowling Green University Popular Press, 1984.

Sneh, Itai. "Achille Lauro (1985)." In *Counterterrorism: From the Cold War to the War on Terror,* vol. 2, edited by Frank Shanty, 112–15. Santa Barbara, Calif.: ABC-CLIO/Praeger Security International, 2012.

—. "Terrorism, War and Revolution in the Middle East: Problems for U.S. Foreign Policy." In *Counterterrorism: From the Cold War to the War on Terror,* vol. 1, edited by Frank Shanty, 453–61. Santa Barbara, Calif.: ABC-CLIO/Praeger Security International, 2012.

Stern, Jessica. *Terror in the Name of God: Why Religious Militants Kill.* New York: HarperCollins, 2003.

Tattelbaum, Rabbi Harvey M. *Tales of the Village Rabbi: A Manhattan Chronicle.* New York: E-Rights/E-Reads, 2009.

United Nations Department of Public Information. *Yearbook of the United Nations 1985, Volume 39.* Dordrecht, Neth.: Martinus Nijhoff, 1989.

Uris, Leon. *Exodus.* New York: Doubleday, 1958.

Vitor, Francisco. Navigation—Cruiseline and Maritime Themes blogspot. http://vmf-cruiseshipsandliners.blogspot.com/2011/12/willem-ruys-becomes-achille-lauro.html.

Walsh, Lawrence E. *Iran-Contra: The Final Report.* New York: Times Books, 1994.

Wills, David C. *The First War on Terrorism: Counter-Terrorism Policy During the Reagan Administration.* Lanham, Md.: Rowman and Littlefield, 2003.

Woodward, Bob. *Veil: The Secret Wars of the CIA, 1982–1987.* New York: Simon and Schuster, 1987.

Index

Palestinian-Israeli conflict, 54, 84, 214,
217–18, 221–22, 224–25, 230
Palestinian Liberation Front (PLF)
and Abu al-Abbas, 3–5, 17, 36, 43, 47,
50, 83–84, 115, 138, 142,
200–201, 239, 244–45, 247–49,
259, 261, 266–67
and Yasser Arafat, 203, 266
and Bassam al-Ashker, 17–18, 266
and funeral of Abu al-Abbas, 272–73
and hijackers' trials, 196, 198
and Monzer al-Kassar, 277
and Nahariyya commando raid, 177
and Muammar el-Qaddafi, 243–44
training of terror squads by, 266
Palestinian National Authority, 249–50
Palestinian national movement, 14, 16,
39–40, 42, 240
Pam Am Flight 103 bombing, 242
Pammatone Hospital, 187
Peace Corps, 280
Peres, Shimon, 135, 167–68, 202, 229,
250–52, 290
Persian Gulf War, 214, 235, 245
Petrarch, 180
Pisacane, Carlo, 195
Planned Parenthood, 148
Poindexter, John M., 60, 103–4
Popular Front for the Liberation of Pales-
tine (PFLP), 42, 45, 162, 202, 252
Port Said, Egypt
and *Achille Lauro* hijacking, 27, 82–83,
85–86, 88, 91, 96, 98, 129,
134–35, 138, 185
and *Achille Lauro* passengers' Pyramid ex-
cursion, 8, 11, 21
and Mossad agents' boarding *Achille
Lauro,* 21–22
Pusillo, Edoardo, 255–56

Qaddafi, Muammar el-, 241–44, 280

Rabb, Maxwell, 85, 113–14, 141
Rabin, Leah, 251
Rabin, Yitzhak, 98, 248–51, 264, 290
Radio Gothenburg, 60
Radio Monte Carlo, 82–83
Rakoff, Jed S., 286
Reagan, Nancy, 125–27, 166

Reagan, Ronald
and Abu al-Abbas's NBC interview, 176,
202
and *Achille Lauro* hijacking, 60–61, 85,
91, 124–25, 167
as anti-Soviet Union, 53, 55–56, 135
foreign policy team of, 52–55
and Saddam Hussein, 200–201
and Iran-Contra affair, 58, 209
and Israeli bombing of Hamman Chott
PLO headquarters, 97, 167–68
and Italian custody of Abu al-Abbas,
141, 144, 240
and killing of Alex Odeh, 124, 149–50
and Klinghoffer family, 125–28, 161,
164–67, 174
1980 presidential campaign, 51–52
and pursuit of escaping hijackers, 103–5,
114–15, 124, 240
and terrorism, 51–56, 59–61
and U.S. involvement in Lebanon,
56–59
Red Brigades, 84, 181, 186–87, 242
Revolutionary Armed Forces of Colombia,
276
Rimer, Sara, 77–80, 91–93, 127
Rockwell, John, 215–16
Rogledi, Cristina, 257
Romney, Mitt, 162
Rosenthal, Abe, 78
Ross, Alex, 297
Roth, Philip, 210
Rothschild, Jacob, 39
Rothstein, Edward, 218
Roto-Broil 400, 30–31
Rubin, Irv, 149, 299
Ruggiero, Renato, 136, 139
Ruys, Willem, 6

Sabra refugee camp, 17, 47
Sadat, Anwar el-, 84
Said, Edward, 218
Said, Gandura, 181, 198
San Francisco Opera, 210, 225
San Francisco Symphony, 220
Saratoga (ship), 106–7, 109
Saudi Arabia, 15, 41, 110, 144, 200, 291
Schneerson, Menachem, 163
Schumacher-Matos, Edward, 146

About the Author

Author and journalist Julie Salamon has written several notable books, among them the Hollywood classic *The Devil's Candy* and the *New York Times* bestselling biography of Wendy Wasserstein, *Wendy and the Lost Boys*. Her ten previous works, which have been translated into several languages, include the international bestseller *The Christmas Tree*, one of three collaborations with illustrator Jill Weber. For many years Salamon was a reporter and critic for the *Wall Street Journal* and the *New York Times*. She is board chair of BRC, a leading nonprofit organization in New York City that provides housing and treatment services to thousands of homeless adults. Raised in rural Ohio, Salamon lives with her family in New York City.